Guarantee of the rights of man and of the citizen necessitates a public force. This force, then, is instituted for the advantage of all, and not for the particular use of those to whom it is confided.—ARTICLE XII OF THE DECLARATION OF THE RIGHTS OF MAN.

THE ARMY
AND THE
FIFTH REPUBLIC

By

ORVILLE D. MENARD

UNIVERSITY OF NEBRASKA PRESS · LINCOLN

Some of the material in Chapter V first appeared in different form in "The French Army Above the State," *Military Affairs*, xxviii (Fall, 1964), pp. 123–129.

Copyright © 1967 by the University of Nebraska Press

All rights reserved

Library of Congress Catalog Card Number: 67–18269

Manufactured in the United States of America

For Darlene

Preface

DURING THE MONTH of May, 1958, French army troops and tanks appeared in Paris, a novel and conspicuous sight on the Parisian boulevards and squares. They had been ordered into position by the government to meet the threat of invasion posed by French army units in Algeria. However, it was not clear whether the defenders would fight the invaders if they came or join them, for France's army was no longer trustworthy. The meeting never took place; the government fell without an invasion and the army's choice, Charles de Gaulle, assumed the leadership of France.

Civilian control of the military had been a well-established tradition in France, yet in 1958, the army was instrumental in the destruction of the Fourth Republic and later attempted to dictate policy to its successor. Ultimately, activist elements of the army, spurred by the despair born of observing De Gaulle adopt a course contrary to their interpretation of the national interest, rose against the Fifth Republic in a futile but spectacular putsch in 1961.

"What happened in France," one is impelled to ask, "to lead the army from its apolitical tradition to overt political action? How did it attempt to influence, even direct, French policy?" Politically ambitious and active armies are generally associated with underdeveloped nations, but France's experience suggests that the technologically backward and politically unsophisticated are not unique in falling prey to overt military political action. Under what conditions, then, may a politically pretentious army appear in a modern nation? What will drive military men to defy their civilian masters? Once having developed a political consciousness, how will they attempt to influence national policy? What factors and conditions will affect achievement or failure of an army's political initiatives? These questions are basic concerns of this book, the first half of which searches for the reasons behind the development of the French army's political consciousness, while the second half is devoted to the means adopted by the army to realize its political goals.

Civil-military relations were strained in many nations in the 1950's and 1960's—in advanced states (recall the Truman-MacArthur episode in the United States) as well as in technologically and politically backward ones. Moreover, one is struck by certain similarities in French and American experience: militant communism identified as the motive force of international strife; limited conflicts fought in far-off lands without widespread homefront attention or enthusiasm; dissenting voices within the homeland questioning the validity, morality, and worth of the struggles; subversive wars recognized as being more than military contests, with the consequent necessity for an army prepared to wage war politically, economically, and socially.

For Americans, the French army's experiences from the end of World War II to Algerian independence in 1962 should be of particular interest, from the strategic and tactical aspects in addition to the civil-military perspective broached above. After great expenditure of effort and lives, the French army was forced to withdraw from Indochina in 1954, beaten by a foe inferior in weapons and numbers, the Vietminh. Attempting to learn from their ignominious defeat, French officers studied the enemy's methods and developed the theory and technique of revolutionary war. Applying these techniques to the uprising in Algeria, the French again were defeated in spite of their superiority in manpower and machines, in spite of their civic actions, their educational and health programs, their fortified hamlets, and in spite of additional French bloodshed and the loss of thousands of Algerian lives, both European and Moslem.

Where did the French go wrong in Indochina and Algeria? Are their failures to be attributed to errors of strategy and tactics; to lack of homeland support; to lack of political direction? Or was France fighting the wrong wars, in the wrong places, at the wrong times? Voices raised in the United States in the mid-1960's concerning American involvement in Vietnam, both for and against, are like echoes from France, resounding from her trials in Indochina and Algeria. Reading and listening to views on subversive war expressed in the United States in the sixties leave one with the feeling of having gone over that ground once before. Ah yes, in the French journals of an earlier decade.

Do these parallels portend increased civil-military stresses for the United States? Are Americans embarking upon a period which will produce enhanced tensions between civilian and military leaders? With the conclusion of the Algerian war, it may be that France has weathered her most virulent civil-military crisis. The United States, on the other hand, standing almost alone as the international fireman, prepared to extinguish brush-fire wars wherever they may threaten the free world, may be facing an era of fitful civil-military confrontations. By examining France's army, perhaps we shall be led to a better understanding of politically active armies, the conditions creating them, the forces mitigating them, and be better equipped to answer the questions just raised.

Finally, may I add that while I sympathize with some officers of the French army, sympathy is not synonymous with approval. As concerns Algeria, France and her responsible leadership finally recognized a changing situation in a changing world. Elements of the army, locked in their dogmatic prejudices and in a blind devotion to the lost cause of *Algérie française*, found themselves where dogma inevitably ends—in conflict with the unbelievers, in attempts to assert and impose their own will, in grudging defeat in the face of more enlightened forces.

As for acknowledgments, the usual procedure is to conclude with a last-but-not-least reference to one's spouse. I wish instead to mention first and foremost my wife, without whose encouragement, efforts and patience this study would indeed not have been possible. I owe too a debt of gratitude to Professor Carl J. Schneider, formerly of the University of Nebraska, who directed me to the fascinating and significant field of French civil-military relations. To Professor Raphael Zariski of the University of Nebraska, I express my great thanks. With his incisive and penetrating comments, Professor Zariski, teacher and friend, rendered me an invaluable service. Mrs. Leona Mason of the University of Nebraska Library and Miss Ella Jane Dougherty of the University of Omaha Library aided me immeasurably in so ably fulfilling my many requests for materials. I am also indebted to the editor of *Military Affairs* for his permission to incorporate in slightly revised form my article which appeared in the Fall, 1964, issue of the journal. Admiring the strengths of the French, attempting to understand their weaknesses, I believe "eternal France, whose death is feared at any moment," will survive her present and future difficulties as she has done so many times in the past.

ORVILLE D. MENARD

Contents

A section of illustrations follows page 114.

Abbreviations Used

CANAC   Veterans Action Committee
CPS   Committee of Public Safety
CRS   Republican Security Company
EDC   European Defense Community
FLN   National Liberation Front
FFI   French Forces of the Interior
FNF   French National Front
GG   Government General Building
GPRA   Provisional Government of the Algerian Republic
MP 13   Popular Movement of May 13
MRP   Popular Republican Movement
NATO   North Atlantic Treaty Organization
OAS   Secret Army Organization
RPF   Rally of the French People
SAS   Special Administrative Section
SAU   Urban Administrative Section
UNR   Union for the New Republic
USRAF   Union for the Safety and the Resurrection of French Algeria
UT   Territorial Unit (Home Guard)

1st REP   First Foreign Legion Paratroop Regiment
10th DP   Tenth Paratroop Division

THE ARMY AND THE FIFTH REPUBLIC

CHAPTER I

The Guardians

Quis custodiet ipsos custodes?—JUVENAL.

"WHO SHALL keep guard over the guardians themselves?" Such is one of the oldest questions posed for society, yet it is one which is ever reborn and is as current as today. The problem of the military's place and role in a political community may be found in Plato, or one may turn to the daily paper for more recent evidence. Not unfamiliar words are coup d'état, pronunciamento, or praetorianism. The spectacle of military involvement in a nation's political affairs has been common in Latin America;[1] and in the post-World War II era, armies have played important political roles in the underdeveloped countries as well as in the advanced nations of the West.[2]

The sanction of force is familiar in man's ordering of his societal affairs, and although it is but one of the elements of a political community, it is omnipresent. As Michael Howard has phrased it: "At the root of all save the most primitive or the most celestial of social organizations, there must be the sanction of force: force not to create right but uphold it; force to assure order, to cow rebellion at home and to subdue enemies abroad."[3] To cow and to subdue are not tasks for all the

[1] For a description of militarism in Latin America, see Edwin Lieuwen, *Arms and Politics in Latin America* (New York: Frederick A. Praeger, 1960), and by the same author, *Generals vs. Presidents* (New York: Frederick A. Praeger, 1964).

[2] On this aspect, see John J. Johnson, ed., *The Role of the Military in Underdeveloped Countries* (Princeton: Princeton University Press, 1962), in particular the chapter by Lucien Pye, "Armies in the Process of Political Modernization," pp. 69–89, wherein Pye discusses the army as a factor of progress and modernization in underdeveloped nations.

[3] Michael Howard, ed., *Soldiers and Governments* (London: Eyre and Spottiswoode, 1957), p. 11.

members of a community, but are confided to a special group of armed men.

The masses, the unarmed, must therefore establish the safeguards which will restrain their protectors from becoming their masters. "When this danger is viewed in connection with the habitual drive of all groups in society, including the military, to enlarge their influence and maximize their share of the available goods and values," writes Louis Smith, "it may be readily seen how grave the problem of civil-military relations can become." [4] Recognizing the problem of the relation of the armed to the unarmed, a French writer in 1910 told his readers that keeping an army subordinate to civil authority and preventing it from becoming oppressive were extremely delicate tasks. [5]

Inherent in the above statements is the proposition that force is instrumental. The men who bear the legitimate responsibility for using force constitute one of many groups in society, yet in spite of their monopoly of force, these weapon-bearing warriors are to execute the demands of weaponless society. Little wonder that problems of civilian control of the military emerge, perhaps great wonder that there is civilian control at all. To dispose as civil authorities propose is the proper role of the armed instrument. Whether one is a democrat or an autocrat, the instrumental principle of civilian control of the military emphasizes the primacy of the statesman over the soldier in political affairs. [6]

In a study devoted to military science, one finds a clear expression of military subordination to civil authority. Clausewitz's famous dictum, "War is nothing but a continuation of political intercourse, with a mixture of other means," is an affirmation of the political nature of war. [7] Armed conflict is the substitution of bullets for diplomatic notes,

---

[4] Louis Smith, *American Democracy and Military Power* (Chicago: University of Chicago Press, 1951), p. 2. This danger is also discussed by Alfred Vagts in his invaluable *A History of Militarism* (New York: W. W. Norton, 1937), p. 14, as he states: "Armies may protect society if they prepare intelligently for defense; they may threaten it if they lose a sense of proportion between their own interests and those of the rest of society." Or again on p. 320: "The natural tendency of armies is not only towards a self-government brooking no outside influence, but also towards the extension of their power beyond their own needs."

[5] Maurice Hauriou, *Principes de droit public* (Paris: Recueil Sirey, 1910), p. 370.

[6] For a brief discussion of this principle, see Harry L. Coles, ed., *Total War and Cold War* (Columbus: Ohio State University Press, 1962), p. 4.

[7] Karl von Clausewitz, *On War* (4 vols.; London: Kegan Paul, Trench, Trubner, and Co., 1940), III, 121.

but the bullets, like the diplomatic notes, are an expression of policy, the "representative of the interests generally of the whole community." War is but another form of international relations wherein the military becomes the instrumental means to realize national goals. Not for the soldier to judge are the political objectives of the statesman, and the desires of the statesman must prevail. From Clausewitz, a military theorist, comes one of the first justifications for civilian control of the military:

> The subordination of the political point of view to the military would be contrary to common sense, for policy has declared the war; it is the intelligent faculty, war only the instrument, and not the reverse. The subordination of the military point of view to the political is, therefore, the only thing which is possible.[8]

But there is another justification for military subordination to civilian control—the conception, rooted in the democratic tradition, that government action shall be an expression of the general will, that sovereignty rests with the entire people. Within the democratic framework, we again find the military obeying civilian masters. A political system based on the principle that ultimate power is vested in the whole people operates on the postulate that special groups of the body politic, even those holding weapons, will be subordinate to the ultimate power.

Therefore, the vindication for civilian control of the military rests upon two principles: (1) the striking force has a guiding hand which directs its blows, and (2) the democratic concept that the people are sovereign. In the context of the former, the military is not to transcend its instrumental role and dictate to the civilian directors, a relationship which is applicable to all forms of government. In the latter case, no group, not even the armed group of society, has the right to impose its will on the majority of the citizenry.

In the preceding discussion, I have used phrases which are frequently encountered yet rarely defined: "civil-military relations" and "civilian control." The basic issue of the civil-military relationship is whether the civilians or the military will make policy. The words "civilian control" indicate that civil-military relations are not to be an equilibrium but an imbalance in favor of the civilian elements of the state. As Professor Samuel Huntington has asserted, all civilians are not immediately referred to, but only those of the governmental leadership. It then

---

[8] *Ibid.*, p. 125.

follows that "civilian control of the military is government control of the military."[9] Civilian control will be realized in the measure that military "leadership groups and through them the armed forces as a whole respond to the direction of the civilian leaders of government."[10] Civilian control will be eroded to the extent the military is able to impose its desires on and give directions to civilian political leaders. The greater the erosion, the weaker civilian control becomes and the closer the state moves toward militarism or military government.

The means used by the military to play a political role are often similar to the methods used by civilians. To make its views known, the military uses its civilian contacts, for example, veterans' groups, service associations, and sympathetic individuals, its public information programs and legislative liaison personnel, and its specialists who provide expert advice to government leaders. Functioning much like any other bureaucracy or pressure group the military remains within the constitutional, legitimate framework. The armed forces may attempt to influence policy, but ultimately accept their subordinate role, recognizing the responsibility of their civilian superiors to make final decisions.

However, stressing its viewpoints in the name of national security in a world of constant threats, intertwining itself with foreign policy, becoming enmeshed with domestic affairs in demands on the economy and manpower, the military is encouraged to play a more active political role. Although still operating under the cover of existing institutions, great pressure is exerted to impose the course of action desired by the military.

Deeper penetration into a nation's life occurs when the military openly abandons its instrumental role and publicly assumes that of policymaker. Just as civilian groups vie to occupy positions of political power, so too the military may attempt to place its favorites in key decision-making public posts. Having upset the balance of civil-military power (as a civilian group may upset the balance between itself and other civilian groups), the military now dictates its desires to the nation through civilian leadership of its choice or, more rarely, places men of the military establishment in civil leadership positions. After a coup d'état, the latter situation may appear briefly, but usually the

9 Samuel P. Huntington, "Civilian Control of the Military: A Theoretical Statement," in Heinz Eulau, Samuel J. Eldersveld, and Morris Janowitz, eds., *Political Behavior: A Reader in Theory and Research* (Glencoe: The Free Press, 1956), p. 380.
   10 *Ibid.*

soldiers step aside, replace themselves with a civil façade and remain in the wings, prepared to intervene again when necessary.[11]

It seems to be a truism that the degree of military political involvement and the forms it assumes are a reflection of a nation's political situation. Military subordination to civil authority—or the absence thereof—is a result of the general political atmosphere.[12] With his usual perceptiveness, Alexis de Tocqueville went to the heart of the matter when he wrote: "The remedy for the vices of the army is not to be found in the army itself, but in the country."[13] A more recent observer informs us that when an army becomes involved in politics, it is the symbol of the country's "disintegration."[14] An army assuming political power in a state is not an indication that the army has slain the previous regime; it is the signal that the predecessor died of a self-inflicted wound.

An army is an emanation of the nation it serves, reflecting social, political, and technological foundations. To study an army is to gain insights into the nation it serves because a nation and its army are interdependent.[15] An army is not a mirror image of the nation, nor a

[11] On military intervention and methods of intervention, see Samuel E. Finer, *The Man on Horseback* (New York: Frederick A. Praeger, 1962), pp. 86–87 and 140–63, and a very interesting article by Jean Meynaud, "Les militaires et le pouvoir," *Revue française de sociologie*, II (April–June, 1961), 75–87, esp. pp. 79–81. For a description of the political strengths of the military (superior organization, symbolic status, and monopoly of arms) and political weaknesses (technical inability of administering any but primitive communities and lack of legitimacy), see Finer, *The Man on Horseback*, pp. 6–22. On direct and indirect methods of military intervention see Lewis J. Edinger, "Military Leaders and Foreign Policy Making," *American Political Science Review*, LVII (June, 1963), 398–99.

[12] According to Finer, "where public attachment to civilian institutions is strong, military intervention in politics will be weak. It will take the form, if it occurs at all, of working upon or from behind these institutions—be they throne or parliament— according to the political formula current. By the same token, where public attachment to civilian institutions is weak or nonexistent, military intervention in politics will find wide scope—both in manner and substance." Finer, *The Man on Horseback*, p. 20.

[13] Alexis de Tocqueville, *Democracy in America* (2 vols.; Boston: John Allyn, 1873), II, 331.

[14] Giles Perrault, *Les parachutistes* (Paris: Editions du Seuil, 1961), p. 77.

[15] See René Rémond, "La politique et l'armée," in René Rémond, *et al.*, *L'Armée et la nation* (Paris: Arthème Fayard, 1960), p. 11. For a further examination of the study of military institutions as an element of political analysis see David C. Rapoport, "A Comparative Theory of Military and Political Types," in Samuel P. Huntington, ed., *Changing Patterns of Military Politics* (New York: The Free Press

microcosm—the nation writ small; it is, in organization, purposes, attitudes, and behavior, conditioned by the sustaining state. In the less-advanced political cultures, where the division of labor is fluid, the civil-military boundaries are ill distinguished and frequently crossed. Thus there are mixed roles, and less adhesion and attachment to institutional perquisites. The result is the phenomenon of an army trespassing in political territory, performing tasks not properly military, but occasioning little surprise in the less-advanced state.[16]

In the advanced political culture, where there is a highly developed role structure, the military's political role may be expected to be less than in the politically underdeveloped state—but not altogether absent. That it will participate in the political processes is necessary, but that it will attempt to dictate to or overthrow the government is considered a remote possibility. Hence, it is in the advanced state that overt military political activity, as occurred in France in the late 1950's and early 1960's, is most shocking.

Since the time of Napoleon Bonaparte the French army had been an apolitical force, accepting the role of governmental instrument. The French army's tradition of serving civilian masters faithfully and

---

of Glencoe, 1962), pp. 71–101. See also the study of "ideal types" of societal principles and the military organizations derived therefrom by M. D. Feld, "A Typology of Military Organization," in Carl J. Friedrich and Seymour E. Harris, eds., *Public Policy* (Cambridge: Graduate School of Public Administration, 1958), VIII, 3–40. According to Feld, "differences in the missions for which armies are organized provide an essential criterion in the analysis and description of political types, as well as military systems. In the kindred fields of politics and war, the army and the state interact on and influence one another." The quotation is from p. 3. Harold Lasswell's garrison state construct is based on an appreciation of army-state interaction and influence upon one another. See Harold Lasswell, "The Garrison State and Specialists on Violence," *American Journal of Sociology*, XLVI (January, 1941), 455–68, and "The Garrison State Hypothesis Today," in Huntington, *Changing Patterns of Military Politics*, pp. 51–70.

[16] Gabriel Almond writes that in a preindustrial society, "because of the absence of a stable and explicit role structure, there is likely to be a high degree of *substitutability* of roles. Thus bureaucracies may take over the legislative function, and armies may do the same." The more advanced the political system and the more stable and explicit the role structure, the less will be the substitutability of roles. See Gabriel Almond, "Comparative Political Systems," *Journal of Politics*, XVIII (August, 1956), 391–409; the quotation is from p. 402. Georges Vedel expresses the view that the distinction between civilian and military pertains to the division of labor in a society, but that politically there can be but one power—the civilian. The distinction is a result of political maturity, concludes Vedel. See *Le Monde*, July 2, 1960.

without protest had earned for it the nickname, the Great Mute (*la Grande Muette*). However, between 1958 and 1962 France underwent the shock of the Great Mute forsaking its silence and openly engaging in French political life, bringing down one Republic, the Fourth, and seriously threatening the Fifth, the one to which it played midwife. The French army had cast off its instrumental role and assumed the task of prescribing and dictating—it had become a political army.

Men who had fought heroically and faithfully under the French flag for twenty years were to find themselves before national tribunals. Their blouses adorned with the medals attesting to their valor and devotion to France, the most professional fighting men in the world sat on the bench of the accused for conspiring against and attempting to overthrow their government, swearing that in their loyalty to France, they turned upon her government.

What happened to turn France's army into a political army? Why did the army enter the political crisis of May, 1958, when it had refrained from intervention for over a century, a century which witnessed many government crises in France? Why was the army successful in its May, 1958, coup, but progressively less effective thereafter? As for the former problem, the key seems to be that the French army had become an alienated army, led to think in its own terms and to provide its own solutions to national problems.[17]

Nineteenth-century France had created a certain state of mind in the French army, one placing the army above factional political strife, permitting it to serve obediently all governments, no matter how often changed or of what political complexion, since the army's mission, the defense of the fatherland, did not include political involvement. For years the French army, in social background and political attitudes, had been a conservative institution, lukewarm at best to the Third Republic. Nonetheless, the army of these years was content to leave politics to the politicians, to let "fools" contest for forms of government while the army, the sanctuary and safeguard of national values, remained above such controversy. The civilians could pass the country from government to government, but the army would stand constant in its devotion to France, serving the men in power who, at least temporarily, governed France. A reciprocally satisfying relationship existed between army and nation.

[17] See John S. Ambler, *The French Army in Politics* (Columbus: Ohio State University Press, 1966), pp. 42–45; and George A. Kelly, *Lost Soldiers* (Cambridge: The M.I.T. Press, 1965), pp. 15–16.

But under the Fourth Republic, France and her army became strangers and the army assumed the role of diagnostician of and prescriber for French political ills. Events following World War II built a wall of separation between France and her protectors. In the post-World War II years, the French army, fighting in lands outside continental France for extended periods, became separated from France, not only by miles and time, but also in heart and mind. In addition, although France was on the victorious side at the end of World War II, the French contribution to victory did not wash away the stigma of 1940. And in spite of the heroic efforts of France's fighting men, further defeats and humiliations followed, and the Empire, the army's pride and glory, was slowly reduced in size.

Men of the army, long absent from France, lost contact with their homeland. They wore the uniform of France's fighting men, but they no longer knew the country for which they were fighting. They felt betrayed by the politicians of the Palais Bourbon, who sent them to fight and then made peace, who failed to give them clear policies, who made them abandon territories brave men had given their lives to keep French. Humiliation, a sense of abandonment, prolonged absence from the homeland, a sense of being second-class citizens—these became a wall between France and her guardians.

The answer to why the army was successful in 1958 but progressively less effective thereafter, is that for those few days in May, 1958, the alienated French army was at one with the civilians of France in a common desire to bring an end to the *immobilisme* of the Fourth Republic. The military's success registered civilian disillusionment. Thereafter, alienation resulted in continued army attempts to play a political role, but paradoxically it condemned the attempts to failure as the nation rallied to the new government and refused to follow subsequent counsels of the praetorians. From May, 1958, the French army, "by a sort of inverse transfusion, an army which no longer received anything from the nation, was going to try to force the nation to receive its values."[18] But the nation, the donors discovered, was not prepared to receive because it was now following the General, not the generals.

Alienation led the army to prescribe for France, but it also determined the army's failure, except in 1958, when civilians shared the army's disgust with the Fourth Republic. Afterward, the French army could have satisfied its political aspirations only if it had embarked upon the conquest of France and forcibly imposed its will with the tips of the

18 Perrault, *Les parachutistes*, p. 78.

"para" (paratrooper) bayonets. Fortunately for France, most of the army perceived the folly of such a course and its inherent contradiction (saving France would have meant destroying Frenchmen) and bowed to the will of the civilians, whom the army did not understand and who did not understand the army.

Since the days of May, when the French army learned of its political power, a struggle to restore the balance of civil-military relations has gone on in France. An exceptional opportunity to study a politically disposed and active army is afforded by the infant years of the Fifth Republic. Thereby, a greater understanding not only of political armies and their patterns of operation may be gained, but also of the conditions giving birth to such armies.

CHAPTER II

La Grande Muette

*Ma politique? Monsieur, je suis un soldat, je ne fais pas de
politique.*—GENERAL HENRI GIRAUD.

THE FRENCH ARMY in the nineteenth century and the first half of the
twentieth century played the role of a politically neutral and passive
instrument. Two principles governed the army's relations with civil
authority: the complete subordination of the army to civilian government and noninterference in political matters. The Great Mute was an
army that had no politics; its function was to execute the orders of the
government without reflection. To obey was the duty of the soldier, and
the chain of command ultimately reached the civilian Chief of State.
"Neutrality or more exactly political passivity," Professor Raoul
Girardet points out, "became one of the essential dogmas of the military
ethic."[1]

Throughout the Restoration, the reign of Louis Philippe, the Second
Republic, the Second Empire, and the Third Republic, this dogma
remained intact. Individual officers (for example, Generals Georges
Boulanger and Maxime Weygand, and Marshal Patrice de MacMahon)
became politically involved, but the military establishment was neither
party to nor part of their schemes.[2]

[1] Raoul Girardet, *La Société militaire dans la France contemporaine* (Paris: Plon,
1953), p. 119.

[2] According to Professor Girardet, "it is necessary to distinguish between the
person of a military chief, occasionally tempted by political adventure . . . and the
institution of which he is a part, the social body from which he practically separates
himself." *Ibid.*, pp. 253–54. Professor Meisel writes: "But there is still that difference
which must be kept in mind between a military interference which has been solicited
by helpless politicians, and which makes it possible for them to stay in power, and
an act of military usurpation, which removes the civil government and gives all
power to the army. The question then, that must be asked in any single case of

Napoleon Bonaparte overthrew the government of the Directory in November, 1799, with the aid of French troops, bringing to an end an inefficient and discredited government which had little support from the nation. Accomplished by the army with the aid of civilian politicians, the overthrow of the government opened the way for the military dictatorship of the First Consul, later the Emperor of the French, Napoleon Bonaparte. In his efforts to bring "order" and "security" to Europe, Napoleon extended and perfected the nation in arms, compulsory service system bequeathed to him by the Revolutionary period. Preaching to his armies their mission and destiny of extending liberty, equality, and fraternity, Napoleon marched them across Europe. But as the zeal and enthusiasm of France waned, Napoleon relied more and more heavily on conscription, the annual draft rising from sixty thousand in 1804 to 1,140,000 in 1813.[3] When Napoleon sailed for St. Helena, he left behind an exhausted and war-weary France.

With the Bourbon Restoration, France relegated the soldier to a low point of national esteem. The army, the instrument of revolution and destroyer of monarchies, could scarcely be expected to be highly regarded by the nobility. Interested in economic progress, the businessman was hostile to the military, for he considered it economically wasteful. Remembering their heavy losses and the burdens imposed by conscription, the lower classes desired freedom from military obligations.

A small part of the nation, however, continued to favor the army. The two groups most opposed to the Bourbon regime, the Bonapartists, who contrasted Louis XVIII's uninspiring, quasi-parliamentarianism with the glories of the Empire, and the sincere republicans, who considered the army "the necessary instrument of the future triumph of the cause of liberty and of universal democracy," both looked to the army as the means of fulfilling their respective dreams.[4]

military intervention, is: have the military taken the initiative, are they the masters or the servants of the situation, are they making use of it for their own purposes, or are they merely being used?" James H. Meisel, *The Fall of the Republic* (Ann Arbor: The University of Michigan Press, 1962), p. 150. Another author defines military intervention as "*the armed forces' constrained substitution of their own policies and/or their persons, for those of the recognized civilian authorities.*" Samuel E. Finer, *The Man on Horseback* (New York: Frederick A. Praeger, 1962), p. 23; (italics in the original).

[3] Carlton J. H. Hayes, *A Political and Cultural History of Modern Europe* (New York: Macmillan, 1952), p. 669.

[4] Girardet, *La Société militaire*, p. 22; also pp. 8–12 and 20–23. See Lieutenant Colonel MacCarthy, "L'armée française et la politique, 1ère partie: de 1815 à 1870," *L'Armée*, No. 1 (February, 1960), 31–33.

But the army, its officer corps a composite of returned nobles and veterans of the *Grande Armée*, remained foreign to political involvement. Most Frenchmen had little interest in their military forces during the Restoration period as the army, ill paid and little respected, began its retreat into silence. After the military irregularities of the Revolutionary and Empire periods, officers sought discipline and obedience. Performing as ordered, without reflection, became the cult and the sign of the effective officer of the Restoration army. Colonel Victor de Castellane described the atmosphere when he remarked: "If you order me to put the soldiers in slippers, tomorrow they will be in slippers."[5]

Rules were added to rules in the Restoration army. Initiative, courage, and resourcefulness had characterized the officers of the *Grande Armée*, but after 1815 leadership became identified with giving and faithfully executing orders in passive obedience to the chain of command which embodied the power of the military and above it, the state organization. The civilian masters desired that the army confine itself strictly to military tasks and leave the civilian sectors to tend to theirs, free of military interference. In return, the army was permitted to control its own internal affairs.

When Charles X attempted a royal coup d'état, he succeeded only in provoking the "glorious days" of July, 1830. Remaining loyal to the king, the small Paris garrison (in order to ensure the surprise of his coup, Charles had not sent for reinforcements) rejected overtures to rally to the forces opposing Charles, and instead sought to defend him on July 28 and 29. However, by the evening of the twenty-ninth, the rebels had virtually cleared Paris of royal troops. Two regiments did defect, but by then there was little question of the fate of Charles' regime. The impulse for the change was not of army origin, and as defenders of the government, the army clashed with the rebels. But when Paris successfully showed that the Bourbons' time had run out, the army obediently accepted the verdict.

A few mild disturbances and the resignation of two thousand officers true to the Bourbons were the extent of army opposition as the Orléanist Louis Philippe replaced the Bourbon Charles X. The attitude of most officers is manifest in an episode related by Professor Girardet: To demonstrate allegiance to the new regime, a regiment discarded all its equipment that bore the fleur de lis. De Castellane, by now a general, who had been lukewarm toward the Bourbons and who readily accepted the new government, came to inspect the unit. Immediately he had the

[5] Quoted by Girardet, *La Société militaire*, p. 100.

fleur de lis restored, announcing that "nothing . . . must be changed in the uniform without an order from the Minister of War."[6] Within a year, officers were toasting the birthday of Louis Philippe just as they had toasted the birthdays of their previous sovereigns.

After 1830, the theme of François Guizot, "*enrichissez-vous*" (get rich), accorded ill with the military profession, since the soldier was generally regarded as unproductive and a burden on the economy. France's other interests were obvious in her lack of interest in the army. Indicative of the national attitude toward the army during the Restoration and Louis Philippe's citizen-king years was the recruitment policy. After the burdens of conscription imposed by Napoleon, France resorted to a system of drawing lots for military service under the Bourbons and Louis Philippe. Those who drew a "bad" number were eligible for duty; however, the man who was able to afford it could hire a substitute and remain a civilian. Therefore, the weight of serving in the ranks fell upon the lower-class individual, who either could not afford a replacement or who sold himself into service.[7] Moreover, after 1815, the nobility and the middle and upper classes sent few of their sons to the military schools, so that the individuals who rose from the enlisted ranks became the backbone of the officer corps. Since the term of conscription in the enlisted ranks was of long duration (seven years), and since the military as a career was a growing concept in the officer corps, the army was becoming a professional force, the form the nation cast for it.

A slight reversal of attitudes concerning the army was noticeable in the French Left and Right after 1830. (Both Left and Right are used here without any attempt to explain nuances or identify groupings within either orientation. Generally speaking, the Left was the refuge of believers in the Revolution of 1789. Republicanism, egalitarianism, anticlericalism—opposition to the traditional political and social order —were characteristics of the Left. On the Right were found the royalists, the authoritarians, the guardians of social privilege and defenders of the church.) The Left, which had considered the army an instrument of rebirth and revolution, had witnessed the army firing on insurgents in

[6] *Ibid.*, pp. 129–30.

[7] Adolphe Thiers defended this system by asserting that the peasant was better off in the army, while for the man destined for a career in business or other civil pursuits of high station, the military was an intolerable burden. A bourgeois who desired a military career could go to a military school and become an officer. See Joseph Monteilhet, *Les institutions militaires de la France* (Paris: Felix Alcan, 1932), p. 30.

the streets of Paris. As a result, antimilitarism appeared in leftist circles, but not in great measure, for most republicans retained their faith in the army. On the other hand, the Right, which had feared the military for the same reasons the Left had supported it, now began to wonder whether the army might be a trustworthy force for order, a protector against boulevard disturbances.

Under the Orléans monarchy, while campaigns in Algeria busied the army and gained attention from the nation, the officer's material position was bettered. Louis Philippe's army was a faithful force and the regime enjoyed a popularity in military circles which the Restoration monarchs had never experienced. When Paris again rose against the government in February, 1848, the army dutifully fired on the insurgents. Nonetheless, when Louis Philippe wrote out his abdication, ignoring Adolphe Thiers' advice to raise an army and besiege Paris, the army bowed before the results of the revolution and passed under the control of the nation's new masters. Although the army disliked the nascent regime, it obediently responded as the government's servant when ordered to put down workers' riots in June. In contrast to what followed the 1830 change of government, almost no resignations were submitted by army officers after the Revolution of 1848.

But in the years between 1848 and 1851, the army did become a factor in political struggles. Disliking the new regime for being weak and ineffective, for having acted against the army in disarming Paris troops after the February uprising, and for retiring thirty-seven generals in April, 1848, officers gravitated to the support of Louis Napoleon in his differences with the legislative branch. The Assembly, with a conservative majority, desired a monarchical restoration. Louis Napoleon preferred to re-establish the Empire. Between these forces stood the army, solicited by both parties and thus in a position to determine the country's political future.

Accordingly, in December, 1851, the army played the key role in Louis Napoleon's coup by supporting him. In doing so, the army remained in obedience to legal civil authority. Aware of the army's fetish for discipline and hierarchy, Napoleon had appointed trustworthy officers to important posts and removed those cool to his schemes. He thereby created a faithful chain of command and assured the success of his movement. In December, 1851, the army followed the orders of its lawful civilian superior, Louis Napoleon, orders passed to them through the legal civil-military hierarchy. Passive obedience to constituted authority justified the military's support of the President. The day after the coup, General Emile Fleury, Louis Napoleon's aide-de-camp, informed a group of parliamentarians: "We are soldiers; we only know our orders."[8]

Even though the army played a vitally important part in Louis Napoleon's success, it was not the instigator of the coup; there was no pronunciamento. The change of regimes was certainly acceptable to the army, but it was neither the initiator nor the cause of the Second Republic's overthrow. The growing tradition of political neutrality remained intact as the army obeyed legally transmitted orders.[9]

Although the new regime owed much to the army, Louis Napoleon, crowned Napoleon III, did not intend to preside over a military-dominated government. Under Napoleon III, the army continued in its passive role, and the Second Emperor of the French provided the military with no great opportunity to be influential in the conduct of national affairs. In short, the army was permitted to play no political role in the Second Empire.[10]

The army did gain glory and honor, and a strong, stable government to serve, suited to its taste. The discredit that the army had suffered since 1815 was removed by Napoleon III. During his long reign, the army was exalted and parades and military spectacles attracted the nation's attention and won the gratitude of the army. In the Crimea, in the Orient, in Mexico and in Italy, Napoleon opened the way to military glory and the raising of the army's prestige. Victory, popular acceptance, flattery from the crowds and the government—all were again enjoyed by the soldier.

The mystique of order and discipline in the French army reached new heights in the last half of the nineteenth century. Order, obedience, and abnegation became the military man's hallowed trilogy. In its hierarchy

[8] Girardet, *La Société militaire*, p. 142.

[9] On the army and the 1851 coup d'état see *ibid.*, pp. 133–42; Eugene Carrias, *La Pensée militaire française* (Paris: Presses Universitaires de France, 1960), p. 238. One commentator sums up the army role thus: "Without doubt, at the time of the coup d'état, it [the army] was still legally only the 'servant of civil power,' but this time assuredly an enthusiastic servant," Monteilhet, *Les institutions militaire*, p. 32. General André Zeller wrote that the army "facilitated" the change of regimes to gain advantages it felt Napoleon would bring to the army and not from political motivations. "Armée et politique," *Revue de Défense nationale* (April 13, 1951), p. 516; see Meisel, *The Fall of the Republic*, pp. 25–26.

[10] See Girardet, *La Société militaire*, p. 143; MacCarthy, "L'armée française et la politique," p. 39; François Kuntz, *L'officier français dans la nation* (Paris: Charles-Lavauzelle et Cie., 1960), p. 46.

and in the material discomforts of the soldiers' life, the profession was compared with the church, which shared these virtues and which was also a symbol of order and authority. It is therefore not surprising that in this period the traditional conservative milieus (the old aristocracy), found shelter in the uniform and the robe. Besides, the military career had regained its attractiveness, and it was no longer considered a social error to send a son to Saint-Cyr, France's foremost military academy.[11]

In the course of Louis Napoleon's pompous, grandiloquent reign, the professionalization of the army continued. From 1855, the Second Empire offered re-enlistment bonuses to keep the trained men who constituted the core of the army. The army felt that strength was found in quality and not in mere numbers, and long-term service in a professional army was considered to be the basis of military power. The process of the lottery remained in use to select enlisted men, and the poor continued to provide the men of the ranks, since others could still buy their way out by payment of the "fee of exoneration."[12] At the same time, France's bourgeois elements accepted the professional army, because it left them free from military obligations. If a "bad" number was unfortunately drawn, a substitute could be bought as a replacement. The army, organized in a manner reflecting national preferences, continued in its role of obedience to civil authority.[13]

The fears entertained by a few on the Left and the hopes held by some on the Right after 1830 were realized in 1848. The army was now definitely understood to be the force of order, the instrument of quelling rebellion, the rampart against revolution. The positions of 1815 had been reversed. The Left had then exalted the army as the symbol of revolution and had considered it the instrument of national rebirth, while the Right had feared it as the destroyer of monarchy and traditional society. After 1848 the Left turned to antimilitarism; the Right embraced the army as the social order's protector and it became the symbol of constituted authority, not of revolution. Hence, the Right became the army's defenders while the Left, increasingly throughout the Second Empire, emerged as its assailant. The army's revolutionary tradition died hard, and attacks against the army from the Left became

[11] Girardet, *La Société militaire*, pp. 26, 75–76; John Terraine, "The Army in Modern France," *History Today*, XI (November, 1961), 735–36.

[12] Arpad Kovacs, "French Military Legislation in the Third Republic, 1871–1940," *Military Affairs*, XIII (Spring, 1949), 1–2.

[13] Kovacs adds that the maintenance of a professional army was a political maneuver of Napoleon III, since he deemed that the bourgeoisie if not burdened with military duties would tolerate his rule. *Ibid.*, p. 1.

numerous only in the last years of the reign of Napoleon III. By then, there had appeared a generation of republicans who had no recollection of the Revolution and Napoleonic armies and who were more prone to criticize an army which to them was clearly associated with the status quo.

Their themes centered on the army as a school of vice, as a sure path to moral degradation, and as a menace to prosperity. The horrors of war were decried, and even the Revolutionary period was condemned, for the army had been engaged in wars of conquest rather than confined to defense of the national territory. In 1867, Léon Gambetta, then a young man of the radical Left, proposed the abolition of professional armies, scoring them as a "source of financial ruin" and "hate among peoples." To replace the professional armies, the Left called for the creation of citizen armies, whose sole purpose would be the defense of the nation. The army composed of professionals, representative of war and repression, would have to be replaced by the army of the people.[14]

Then came 1870, and the massive Prussian army jolted the proud professional French army with a powerful shock. On September 1, 1870, MacMahon's forces at Sedan broke after weak resistance against the invader. Three days later, Napoleon's empire collapsed before crowds demonstrating in favor of the proclamation of a republic. The army, which the Emperor had favored and fostered, found neither voice nor will nor regiments to defend Napoleon III or uphold his rule. Passing under the orders of the provisional government, the army again followed the lead of the nation and submitted to new civilian superiors.

In spite of the feverish efforts of the Minister of War, the fiery and colorful Gambetta, to raise a nation in arms, the units sent into battle were no match for the Prussians, and France was forced to capitulate. In February, 1871, France elected an assembly which reluctantly accepted peace terms on March 1. Later in the same month, the assembly faced new difficulties when its authority was challenged and a civil war began which racked and ravaged the French capital for sixty-two days, in the battle known as the Commune of Paris. Obedient to France's new leaders, the army followed government orders and finally, after the loss of twenty thousand lives in the repression of the uprising, restored order.

After the tumult and fearful experiences of 1870 and 1871, France faced the problem of recasting her political and military institutions.

---

[14] The antimilitarism of the Left during the Second Empire is frequently referred to by Girardet, *La Société militaire*, pp. 33–45.

Politically, a compromise Third Republic emerged out of a welter of conflicting factions, none individually powerful enough to dictate what the political order should be. Militarily, it had been learned that mass armies were necessary to defeat mass armies. Therefore, the principle of universal military service had few opponents in France after 1872. In addition, because of the bloody crushing of the Commune, the Left saw its fears of the professional military as an agent of repression realized. The Right, on the other hand, had its faith in the army as a dutiful defender of order sustained.

Yet in spite of these differences concerning the army, France's military forces became the object of veneration and respect in the quarter century following 1870. The spirit of *revanche* (revenge) was more powerful than disagreements over the army's internal role and it became an institution placed above factional strife, acclaimed from all sides. The army was hailed as the "common denominator" of the nation, honored as the symbol of revenge for the lost provinces of Alsace and Lorraine, and promoted as the means of obliterating the shame of the Franco-Prussian war. Applications for Saint-Cyr tripled, and to be an officer was to be a member of a highly honored and respected profession. To have a son at Saint-Cyr during this period was an "indisputable criterion of respectability."[15]

A sacrosanct aura as the symbol of national rebirth encircled the army. In its exalted position, the army gained support from both the Right and the Left in the years following 1870. The former continued to regard the army as a defender against internal disturbances and as a school of social discipline. The latter, with the adoption of universal conscription, viewed the army as the expression of its equalitarian ideas and looked upon it as a school of citizenship and preparation for public service.[16]

In the early years of the Third Republic, the aristocrats continued to provide officers for the army. The Empire's prestige and glory had earlier attracted them, while after 1870 the closing of the political and administrative avenues to these conservative elements by the republicans channeled them into the military. An army preference for an authoritarian regime was inherited from Napoleon III's empire, in which many

---

[15] Lieutenant Colonel MacCarthy, "L'armée française et la politique, 2è partie: 1870 à nos jours," *L'Armée*, No. 2 (March 2, 1960), 40.

[16] *Ibid.*, p. 39; Girardet, *La Société militaire*, pp. 172–81; Edward Behr, "The French Army as a Political and Social Factor," *International Affairs*, XXXV (October, 1959), 439.

officers of the Third Republic had served. Like their superiors, the young men from the traditional backgrounds who entered the officer corps after 1870 favored a government of autocratic order and stability.

However, this bias of the military was an attitude and not an active political position. A stronger sentiment in the army was the desire to be autonomous within the nation (hence the difficulties in the Dreyfus case) in an isolated, particular profession. Above civil strife and bourgeois values, the officer considered himself part of a special corps distinct from society, and he distrusted any fellow officer who had contacts with the outside civilian world. Promotion boards looked with favor upon the officer who remained indifferent to politics, and askance upon the one who had political preferences. By means of their professional particularism, officers were able to attach themselves to their own society and mores, and military men were able to serve any government, for the officers' allegiance was to the army and to the nation, the latter considered distinct from and superior to transient and ephemeral governments.[17]

Passive obedience to the orders of civilian superiors was also part of the military heritage received from the Second Empire. Stronger than rightist sentiment, the cult of discipline fostered the tradition of the Great Mute. While it may have mentally opposed republican measures and government, no conspiracy against the Republic was evident, not even in the height of army discontent, between 1900 and 1911. Reference to the army as a potential threat to government, but also to the army's restraining discipline, are both contained in the following words of Felix Faure, President of France from 1895 to 1899:

> There is much talk of a military coup d'état. If one were to occur, an attempt will be made to arrest me in my office. Some general enters, sword in hand, followed by his officers. I look him squarely in the eye and tell him: "General, fifteen days of confinement in a fortress!"
>
> He puts the sword back into its sheath.
>
> That's the end of the coup d'état.[18]

That antirepublican sentiments were indeed extant in the army during this period is demonstrated in the *fiches de Gambetta* (Gambetta's

[17] Girardet, *La Société militaire*, pp. 248–56; MacCarthy, "L'armée française et la politique, 2è partie," pp. 42–43.

[18] Quoted by Nathan Leites, *On the Game of Politics in France* (Stanford: Stanford University Press, 1959), p. 149.

notes). While working with the Gambetta papers in the archives of the French Foreign Affairs Ministry, François Bédarida discovered two notebooks, secret dossiers on the French army compiled in the first years of the Third Republic.[19] Apparently gathered by republican informers in liaison with the Freemasons, the two notebooks contained information on the political attitudes of French officers, in addition to their professional competency.

One notebook, presumably compiled in 1876, is concerned with officers serving in the army's line elements; the second source, put together in 1878 according to Bédarida, contains information on officers who were serving in French military schools. The *fiches* disclose that the officers of the "fighting" army were predominantly antirepublican in their political orientation while those of the "study" army were, in the majority, republican. As to the former, Bédarida concludes, "The French army, at its different echelons . . . was directed by leaders whose opinions were, at least for three-quarters of them, unfavorable to the republican regime. . . ."[20] However, the second group's importance must not be overlooked, since the men in the military schools, found to be three-out-of-five republican in their orientation, were training the young men who would be the officers of the future "fighting" army.[21]

Organizationally, after 1870 the French army changed from a body of long-term professionals to one based on short-term conscription. A professional training cadre and the steady flow of draftees turned the army into a mixture of career soldiers and those who briefly passed under their tutelage (a cadre-conscript army). After the fall of the Second Empire, the main issue concerning military legislation was how long the draftee would serve. The Right preferred a relatively long tour

[19] François Bédarida, "L'Armée et la République," *Revue Historique*, CCXXXII (July–September, 1964), 119–64.

[20] *Ibid.*, p. 145.

[21] Notebook no. 1 includes information on 187 out of 234 general officers exercising command responsibilities in 1876. Of the 187, 70 percent were found to be antirepublican in political orientation (antirepublican being those considered to be Bonapartists, royalists—either legitimists or Orléanists—and conservatives, sometimes called reactionaries in the *fiches*); 8 percent were found to be republican, 2 percent neutral, and 2 percent unknown as to their political viewpoints. Notebook no. 2 demonstrated that of the 311 officers at the military schools (ranging in grade from lieutenant to general) only 32 percent were antirepublican, while 63 percent were prorepublican, with 4 percent neutral and 1 percent unknown. See the charts in *ibid.*, pp. 142 and 147.

of duty, the Left a shorter one. Supported by the Right, the generals stressed that a large force composed of experienced men was necessary to ward off aggression. The Left argued for an army based on trained citizens available for military service in an emergency. Earlier the Left's position had been advanced as a means of weakening the autocratic regime of Napoleon III; now it was advocated on the grounds that it would create an army loyal to the Republic, since the army would become a school for the nation, a school of citizenship.[22]

In the national legislature, Thiers was the champion of the conservative viewpoint, placing his faith in a semiprofessional army capable of putting down uprisings such as the Commune of Paris. On the Left, the leader was Gambetta, who led the fight for a national army of large reserves. In July, 1872, a compromise was reached. While Thiers had argued for seven years' service, the actual commitment was set for some at five years. The Left, which had desired short-term universal and equal military service, was also satisfied only partially. The prospective draftees were divided into two classes, one-half to serve five years, the other half to serve one year, with the division established by the old method of drawing lots. Furthermore, the holders of a university degree could, on the payment of fifteen hundred francs, contract for one year.[23] Not until 1889 was equal military service made a reality; at that time the service commitment became three years for all, seminarists and priests excepted.[24]

During the last years of the nineteenth century, the army's period of acclamation and of being a symbol of national unity came to an end. The army remained in the foreground, but now it symbolized division rather than unity as the differences between the Left and Right were amplified and the latter rallied to defend the army while the former returned to the attack. By appearing for a time to be in a position to threaten the Republic, General Boulanger and the affair that bears his name resurrected the fears of the Left concerning the army.

[22] Kovacs, "French Military Legislation," pp. 3–4; Richard D. Challener, *The French Theory of the Nation in Arms 1866–1939* (New York: Columbia University Press, 1955), p. 52.

[23] See Kovacs, "French Military Legislation," pp. 3–4; Kuntz, *L'officier français*, p. 59; Ernest Lavisse, *Histoire de France contemporaine* (10 vols.; Paris: Hachette, 1921), III, 330–32; and the account of the background and conflict over the July, 1872, draft law in Gabriel Hanotaux, *Contemporary France* (4 vols.; New York: Putnam, 1903), I, 452–69.

[24] Kuntz, *L'officier français*, p. 60; Kovacs, "French Military Legislation," p. 5.

Boulanger had won a series of by-elections to the Chamber of Deputies in 1887 and 1888, and then soundly defeated a strong republican candidate in a Paris by-election in January, 1889. With evidence of such popularity, many of Boulanger's backers believed the moment was ripe for a coup d'état, but the General preferred to wait for the general elections, when he believed he would be voted into power in a nation-wide burst of enthusiasm. Boulanger's plan was to head a list in every district in France, and on the basis of his expected widespread election strength, assume the leadership of the nation. However, his plans ignominiously collapsed. Believing that the government was going to try him for treason, Boulanger fled to Belgium. In the general elections held in September, the failure of the Boulanger movement was demonstrated as only a handful of his followers won seats in the Chamber of Deputies, ending Boulanger's political aspirations.

Although the Boulanger affair restored the Left's fears concerning the army, the military establishment had little to do with the movement. Civilians provided the General's support, notably from monarchist and Bonapartist circles. The army held itself aloof from both Boulanger and political controversy concerning the aspiring Caesar. Individual ambition, not army political designs, mark the Boulanger affair. However, the General's short but dazzling successes troubled the republicans, for they observed in certain circles the desire to return to authoritarian government and a distaste for the parliamentary regime. Boulanger's contacts with rightist elements made the Right an even greater target of suspicion; the fact that he was a general made the army such a target.[25]

The affair enhanced republican distrust of the army, and the Left determined to remove from the army all possibilities of threatening the Republic. The solution, it was thought, was to republicanize the army, long the stronghold of conservative thought and support. The Dreyfus affair afforded the Left an opportunity to put its program into effect.

The details of the Dreyfus affair have been frequently recounted, so they shall not be retold here.[26] It suffices to point out that in this alleged

[25] Girardet, *La Société militaire*, p. 178; Michael Howard, ed., *Soldiers and Governments* (London: Eyre and Spottiswoode, 1957), p. 59; Paul-Marie de la Gorce, *The French Army* (New York: George Braziller, 1963), pp. 18–19; René Rémond, "La politique et l'armée," in René Rémond, *et al.*, *L'Armée et la nation* (Paris: Arthème Fayard, 1960), p. 13.

[26] See the excellent account by Guy Chapman, *The Dreyfus Case* (New York: Reynal and Co., 1955).

case of treason, the question ultimately centered on the army's right to function as an autonomous organization free from civilian interference —the key issue was the relation of a democratic state to its army. The army considered civilian and military justice to be separate, and the army's resistance against civilian interference into what officers considered their jurisdiction won the army allies in rightist circles. The attempt to break down the military attitude of separateness was supported by the Left, and from 1898 the military became the object of leftist attacks, particularly from the Socialists. An effect of these antimilitary sallies was to enhance mutual suspicions among civilians and officers.[27]

Although the army suffered a barrage of criticism during the Dreyfus affair and it felt its honor was impugned, there seems to be no evidence of any plans for political disobedience or a coup d'état. Resentful and embittered, the army nonetheless remained obedient. When the army's twice-found verdict of Dreyfus' guilt was reversed by a civilian court in 1906, the military accepted the judgment. Paul-Marie de la Gorce has observed, "The underlying significance of the Dreyfus Affair, grave as it appeared at the time, is that nevertheless neither the Army nor the Nation had any serious thought of challenging the basis of their relationship. Not a trace can be found in military circles at that time of any attempt to overthrow the regime."[28]

But the French army now entered a period of *malaise* and of difficulties which would last to the eve of World War I. Contributing factors to this condition were the Boulanger affair and the Dreyfus situation. In addition, after 1900, France experienced a current of pacifism and a feeling of repugnance toward a profession regarded as brutish and unprofitable. The army lost its career appeal, and Saint-Cyr's reduced enrollments reflected the decline in the officer's prestige. Once again the army had fallen into national disfavor.

Another factor in the military discontent of these years was the anti-clerical actions of the Radicals, who assumed power in 1899, dominating the cabinet of the moderate René Waldeck-Rousseau. Waldeck-Rousseau initiated the attack on the church, aimed at expelling those religious orders which had been most involved in the anti-Dreyfus circles (the Assumptionists and the Jesuits). However, the Dreyfusards

[27] *Ibid.*, pp. 322–23. Chapman mentions in particular as antimilitarist writers the journalist Urbain Gohier, the schoolmaster Gustave Hervé, and the political theorist Georges Sorel. See also Howard, *Soldiers and Governments*, p. 62.

[28] De la Gorce, *The French Army*, p. 2; see Chapman, *The Dreyfus Case*, p. 200; Terraine, "The Army in Modern France," p. 738.

in the Chamber, convinced the church had been involved in an anti-republican plot with the military in the Dreyfus affair, amended the Waldeck-Rousseau bill to exclude all religious orders not authorized by Parliament.

Emile Combes, who succeeded Waldeck-Rousseau as Premier in 1902, carried the antichurch measures much further. In 1905 several laws were passed separating church and state in France. Priests and bishops no longer would be paid by the state, and title to church property was transferred to the state. When civil servants went to inventory church property they were often met by parishioners unwilling to grant the state's representative entrance to their church. To disperse the crowds, the army was frequently called upon, an army commanded by officers many of whom, being from conservative families, had been raised in the Catholic faith. Officers underwent a crisis of conscience as they were ordered to enforce the edicts of the state against their church. Those who refused to carry out their orders were broken; others resigned rather than execute their orders; many obeyed, but with bitterness.

Meanwhile, the leftist plan to republicanize the army was put into effect between 1899 and 1905. Waldeck-Rousseau's first Minister of War, General Gaston Galliffet, took the first step when he suppressed the Commissions of Classification. These commissions were responsible for making nominations for promotions in the officer grades and were staffed by generals; the system of promotion was thus one of co-option. Galliffet transferred this power from the generals to the Minister of War, the representative of the government. Advancement was thereby placed in the hands of civil authority, and promotions became a weapon in the republicanization of the army.[29]

Galliffet's successor continued the mission of breaking the conservatives' hold on the army. General Louis André, who served under both Waldeck-Rousseau and Combes (from June, 1900, to November, 1904), in his attempts to promote "reliable" officers, sought information on the politics and religion of army officers. Since André felt he could not rely for information on officers who might themselves be antirepublican or Catholic (regarded as conservative and authoritarian), he turned to the Radical party. With the help of his allies, in four years André accumulated twenty-five thousand notes (*fiches*), containing personal information about French officers. To stop an officer's

[29] MacCarthy, "L'armée française et la politique, 2è partie," p. 45.

advancement, a *fiche* had only to mention that "he goes to mass" or "his wife goes to mass" or "he put his children in a Jesuit school."[30]

On December 28, 1904, a rightist deputy, Guyot de Villeneuve, publicly denounced the system and produced incriminating documents delivered to him by an employee of the Freemasons, whose Paris head-quarters had served as a *fiches* collection center. André resigned as Minister of War, but his leaving did not stop the furor, since every promotion of his four-year tenure as minister was brought under suspicion. But by the time André's spynet was exposed, he had made enough changes to ensure that the high command was no longer a clerical-monarchical stronghold.

Conscription policy also demonstrated the ardor of the Left's attack on the army. In 1905 the term of military service was reduced to two years; the army, as the republicans had long desired, was to become a vast classroom to teach republicanism to the young men who entered the barracks for a brief period of their lives. Officers were to be teachers of republican ideals, imbuing the recruits with the virtues of citizenship. In place of the military's blind discipline would be obedience drawn from republican convictions, learned not from the martinets of old but from teachers of civic responsibility.

However, when the threat of war loomed in Europe, the term of service was re-established at three years (in 1913), in answer to the generals' demands for soldiers on hand rather than in reserve. Military ideals of obedience returned and triumphed over the civilian attitudes that had penetrated the army a few years before, and the old soldier of the traditional mold again became the model. Confronted with the threat of imminent war, the nation returned the army to the army.

The Boulanger affair, the Dreyfus controversy, the church-state dif-ficulties, and the efforts to republicanize it, produced in the French army in the late nineteenth and early twentieth centuries a period of crisis. Yet for all of its difficulties, the army remained subordinate and in the tradition of political passivity. The tradition of obeying the civilian leadership, embodied in whatever system, is well expressed in the following words: "The day after the reversals of legality, changes of regime, we see him [the soldier] pass with a gloomy fatalism to the side

[30] Quoted by Girardet, *La Société militaire*, p. 261; on the *affaire des fiches* see *ibid.*, pp. 257–58; Chapman, *The Dreyfus Case*, pp. 335–40.

of the rebels, fought the night before, but who have now become the legal masters of the country."[31]

As World War I approached, the nation once more looked favorably upon its army. Antimilitarism declined, patriotism gripped French hearts, and the army resumed its status as the symbol of national unity. The officer regained his prestige and sense of usefulness as the nation, in the face of external danger, restored the army to a position above factional controversy.

When World War I came, France put herself under the virtual military dictatorship of Marshal Joseph Joffre. National leadership passed back to Parliament, however, when the General failed to win the expected quick victory, and Joffre was replaced by General Robert Nivelle in late 1916. Nivelle was no more successful than Joffre, and he was finally ruined by the Chemin des Dames offensive in 1917 (which was followed by mutinies in the French army).[32] Nivelle had been Parliament's man, and now both the military and the legislative body had lost face. When the Paul Painlevé Cabinet fell in November, 1917, President Raymond Poincaré called Georges Clemenceau to be Premier. With Clemenceau's elevation to the head of the government, France found herself under a civilian dictatorship headed by a man "whose name symbolized the will to victory." The army, which had exercised the leadership of France in the early days of the conflict, retreated to its subordinate role.[33]

With the return of peace, the army as a whole remained the Great Mute, except for two officers who engaged in political affairs in the immediate postwar years. One of these was Marshal Ferdinand Foch (Commander in Chief of the Allied armies), who protested against several articles of the peace treaty and threatened to resign as Commander in Chief if the Rhine were not made the French military frontier. The other officer was General Charles Mangin, who became involved in separatist efforts for an independent Rhineland. Both Foch and Mangin felt that French security dictated the necessity of separating the Rhineland from Germany. For his efforts, Mangin was relieved of

[31] Pierre Chalmin, *L'Officier français de 1815 à 1870* (Paris: Marcel Rivière et Cie., 1957), p. 361.

[32] For an account of the mutinies, see Richard M. Watt, *Dare Call it Treason* (New York: Simon and Schuster, 1963).

[33] On the conflicts between the army and the government and the evolution from military dictatorship to civilian dictatorship see Jere Clemens King, *Generals and Politicians* (Berkeley and Los Angeles: University of California Press, 1951). The quotation is from p. 192.

his command and ordered by the Minister of War to limit himself to military matters. Foch did not resign, but neither did his views prevail.[34]

With Foch and Mangin we are again dealing with individual involvement in politics and not institutional involvement. The army was not behaving politically; two officers were. Neither of them had organized army support, nor did the army attempt to use its influence to back either the Marshal or the General. They acted alone, and alone they failed.

Unlike the defeat of 1870, the victory of 1918 brought no national rallying to the army. Morale and prestige in the army dropped as France, in weariness and dread of war, became increasingly pacifist and the national concerns became economy, security, and peace. Army theorists devoted themselves to defensive doctrines, and the Maginot line, the symbol of defense, resulted. Military service was cut to one year by the 1927–1928 measure which also provided the funds for the Maginot line. The state of the active army reached the point where one writer could observe that "there was no more standing army, unless the garrisons of the Maginot line could be considered such."[35]

In the twenties and thirties the army experienced another time of doldrums, and the seeds of alienation were planted in an army ignored and forgotten by the nation. Paul-Marie de la Gorce, speaking of the trials of France and her army in these years, particularly after the stock market crash of 1929, states:

> No one could have foreseen that in a mere ten years a total situation would develop which would split Army and country, rupture the unity of the traditional state and yet, in the long run, be only the preliminary to a revolution that would convert the Army into a political force. The road that led to May 13, 1958, and the French uprising in Algeria, can be traced back to the stresses of the thirties.[36]

In 1940, France was easily defeated by a vibrant German army. A few officers and politicians, such as Charles de Gaulle and Paul Reynaud, had argued that France needed a mechanized army manned by

[34] On Foch's and Mangin's attempts to influence the Versailles Treaty see De la Gorce, *The French Army*, pp. 147–71; and Alfred Vagts, *A History of Militarism* (New York: W. W. Norton, 1937), p. 312.

[35] Kovacs, "French Military Legislation," p. 12.

[36] De la Gorce, *The French Army*, p. 218.

professionals, but the venerated Marshal Henri Pétain and General Maxime Weygand, France's most influential military figures, continued to think in the static terms of Verdun's trenches. When the Germans finally attacked after the winter of the phony war (1939–1940), the French army, which had been thought to be a well-trained and well-equipped force, was no match for the German Panzer divisions.

As the situation crumbled around them, Weygand, who had been recalled from Syria to become Commander in Chief of French forces, clashed with Premier Paul Reynaud, who had taken office in March.[37] As German troops marched over France, Weygand exceeded his military role and entered the political realm, taking a position in opposition to the course desired by Reynaud. The Premier thought that French forces in contact with the enemy should surrender, but with the government retaining its right to continue the fight elsewhere. Weygand angrily refused to consider a purely military surrender. In his opinion, to do so would cast shame upon the army, and for Weygand, any field of battle other than France was inconceivable. Germany had beaten France; France must leave the war. Weygand declared that he would not leave for overseas even if put in chains.

According to Weygand, the government's only choice was to capitulate and sign an armistice. The war would then be over and although France would be partially occupied, part of the army, the symbol of order, would remain free. Reynaud's course, warned Weygand, led to occupation and the direct control of France by the Germans. As Winston Churchill observed:

> This was a substantial argument, but it belonged to the Government of the Republic and not to the Commander-in-Chief of the Army to decide upon it. Weygand's position that because the army under his orders would in his opinion fight no more, the French Republic must give in and order its armed forces to obey an order which he was certainly willing to carry out, finds no foundation in the law and practice of civilized states or in the professional honor of the soldier. In theory at least the Prime Minister had his remedy. He could have replied: "You are affronting the Constitution of the

[37] General Weygand was an antirepublican. As a young captain he had contributed to a monument built for Colonel Hubert Henry, the General Staff officer whose forged letter helped condemn Dreyfus. Saul K. Padover, "France in Defeat: Causes and Consequences," *World Politics*, II (April, 1950), 312. Padover attributes France's defeat to three causes: men, materials, and morale, classified as inept, inadequate, and low.

Republic. You are dismissed from this moment from your command. I will obtain the necessary sanction from the President."[38]

But Reynaud was in no position to take such action. Weygand was backed by the prestigious figure of Marshal Pétain, who was at the center of a circle of defeatist ministers. Weygand's view, shared by Pierre Laval, who desired not only peace with Germany but also collaboration, prevailed and on June 22, 1940, France left the war.

It has been written that Weygand's "aim was to preserve both the military hierarchy and the state, for which he was willing to pay the price of an armistice with Germany."[39] Was it Weygand's aim or the army's aim? Individual or institutional involvement? Weygand's challenge to Reynaud appears to be another instance of individual political action, for "prior to June 16, when Paul Reynaud resigned, there was no indication of a general movement among the totality of the military leaders, in favor of an armistice."[40]

Suggesting that Marshal Pétain should replace him, Reynaud resigned after a majority of his Cabinet voted to ask Germany's armistice terms. The principle of passive obedience dictated that the army would pass under the new government to be formed by the aged hero of Verdun. However, instead of adherence to the tradition of obedience came a call to disobedience. On the morning of the seventeenth, General Charles de Gaulle left Bordeaux for England and the very next evening, speaking over the BBC, asked the army to join him in disobeying France's legally constituted government. In his "call to honor," he announced:

> I, General de Gaulle, now in London, call on all French officers and men who are at present on British soil or may be in the future, with or without arms . . . to get in touch with me.[41]

With his summons, De Gaulle offered a torturous choice to the French army's men and officers: whether to remain faithful to the

[38] Winston Churchill, *Their Finest Hour* (Boston: Houghton Mifflin Co., 1949), p. 202. On Weygand's intervention during the June crisis see *ibid.*, pp. 200–215; De la Gorce, *The French Army*, pp. 296–306; Phillip Bankwitz, "Maxime Weygand: A Study in Civil-Military Relations," *The Journal of Modern History*, XXXI (September, 1959), 225–42.

[39] De la Gorce, *The French Army*, p. 304.

[40] *Ibid.*, p. 306.

[41] Charles de Gaulle, *The Call to Honour* (New York: The Viking Press, 1955), p. 84.

tradition of obedience or continue the struggle against Germany. Most remained with Pétain; some answered De Gaulle's call and joined the Free French. Many, after the dissolution of the armistice army in November, 1942 (the armistice army, composed of units which had not been demobilized, had served as a force of internal order and amounted to about 100,000 men), then joined the Resistance. The divided army clashed in Syria and Frenchmen fought Frenchmen, with one thousand Vichy French slain and eight hundred Free French. Concerning the difficulties of the World War II years, it has been said that "by some it has never been forgiven; by none has it been forgotten."[42]

Following World War II, after brief exaltation and praise of the army, a negative attitude toward the military again swept France. The defeat of 1940 had smashed the glorious tradition of the army and the small contribution of Free France to the Allied victory could not wash away the blot on the army's honor. Its prestige fell further as the once-proud French army, which had been the symbol of national greatness, was unable to match the world's great powers in the development of modern weapons and it had to rely on a foreign power, the United States, to bolster military budgets.[43]

Civilians and military men engaged in recriminations over the 1940 defeat, the former accusing the officers of stupidity and incompetence, the latter accusing the politicians of having failed to provide adequate equipment.[44] Distrust, doubt, and lack of confidence was the heritage

[42] Terraine, "The Army in Modern France," p. 740. See John S. Ambler's chapter, "Disgrace Through Discipline, 1939–1945," in his *The French Army in Politics* (Columbus: Ohio State University Press, 1966), pp. 56–89.

[43] See Edward L. Katzenbach, "The French Army," *Yale Review*, XLV (Summer, 1956), 504–6.

[44] The conflict still rages. For example, on July 12, 1960, the Socialist Joseph Paul-Boncour at a meeting of the surviving deputies who had voted against investing Pétain with full powers on July 10, 1940, argued, "we had as many, if not more, tanks than Germany . . . it is not their number which was insufficient, it was their use which was defective. It is not the fault of the deputies, nor of the senate. It is that of a too conformist high command which did not listen to the prophetic warnings of Colonel de Gaulle." *Le Monde*, July 12, 1960. Whether France had as many tanks as Germany in 1940 has been a disputed point. One study relates that during the period from May 10 to June 1, 1940, the French were able to engage only 1,520 tanks against the Germans' 2,683. Ten days later the French had brought into action 2,262 modern and 540 obsolete tanks. The difficulty of France seems to have been that she parceled out her tanks to infantry units, thus widely separating her armored strength. The German mechanized divisions thus met few forces able to oppose them. See Major A. Wauquier, "Les forces cuirassées dans la bataille," *Revue d'histoire de la deuxième guerre mondiale*, III (June, 1953), 163–64.

of World War II for civil-military relations in France. In the face of the great powers and their nuclear weapons, a sense of helplessness was added, for it was felt that no matter how much attention was given to the army, it still would not be capable of defending France.

The low popular esteem of the army was reflected in a shying away from a military career by France's young men. The army's lack of prestige, lower than at any time since the 1920's, the general attitude of doubt concerning the military, the army's humiliation after 1940 and yet again in Indochina, contributed to deter Frenchmen from a military career and lead them to other pursuits. Further deterrents, also reflecting the national attitude toward the army, was the low social standing of the officer and his modest rate of pay.

In the postwar period, the officer was relegated to the lower levels of the social scale, and the days when the insignia of command indicated social standing appeared to be over, culminating a decline which had begun after 1918. An indication of the officers' situation is provided by their pay, mediocre in comparison with those of their civilian countrymen and far lower than that of other nations' officers. In 1953, for example, a French major was making three times less than his American counterpart. In that year, a French officer making 95,000 francs a month would have been paid 120,000 francs in England, 220,000 in Russia, and 280,000 in America.[45]

A development in connection with salaries served to increase the military's bitterness toward their civilian masters. It was decided in 1947 to re-classify officers into the civil service hierarchy and create a single pay structure for all state servants. For a profession which had long considered itself a special body of the state, being lumped into the same pay scale with civil servants was a bitter experience. Furthermore, the classifications that were made angered the officers since they felt they were scaled much lower in relation to the civil servants than their training, skills, responsibilities, and experience warranted. For example, a lieutenant colonel with twenty-four years' service was placed in a lower pay classification than a director of the second class in customs.[46]

[45] Raoul Girardet, "Civil and Military Power in the Fourth Republic," in Samuel P. Huntington, ed., *Changing Patterns of Military Politics* (New York: The Free Press of Glencoe, 1962), p. 127; see Capitaines T. and A. "Capitaines, ou bas-officiers? Essai sur la structure sociale de l'armée française," *La nouvelle critique*, No. 107 (June, 1959), 68–69.

[46] De la Gorce, *The French Army*, pp. 353–54; Jean Planchais, *Le Malaise de l'armée* (Paris: Plon, 1958), p. 17; and especially Raoul Girardet, *et al.*, *La Crise militaire française* (Paris: Armand Colin, 1964), pp. 108–28.

Another blow was the government's discharge of thousands of career officers and enlisted men. Immediately after the Liberation, the army was faced with the problem of assimilating the various forces that existed at the end of the war: the Free French, the FFI (*Forces françaises de l'intérieur*), and the Regular army. Finding herself with too many officers, France decided to reduce their number. The reduction in strength, which was instigated in civilian circles to meet reduced military credits, struck 45 percent of the officer corps and 40 percent of the noncommissioned officers during 1946 and 1947, as over 12,000 men were eliminated from the army. Of the officers who became civilians, 53 percent were graduates of Saint-Cyr and 65 percent of the Ecole Polytechnique.

It was left to the army to decide who would be released. Some units asked for volunteers, others arbitrarily reduced retirement ages, while contacts and personal preferences and differences played their inevitable part. As a consequence, "the release of the cadres opened a wound which is not yet closed."[47] The disastrous effects of the discharges struck a few years later when the Indochinese situation siphoned France's experienced military personnel to the Far East, leaving few men to train the steady input of recruits. Another effect was the blow to the officer corps' quality since many Saint-Cyrians and Polytechnicians left the service. Finally, in releasing these men, the state not only reduced the quality and effectiveness of its army, but also earned the suspicion of all military men. By its action, the government cast loose men who had contracted with the state, but the state abrogated the contracts and deprived them of their careers. Both officers and enlisted men —men who had been trained as soldiers and who expected and planned to spend their lives in uniform—suddenly found themselves civilians, feeling that ":the state had gone back on its word."[48]

During the next few years, the army and its leaders came more and more into the political limelight. For example, Admiral Thierry d'Argenlieu, who came to the Far East, "was to prove the chief

---

[47] Planchais, *Le Malaise*, p. 19; De la Gorce, *The French Army*, pp. 352–53. No explanations as to why so many graduates of the military academies left the army have been discovered. One can venture at least two possible reasons. First, many professional officers had remained in the tradition of obedience to legally constituted authority. These Pétainists could then have been a target of the Gaullists. Second, since officers could volunteer for release, many of the technically trained men may have done so to undertake civilian careers.

[48] De la Gorce, *The French Army*, p. 352.

instigator of the 'reconquest' of Indo-China."[49] D'Argenlieu had been appointed High Commissioner of Indochina by De Gaulle in 1945. The admiral soon surrounded himself with a group of conservative advisers, the so-called Saigon clique, who were devoted to a "tough" answer to Vietnamese demands for independence and who feared a relaxation of French control.

Fearing the formation of a left-wing government in Paris as a result of Communist successes in the fall French elections, D'Argenlieu left for Paris in November, 1946, leaving command in the hands of General Jean Valluy. Valluy's instructions from D'Argenlieu "may be guessed from what was to happen in the next few days."[50]

Fighting soon broke out in Haiphong, and although a cease-fire was arranged by a joint French-Vietnamese commission, Colonel Pierre-Louis Dèbes, the local French commander, refused to honor it. When the commission proposed meeting again, General Valluy suggested conditions which the Vietminh could not accept: total evacuation by Vietnamese troops of Haiphong, and total freedom of movement in the city for the French forces. The day before, Valluy had informed Dèbes of his prospective demands, and added that he considered it "indispensable to take advantage of the incidents and to improve our relations at Haiphong."[51]

On the afternoon of November 22, Dèbes again heard from Valluy and was told that the Vietnamese had to be taught a "hard lesson." The next morning, Dèbes' men became more aggressive and fighting again broke out with the Vietnamese troops. Dèbes then called upon the cruiser "Suffren" to bombard the Vietnamese section of the city, with consequent heavy losses among the civilian population there. Valluy's harsh demands were repeated two days later, saying in effect that Haiphong was to come under complete French control.

Although the Indochinese war did not officially start until the Hanoi massacre of December 19–20, the real beginning was in Haiphong three weeks earlier. "Whoever was directly responsible for the Hanoi rebellion of December 19," writes one close student of the subject,

[49] Alexander Werth, "How a War Began," *New Statesman and Nation*, XLIV (September 20, 1952), 311.

[50] Alexander Werth, *France, 1940–1955* (New York: Henry Holt and Co., 1956), p. 338.

[51] Quoted from Philippe Devillers, *Histoire du Vietnam de 1940 à 1952*, p. 335 in *ibid.*, p. 339.

"there is no doubt that the Saigon clique had done everything in its power to create a political and psychological atmosphere, in which an explosion became inevitable."[52] D'Argenlieu, Valluy, and Dèbes are certainly noteworthy examples of military leaders influencing policy. A military man, D'Argenlieu, was given the political-military post of High Commissioner and made the most of it. Valluy and Dèbes apparently shared the admiral's sentiments; in any case, he was their superior.

D'Argenlieu was surrounded by conservative advisers, men who were the *colons* (colonialists) of Indochina. There seems little doubt that he fell in easily with their "tough" policies, for he saw the maintenance of France's grip in the area a necessary element of the rebirth of French prestige in the world. Was D'Argenlieu's promotion of these conservative policies an instance of individual or institutional intervention? Was D'Argenlieu speaking for himself and the Saigon clique and/or the military establishment of which he was a member? It is difficult to say, for certainly he was "used." Yet at the same time he was promoting ideas in which he personally believed; furthermore, many military men shared the sentiment of restoring and maintaining the French presence in the Far East. However, D'Argenlieu's actions do seem more individual than institutional. For example, while the admiral urged the "tough" line, General Jacques-Philippe Leclerc (the military commander in Indochina), like D'Argenlieu of conservative background and a Gaullist, favored a policy of conciliation toward the Vietminh. An indication of the possible individual influence exercised by D'Argenlieu is apparent in Alexander Werth's musing:

> What, one may wonder, would have happened if not Thierry d'Argenlieu but Leclerc had been High Commissioner? . . . In Indo-China, one was carried away by his traditional class reflexes; the other was willing to make allowances for a changing world, in which the rising tide of Asian nationalisms had to be reckoned with, if anything was to be saved for France in Indo-China. Would Leclerc in the end have been overruled—and eliminated—by the pressure of the traditional colonialists? In the long run, perhaps. But it is certain that if Leclerc had been High Commissioner at Saigon in the winter of 1946, there would have been no Haiphong, and consequently, no Hanoi and history might have taken a different course.[53]

---

[52] *Ibid.*, p. 342. See also Phillip Williams and Martin Harrison, *De Gaulle's Republic* (New York: Longmans, Green, and Co., 1961), pp. 24–25. On the background, politics, fighting, and effects on French military thinking of Indochina see George A. Kelly, *Lost Soldiers* (Cambridge: The M.I.T. Press, 1965), pp. 31–104.

[53] Werth, *France, 1940–1955*, pp. 342–43; see pp. 326–43, and De la Gorce, *The French Army*, pp. 375–404.

Taking the course it did, history embroiled France in a long and bloody conflict in Indochina. In the hills and jungles of Indochina, the French army's political appetite was whetted and the army embarked upon a course which would lead it to Algiers and May 13, 1958. Lack of homeland support and criticisms of *la sale guerre* (the dirty war) further divided the army and the nation, with one of the important wedges being *l'affaire des généraux* (the generals' affair). A highly complicated and still clouded series of incidents, the affair began on September 18, 1949, with the arrest of two Indochinese students in Paris, one of whom carried a copy of a report by General Georges Revers, the Chief of the General Staff. In the report, the General advocated that a soldier be appointed as Indochina's High Commissioner, and included was a highly favorable account of Revers' friend, General Charles Mast, a Far Eastern expert and then director of the Institute of High Studies of National Defense. An investigation to determine the theft, or leakage, of the report led to Roger Peyré, the manager of a small import-export business.

Under questioning, Peyré admitted receiving the document from Revers, passing it on to M. Van Co, one of the arrested students, and receiving in exchange two and one-half million francs. Peyré said he gave one million francs to each of the generals, and the rest to a "prominent Socialist ex-minister." However, the government soon issued a statement that was an obvious coverup. Premier Henri Queuille (Radical) announced that only the political parts of the Revers report had been divulged, no military secrets having been released. The Premier, his Minister of Interior, Jules Moch (Socialist), and his Minister of Defense, Paul Ramadier (Socialist), apparently wished to avoid an incident involving their Chief of Staff.

But Paul Coste-Floret (*Mouvement républicain populaire*, MRP), the Overseas Minister, was not content to let the situation drop so easily, and on September 27 he sent a report to the Premier filled with charges of high-level intrigue, especially on the part of and in behalf of the Socialist party, which was allegedly going to profit financially from Mast's appointment as High Commissioner. On October 13, Peyré gave a new statement clearing General Revers of involvement in any plot and then suddenly left for South America on November 30. Nonetheless, on December 7, Revers was released as Chief of Staff. His travails, however, were not over, because in January he was attacked in *Time* magazine for leaking military secrets which purportedly had made their way to the Soviet Union.[54] A legislative commission of inquiry was

[54] *Time*, LV (January 30, 1950), 28.

instituted on January 17, 1950, to concern itself with the business now known in the press as *l'affaire des généraux*.

Although the generals had become closely identified with the sequence of events, it seems that political figures and machinations were at the root of the affair. Revers was influenced by Peyré, the latter having connections in Socialist and Radical circles, parties that wished to place their own man in Indochina (General Mast) in the place of the incumbent Léon Pignon (MRP). In the uproar which followed the exposure of the Revers report, it appeared that the Socialists in the government, Ramadier and Moch, plus the Premier, had gone to some lengths to prevent a full disclosure of the circumstances surrounding the leakage of General Revers' recommendations concerning Indochina. Yet the commission of inquiry report, although it "cannot be described as a whitewash . . . managed to spare the politicians, except Moch, from any charge of criminal culpability."[55] The army, through Generals Revers and Mast, who were forced to retire, was made to take the burden of guilt in an affair which had at its origins a political dispute between the Socialists and the MRP.

While it may be said that we have been again dealing with individuals in uniform who became involved in political affairs, there are certain points to keep in mind regarding Revers and Mast. For one thing, their involvement was apparently invoked by civilian figures for party purposes; for another, while the army's involvement was slight, the effects on the army were great. Revers and Mast had become involved in a political situation, not on behalf of the army, but on behalf of political parties. However, the generals were the ones who suffered, and through them, the army, which felt that its generals had been unjustly dealt with.

The gap between the military and civilian worlds widened as the army accused the civilians of using it to escape from political difficulties by sacrificing high-ranking officers. On the other hand, civilians saw in Revers and Mast political involvement by the army. A consequence of the affair was a spreading feeling in the army that in order to defend itself and its members against the Fourth Republic, political action might become necessary. "The so-called *affaire des généraux* was the first of a series of important events . . . that permanently shattered the already tottering relationship between the government and the army," concludes one student of the incident.[56]

[55] George A. Kelly, "The French Army Re-enters Politics," *Political Science Quarterly*, LXXVI (September, 1961), 380.

[56] *Ibid.*, p. 379. The best account to appear so far is Phillip Williams, "L'Affaire des généraux," *Cambridge Journal*, IV (May, 1951), 469–80. See also *L'Année*

Just a few years later, army involvement in political questions made a definite appearance. On the European Defense Community (EDC) proposal, the military establishment announced its opposition to the surrender of French command to a supranational force. Among the most vocal of the EDC's adversaries was Marshal Alphonse Juin, who, on March 31, 1954, violently attacked the proposal publicly without first having cleared it through channels. As a result, the Joseph Laniel government withdrew Juin from French army functions, although he retained his post as chief of the Central European Section of the North Atlantic Treaty Organization (NATO). Many generals, owing their positions to the government in power, were reticent on the issue of EDC, but the remainder fought the plan "with a greater show of unity than they had ever shown on other issues."[57]

In October, 1956, the Great Mute stirred again, this time to effect a change in policy by engineering the capture of the Algerian rebel leader Ahmed Ben Bella and four other insurgent chieftains. In the fall of 1956, the Guy Mollet government was trying to arrange secret talks with the National Liberation Front (FLN), using as an intermediary the Crown Prince of Morocco, Moulay Hassan. (When Mohammed Khider was captured with Ben Bella in October, documents reportedly were found on the former which pointed to preparations for such talks.)[58]

On the morning of October 22, 1956, Colonel Ducournau and Lieutenant Colonel Branet, Lacoste's military advisers (Robert Lacoste, a Socialist, was the Resident Minister of Algeria), informed Pierre Chaussade, secretary general of Lacoste's Ministry, that an aircraft carrying five rebel leaders was flying over Algeria headed for Tunis. Chaussade refused to act on the officers' suggestion that the plane be

---

politique 1950 (Paris: Presses Universitaires de France, 1951), pp. 6–8, 32–34, 48–50, 277–86; Werth, *France, 1940–1955*, pp. 459–67; Georgette Elgey, *La République des illusions* (Paris: Arthème Fayard, 1965), pp. 467–97.

[57] Katzenbach, "The French Army," p. 510; Pierre Gerbet, "Les rapports entre pouvoir civil et pouvoir militaire en France dans l'élaboration de la politique de défense," unpublished paper delivered at the 1961 Fifth World Congress of the International Association of Political Science, p. 15. Planchais, *Le Malaise*, pp. 54–57. The most comprehensive study of France and EDC remains Daniel Lerner and Raymond Aron, eds., *France Defeats EDC* (New York: Frederick A. Praeger, 1957).

[58] See Richard and Joan Brace, *Ordeal in Algeria* (New York: D. Van Nostrand Co., 1960), pp. 141–47. Tournoux indicates that Mollet had given Moulay Hassan the following message: "We wish to end the war in Algeria. . . . If the F.L.N. representatives in the interior, those who fight us, wish to come to Paris, give me their names. On my word of honor I agree to bring them to France, meet with them, and guarantee their safe return to Algeria." Jean-Raymond Tournoux, *Secrets d'état* (Paris: Plon, 1960), p. 43.

grounded in Algiers. Since Lacoste was absent at the time and could not be reached, Chaussade apparently did not want to assume responsibility for giving the order.

A number of telephone calls were made, and finally a representative of the Minister of Defense was reached who said that the situation was for the Resident Minister to handle. General Henri Lorrillot, the Commander in Chief in Algeria, then contacted Max Lejeune (Socialist), the Secretary of State for War, who agreed that the plane should be intercepted if possible. The army was eager to comply because it was anxious to prevent any move toward negotiations with the FLN rebels, for in their eyes, this could lead only to another abandonment. It is interesting to note that the army took no action until approval was provided by a civilian, thereby covering its action and keeping itself in the chain of command. The army was not yet ready to strike out on its own.

But once the approval of a government official had been received, the army moved swiftly. The aircraft carrying the five rebel leaders was owned by King Mohammed V of Morocco and was piloted by a French crew. As the plane was crossing Oran, Algeria, it was ordered to land "by the orders of the Minister of Defense." Lejeune, it will be recalled, was the Secretary of State for War, and Maurice Bourgès-Maunoury, the Minister of Defense, had not been reached. When this order failed to bring the aircraft to earth, radio Algiers at the airdrome at Maison-Blanche took over.

From radio Algiers the pilot learned that he must land "in the name of the French government, orders given by Lacoste, minister of Algeria." The aircraft commander asked for the message to be repeated. Again he heard that he was ordered to land "in the name of the French government, orders given by Lacoste, minister of Algeria,"[59] although Lacoste, like the Minister of Defense, was unaware of the proceedings. On hearing the message the second time, the pilot landed and his passengers were taken into custody.

Premier Guy Mollet supposedly said when he learned of the incident: "It is not possible. It would be folly." And President René Coty replied: "We are dishonored."[60] In its opposition to government maneuverings toward peace talks, the army succeeded in halting them and did so under the cover of acting in accordance with civilian instructions. Ben Bella's capture assured the army of the opportunity to carry on its task of subduing the revolution.

[59] Quoted by Brace, *Ordeal in Algeria*, pp. 143–44.
[60] *Ibid.*, p. 145.

A clear instance of military intervention is provided by the enforced landing of Ben Bella's aircraft. There is no question in this incident of an individual military chief acting to influence policy. It is rather a case of the army's taking the initiative, acting as master of the situation, and making use of it for its own purpose: to sabotage the government's attempts to meet with the rebels. The attitude of many French officers in Algeria toward the capture of Ben Bella was expressed in the diary of a young lieutenant who noted with satisfaction that the rebels had been "taken during the night like rats. *Joli coup.*" [61]

Shortly after the Ben Bella coup, two more military men, Generals Jacques Faure and Paris de Bollardière, became involved in political questions. General Faure, who had chosen Vichy in 1940, became convinced, while stationed in Algiers in 1956, that the Algerian situation's only salvation was for the army to take power by means of a simultaneous uprising in Algiers and Paris. A naïve plotter, Faure revealed his plans to Paul Teitgen, the secretary general of the Algiers police. Teitgen reported the conversation to Lacoste and on orders from the Resident Minister, secretly recorded the General's words during his next visit. For his conspiracy, Faure was recalled to Paris on December 27, 1956, and given two months' confinement to quarters. Apparently the government feared army reaction if Faure were treated more harshly. Following a brief tour in Germany, he was returned to Algeria, where, shortly after his arrival, he received his third star. [62]

Like Faure, General Paris de Bollardière was in London in 1940 before the French capitulation, but De Bollardière chose the Free French. After the war he served first in the Far East and later was sent to Algeria where, in 1956, while serving as a sector commander, he wrote an order to his subordinates referring to a directive prescribing increased "police" action which he had received from higher headquarters. In his order, the former Free French fighter told his men that "the temptation which the totalitarian countries have not resisted, to consider certain processes as a normal method to obtain information, must be rejected without equivocation, and the processes formally condemned." [63]

[61] Jean-Yves Alquier, *Nous avons pacifié Tazalt* (Paris: Robert Laffont, 1957), p. 32.

[62] Tournoux, *Secrets d'état*, p. 197; Merry and Serge Bromberger, *Les 13 complots du 13 mai* (Paris: Arthème Fayard, 1959), pp. 87–93.

[63] *Le Monde*, October 3, 1961. See Roger Barberot, *Malaventure en Algérie avec le général Paris de Bollardière* (Paris: Plon, 1957), p. 197; see pp. 178–84, 195–214, 220–27.

After several disagreements with General Jacques Massu, the tough paratroop hero who was the Algiers commander, De Bollardière in March, 1957, asked to be relieved of his command. On March 28, Minister of Defense Bourgès-Maunoury announced there was no connection between the General's departure from Algeria and his disapproval of methods that Bourgès-Maunoury professed to be ignorant of.[64] The next day, *L'Express* printed a letter from De Bollardière to the paper's editor, Jean-Jacques Servan-Schreiber, who had served under the General in Algeria. De Bollardière's letter spoke of the great danger "for us to lose sight, under the pretext of immediate effectiveness, of the moral values which till now have been responsible for the grandeur of our civilization and of our army."[65] In April, De Bollardière was given sixty days' confinement to quarters for his "breach of discipline," that is, for taking a stand against the methods being used in Algeria.

De Bollardière was sent to Cameroon, where he served until 1960, his requests to return to Algeria denied, as was promotion. On October 3, 1961, at his request, he retired from active duty. Only one hypothesis has been advanced to explain the refusal to return De Bollardière to Algeria. Both the Fourth and the Fifth Republics may have feared to impose him on the military extremists of Algeria, fearing reactions from men who utilized the methods De Bollardière condemned.[66]

In February, 1958, another army action raised questions concerning the military taking affairs in its own hands and attracted the attention of the world. FLN bands were striking French units in Algeria and then swiftly retreating across the border to Tunisia and sanctuary. Early in 1958, French planes were repeatedly fired on from the Tunisian village of Sakhiet-Sidi-Youssef and warnings of retaliation were given by the French. On February 8, 1958, the threat was carried out and French planes struck the village, hitting no rebels but many civilians, including children.

Whether the attack was carried out on military initiative or whether accomplished in accordance with government orders is an open question. It may be that the government ordered the attack and then used the army as a scapegoat when the raid turned out badly. By not admitting that it gave the order for an armed strike across an international

[64] *Le Monde*, October 3, 1961.
[65] *Ibid.*, and *Le Monde*, August 26, 1960.
[66] *Le Monde*, October 3, 1961.

border, the government made it appear that the army, tired of the Tunisian-based attacks, struck on its own accord.[67]

However, the strike may have been ordered by the army without the government's knowledge. We are then confronted by another case of military intervention. The decision to instigate what was clearly an international incident was one which should have been made by the government, certainly not by the army. If this was the case, that the army struck on its own initiative, the government's reluctance to take adverse action against the army may have been due to a fear of offending an army already showing signs of discontent.[68] In any event, wherever the attack order came from, more ill will was engendered between the nation and the army.

But the *malaise de l'armée* went far deeper than matters of physical existence or reciprocal civil-military suspicions. Both were important contributing factors, but the root cause of the army's despair and alienation was the colonial wars France fought after World War II:

> The Algerian war separated the army—or to be more exact, that which is generally called the army, that is, the average opinion of the officer corps—from the nation, because this nation underwent, for the last fifteen years, the repercussions of an international phenomenon called "decolonization," whereas French officers forged, while undergoing the same phenomenon, an ensemble of political and social ideas which no longer corresponded to those of the majority of the nation, and separated them more and more.[69]

Sacrifice without meaning, humiliation, lost honor, and abandonment were repercussions of these conflicts as were the growing suspicions among army and nation. Two more results of the colonial wars which help to explain the army's disavowal of the tradition of the Great Mute, were the theory of revolutionary war and the assumption by the army of extended civilian functions in Algeria.

[67] For this viewpoint see Brace, *Ordeal in Algeria*, p. 179; *Le Procès d'Edmond Jouhaud* (Paris: Editions Albin Michel, 1962), p. 315.

[68] Williams and Harrison, *De Gaulle's Republic*, pp. 43–44. See General Maxime Weygand's defense of the raid in *Le Monde*, March 6, 1958, and for the view that the attack was approved by General Raoul Salan, the Algerian Commander in Chief, without Premier Felix Gaillard's consent see Alexander Werth, *The De Gaulle Revolution* (London: Robert Hale, 1960), pp. 17–21; Werth, *De Gaulle* (New York: Simon and Schuster, 1965), p. 12; Louis Terrenoire, *De Gaulle et l'Algérie* (Paris: Arthème Fayard, 1964), p. 50.

[69] Henri Azeau, *Révolte militaire* (Paris: Plon, 1961), pp. 6–7.

The theory of revolutionary war deserves separate treatment and is dealt with in Chapter VI. Increased civilian functions handled by the army can be traced back to 1955. From that year, progressively greater administrative and police duties were bequeathed to the army by Lacoste. In April, 1955, General Gaston Parlange was given civil and military authority in the eastern part of Algeria in a section which included 1,200,000 individuals. Dated April 30, 1955, Parlange's orders, signed by Premier Edgar Faure, provided that he was "charged, under the authority and responsibility of the Prefect of Constantine, with the direction of all civil and military actions with the goal of re-establishing order."[70] His task was the reconquest of the area "in depth," and in order to fulfill his mission, he reorganized the area into twelve zones, each having at its center a *bordj* which fulfilled the dual purpose of a fort and administrative headquarters. Officers in charge of each *bordj* were set to the task of improving the lot of the people in their zones and arming them for self-defense.

In order to make contacts with the Moslems in the countryside, Special Administrative Sections (SAS) were established in September, 1955, and in the cities of Algeria the Urban Administrative Sections (SAU) appeared.[71] The special sections were concerned with "human contacts," their function being to work for the social and economic development of the Moslems, especially in the rural areas. The officers of these sections engaged in public works, schoolteaching, administrative tasks, and other duties far removed from the soldier's profession of armed combat. "Preoccupied with the problems of man [the SAS]," announced the *Bulletin d'information du ministère des armées* in March, 1957, "has multiplied human contacts. It has strived to establish or re-establish between the different communities circuits of confidence. It has brought sympathy and received gratitude in exchange."[72] Cap-

[70] Quoted by Claude Paillat, *Deuxième dossier secret de l'Algérie* (Paris: Les presses de la Cité, 1962), pp. 149–50.

[71] The *Bulletin d'information du ministère des armées*, March 20, 1957, gives 1957 as the official beginning of administrative and sociological action, paralleling the classical war efforts of the army. Yet, the same bulletin acknowledges that SAS officers were operating earlier, in January, 1956, when there were 160 SAS officers in Algeria. Quoted in *Le Monde*, March 21, 1959. On the SAS see Ambler, *The French Army in Politics*, pp. 176–77; Kelly, *Lost Soldiers*, pp. 180–82; and Peter Paret, *French Revolutionary Warfare from Indochina to Algeria* (New York: Frederick A. Praeger, 1964), pp. 46–48; 104–6.

[72] Quoted in *Le Monde*, March 21, 1959. Between November, 1957, and March, 1959, the French army in Algeria grouped some 25,000 youths in sporting organiza-

tain Georges Oudinot summed up his five-year role as one of the twelve hundred SAS officers in the following words: "I worked especially to improve the conditions of life . . . I opened roads, schools, dispensaries. . . . I wished to make of the men of the mountains not the enemies of tomorrow, but friends forever." [73]

It should be mentioned that the French army had a long history of social service and construction in the colonies, and the great colonial officers, Louis Lyautey and Joseph Galliéni, had stressed the administrative and political tasks of the colonial warrior. Indeed, the Arab Bureaus created in Algeria in 1833, in Tunisia in 1881, and in Morocco in 1911, were the predecessors of the social service sections which appeared in Algeria during the Algerian rebellion. However, the mission of the pre-World War II colonial army had been the assimilation of colonial areas and the spread of French civilization, and before 1940, colonial officers were but a small segment of the French army, since the main force was in France where the defense of the homeland was centered. Across the Vosges Mountains lurked the enemy, and the typical officer expected to make his career on the eastern frontier, ready to defend *la patrie*. [74]

But in Algeria, the homeland army's tradition of abstention from nonmilitary activity was whittled away by duties which were often more political than military. By 1958, over half the army was stationed in Algeria, and administrative tasks had assumed an unprecedented scale. As the boundaries of their domains blurred, civil and military authorities often clashed over their respective responsibilities. The soldier's expanded horizons were stated by Captain Estoup when he stood

---

tions, and another 3,600 were enrolled in trade schools. Army medical officers' free consultations and care in Algeria rose from 19,000 a month in 1956 to 460,000 in 1957, to over 940,000 in 1959. *Ibid.* In 1958 there were 418 French soldiers teaching 23,000 Moslem students in Algeria: two years later 120,000 such students were being instructed by 1,620 military teachers. *Le Monde*, August 26, 1958, and August 6, 1960.

[73] Maurice Cottaz, ed., *Les Procès du putsch d'Alger et du complot de Paris* (Paris: Nouvelles Editions Latines, 1962), p. 130. On the army's "human contact" activities, see the diary of an SAS lieutenant, Alquier, *Nous avons pacifié Tazalt*, and Jean-Yves Alquier, *et al.*, *Ceux d'Algérie* (Paris: Plon, 1957). For an unfavorable account of SAS activities and accomplishments see Jean-Michel Darboise, *et al.*, *Officiers en Algérie* (Paris: François Maspero, 1960).

[74] On the colonial army see MacCarthy, "L'armée française et la politique, 1ère partie," p. 35; MacCarthy, "L'armée française et la politique, 2è partie," pp. 46–48; Terraine, "The Army in Modern France," p. 735; Katzenbach, "The French Army," p. 502.

before the High Military Tribunal for his role in the April, 1961, putsch attempt:

> They had never taught me at Saint-Cyr to organize the supply of fruits and vegetables for a city like Algiers. On January 2, 1957, I received the order to do so.
> They had never taught me at Saint-Cyr to concern myself with police channels. In February, 1959, I received the order to do so.
> They had never taught me at Saint-Cyr how to exercise the functions of a prefect of police responsible for a population of about 30,000 inhabitants. In January, February, and March, 1957, I received the order to do so.
> They had never taught me at Saint-Cyr to organize a polling place. In December, 1958, I received the order to do so.
> They had never taught me at Saint-Cyr to set up the embryo of a municipality, to open schools, to open a market. In the autumn of 1959, I received the order to do so.
> They had never taught me at Saint-Cyr to prudently disperse insurgent citizens. In February, 1960, I received the order to do so.[75]

The culmination came in January, 1957, when Algiers' civil authorities admitted their incapacity to cope with security problems. The assignment of keeping civil order in Algiers was given to the army on January 7, and all police powers in Algiers were turned over to the Tenth Paratroop Division (10th DP) under the command of the hero of the "paras," General Jacques Massu. Massu's paratroops were given the authority to arrest and hold any Moslem or European without informing civil authorities, and arrests were made on the slightest suspicion. In the first nine months of 1957, three thousand persons disappeared and another five thousand were sent to prisons and concentration camps.[76]

During the Battle of Algiers, all citizens were registered and given identification cards. Search parties could operate at any time, and families, buildings, blocks, and districts were organized into a hierarchy of responsibility. In Simon's *Portrait d'un officier*, Jean de Larsan, the traditional officer, protests being made a policeman to the division chief of staff. He is told that he is not a fireman either, but if a fire were to break out, he would have to help extinguish it, not because he was a

---

[75] Cottaz, *Les Procès du putsch d'Alger*, p. 80.

[76] Jacques Dusquesne, *L'Algérie ou la guerre des mythes* (Paris: Desclée de Brouwer, 1958), p. 25; Joseph Kraft, *The Struggle for Algeria* (Garden City: Doubleday and Co., 1961), pp. 104–5.

fireman but "because he is a soldier and his first duty is to do what the nation commands. It is the same thing if it needs him to run down gangsters."[77]

Using soldier-policemen, imprisonment, torture, and executions, the Battle of Algiers was won by September, 1957. But not all officers and Frenchmen agreed with the methods that had been adopted, and the use of torture became a controversial subject in France and Algeria, particularly after the publication of Henri Alleg's, *The Question*, in which Alleg described his experiences at the electrode-bearing hands of French paratroops in Algiers.[78] In justification of the army's "methods," Claude Paillat relates that Massu, during the Battle of Algiers, wrote: "In a secret war, the 10th D. P. answered with secret methods."[79]

From their involvement in manifold functions, many in the army wondered why, if they were given such extended tasks, they were not given power as well. Incompetent politicians, the argument ran, had proven their ineptness by giving their tasks to the army; having thus abandoned power, it seemed logical that its real wielders should assume leadership. As a consequence of contacts with the Moslems, the army also attributed to itself a sense of mission: that of helping the Moslem masses and raising them to European standards. Their contacts, the work performed, the promises made, intensified the conviction of officers that France must never leave Algeria.

Fear of abandonment was much a part of the *malaise* of the army, to which we must now re-direct our attention. Feeling rejected by the nation and suffering from a loss of prestige, the French army from 1945 increasingly considered itself the victim of political errors. The loss of Indochina, which had been a favorite assignment of many officers who enjoyed the women and the way of life there, the loss of Morocco, the pride of the army which had pacified and governed that land, and finally the loss of Tunisia embittered an army which had fought courageously only to see the Empire slowly slipping away.

The mental anguish induced by feelings of worthless sacrifice, disgust, humiliation, abandonment, and lost honor cut into the army deeply.

---

[77] Pierre-Henri Simon, *Portrait d'un officier* (Paris: Editions du Seuil, 1958), pp. 127–30.

[78] Henri Alleg, *The Question* (New York: George Braziller, 1958).

[79] Quoted by Paillat, *Deuxième dossier secret*, p. 360. On the army's use of torture see also Pierre Leulliette, *St. Michael and the Dragon* (Boston: Houghton Mifflin Co., 1964), pp. 279–97; Pierre Vidal-Naquet, *Torture: Cancer of Democracy* (Baltimore: Penguin Books, 1963); and Kelly, *Lost Soldiers*, pp. 196–205.

Thousands of lives were lost in Indochina, French and non-French fighting under the French flag, and in the army's opinion these men died for nothing since in the end Indochina was lost—lost by the politicians of Paris. The army despondently counted its dead and missing—2,005 officers, 41,070 enlisted French soldiers, legionnaires, and Africans— and blamed the regime for the losses.[80] A former Commander in Chief in Indochina announced that "the real reasons for the defeat . . . are political."[81] His conclusion became a conviction among French officers and deepened the gulf between the army and civilian leadership.

During the seven years of the Indochinese war, France had nineteen governments, replaced the High Commissioner of Indochina five times, and the Commander in Chief six times. Concerning the homeland situation, Colonel Joseph Broizat stated during the Barricades Trials: "We saw our directors incapable of winning this war, an indifferent population, a press accusing us of conducting a dirty war. That led us to defeat, not Dien Bien Phu, but Geneva."[82]

Disgust with politicians, whom the army continued to blame for later reverses in Algeria, was heightened by the sense of useless sacrifice the army felt at fighting for apparently no reason. France's army fought almost continuously from 1940 to 1962, only to find itself repeatedly defeated and humiliated. The one victory achieved, the Suez invasion in the fall of 1956, was snatched from their hands, again by the politicians, and again the army was forced to withdraw. Pierre Leulliette, a young French paratrooper who participated in the Egyptian action, described his own and his comrades' emotions in the following words: "It will take us several weeks to realize fully that, though conquerors, we are also vanquished."[83] The humiliation of steady reverses struck the once-proud French army particularly hard, an army whose military prowess in both battle and theory had always been a source of national pride. To a Frenchman, "there could be no question among right-

[80] Figures from Tournoux, *Secrets d'état*, p. 93.

[81] General Henri Navarre, *L'Agonie de l'Indochine* (Paris: Plon, 1957), p. 319. See Pierre Boyer de Latour, *Le martyre de l'armée française* (Paris: Les presses du Mail, 1961), p. 41.

[82] *Le Monde*, January 14, 1961. On the effect of Indochina on the French army see Raymond Aron, *France, Steadfast and Changing* (Cambridge: Harvard University Press, 1960), pp. 82, 110; Jean-Marie Domenach, "The French Army in Politics," *Foreign Affairs*, XXXIX (January, 1961), 185; Behr, "The French Army as a Political and Social Factor," p. 441; Edward Behr, *The Algerian Problem* (New York: W. W. Norton, 1962), p. 67; Planchais, *Le Malaise*, pp. 9–11.

[83] Leulliette, *St. Michael and the Dragon*, p. 263.

thinking men of whatever nationality that militarily France was *le premier du monde"* (first in the world).[84]

Finally, the army decided that retreat and humiliation had to stop; their last field of battle was Algeria, an integral part of France according to many Frenchmen. Captain Branca, a Foreign Legion officer, expressed his anguish of humiliation in these words:

> I can lose my decorations. Having ardently desired to belong to an army finally victorious, I can not keep them if they must be the symbol of useless deaths and a new defeat. I can lose liberty. That would be very little in relation to the downfall of my soldierly ideal and my country's humiliation.[85]

The saying that the Mediterranean divides France as the Seine divides Paris was familiar, and Algeria was considered by many officers to be as much a part of France as any mainland department. Several men who joined the April putsch in 1961 claimed they did so out of devotion to the goal of keeping Algeria French.[86] General Jacques Faure, speaking of the accused who challenged Paris in 1960 during the Week of the Barricades, stated: "Their trial is that of all those who know Algeria is an integral part of France and have experienced the anguish which comes from abandonment."[87]

In addition to the fear of losing a "part of France," the army was haunted by the specter of broken promises. Major Denoix de Saint-Marc, an exemplary officer until the April, 1961, putsch, explained to his judges why he joined General Maurice Challe in open defiance of De Gaulle:

> I have sacrificed twenty years of my life to France [De Saint-Marc was not yet forty at the time of his trial]. I have been an officer of the legion for fifteen years. I have fought. I have seen legionnaires die, foreigners by the blood of their fathers, but French by the blood they shed. It was in thinking of them that on April 23, at 13:30 hours, I made my free choice.[88]

The thought of abandoning Algeria struck the veterans of Indochina particularly hard. They had made pledges and oaths in Indochina,

---

[84] Watt, *Dare Call it Treason*, p. 3.

[85] Cottaz, *Les Procès du putsch d'Alger*, p. 107.

[86] For examples, see *ibid.*, pp. 11, 20, 28, 47, 51, 62, 81, 111, 194; *Le Procès des généraux Challe et Zeller* (Paris: Nouvelles Editions Latines, 1961), pp. 49–50.

[87] *Le Monde*, January 21, 1961.

[88] Cottaz, *Les Procès du putsch d'Alger*, p. 12.

swearing they would remain and protect France's friends. Several officers have spoken of the mental torture they endured when they were ordered to evacuate and leave to reprisals and vengeance those who had given the French army their confidence. French officers remembered leaving the shores of Indochina and seeing the Indochinese left behind wade into the water, begging to be taken along, only to be swallowed by the sea. A typical reaction to such memories was that of a captain who said:

> With us were 12,000 Thai partisans, who were the most faithful of our friends. At the moment of the armistice of 1954, we had to abandon them on orders, that is, to deliver them to the Viets, who tortured and massacred them. . . . That is what they had me do in Indo-China. Now understand what my state of mind is, what the state of mind is of all my comrades who have known not only treason but disgrace.[89]

More promises were made in Algeria. Promises of continued French presence were given by the social service officers, by the men in command of *harkis* units (composed of Algerian Moslems who took up arms against the FLN), by all the French officers and men devoted to the cause of keeping Algeria French. The agonizing position of the French army was expressed by an SAS lieutenant who stated:

> I think of all those who were massacred in Indo-China for having believed in France, after having won them to France's side, after promising not to abandon them . . . of those of Tunisia, true to the end . . . of those of Morocco.
> And once again, I wonder if, one day, with my comrades, we will not have on our conscience the death of those who rallied to us in Algeria. . . . It is not a question of a speech such as one could make on the floor of parliament. It is a question of the lives of men who are our friends.[90]

Additional oaths were made in Algeria. After operating against the rebels for seven months in 1956, Captain Delacour took an "oath to leave this ground only once the rebellion [was] vanquished," in order that the efforts and losses of his men should not have been in vain.[91]

[89] Quoted by Paul Gerin, *L'Algérie du 13 mai* (Paris: Gallimard, 1958), p. 106. For further expressions of this sentiment see Cottaz, *Les Procès du putsch d'Alger*, pp. 10, 16, 81, 132–33, 136.

[90] Alquier, *Nous avons pacifié Tazalt*, pp. 270–71.

[91] Cottaz, *Les Procès du putsch d'Alger*, p. 152.

A short time later, the captain found the bodies of fourteen of his men who had been killed in an FLN ambush. "Before those dead, I renewed my oath not to abandon the country to the hands of such assassins."[92] Condemned to death by the Military Court of Justice for his Secret Army Organization terrorist activities, Roger Delgueldre, ex-lieutenant, former legionnaire, said to his lawyers shortly before his execution on July 6, 1962: "I ask you to tell my comrades that I am proud to be about to the very end, and to die for having kept the oath which all fighting officers swore at least one time—not to surrender Algeria to the FLN."[93]

The *malaise de l'armée* enveloped an army which had become separated from France psychologically, morally, and physically. The average French infantry officer spent 73 percent of the time between 1946 and 1958 outside France, indicating the extent "of the separation which, during all this period, isolated the military from national life."[94] Developing its own theories and policies, the army was soon engaged in conflict with a France which no longer understood its army and which was not understood in return. "After a separation of eight years," lamented Captain Estoup, "I have the sad feeling of re-discovering a France which no longer knows me and which I no longer know."[95]

The development of the French army from the politically passive force of the nineteenth and early twentieth centuries into an armed force ripe for political action has been followed. Whereas in the earlier periods the army assumed a form and posture which represented a reciprocally satisfying relationship between army and nation, the post-World War II years created a breach in the relationship and an apolitical army became political.

During the years between the reign of Napoleon I and World War II, the army had been the Great Mute. The officer corps' social structure, its professional commitment, and the attitude of the nation, contributed to create an army which placed itself above the state and political battles, devoting itself to the nation's defense. Governments and politicians could come and go, but the army, which I call an elevated army, would serve all without question in the tradition of obedience.[96]

[92] *Ibid.*

[93] Quoted in *Le Monde*, July 7, 1962.

[94] Girardet, *La Crise militaire français*, p. 140; see pp. 134–41 on army nomadism.

[95] Cottaz, *Les Procès du putsch d'Alger*, p. 82.

[96] Another type of army-state relationship may be referred to as the integrated army, an army representative of the nation's social and political foundations. The

Aloof, concerned with itself, the army could serve any government because it served France.

Civilians were pleased with the army's special status, rendering it homage from time to time, attacking it on a few occasions, rallying to it in national crises, but generally leaving it to itself. In return, the army left politics to the civilians. But after World War II, the elevated army became an alienated army. Already considering itself distinct from the state, the army's transition to alienation was facilitated and isolation became estrangement.

The army's low social and economic status, the various repercussions of the colonial wars, especially humiliation and broken pledges, long absence from France, lack of sympathy and understanding between army and nation created an alienated army. Men of the French army found themselves fighting for a country which paid little attention to their efforts, and when it did, it was often critical. In return, intellectuals, politicians, and journalists became particular targets of army scorn, and they were accused of leading France astray, of not understanding the nature of France's and the free world's Communist enemy. If politicians were responsible for the loss of the French empire, if intellectuals and journalists were responsible for undermining the army, then the army's path was clear—remove the politicians and silence the voices of defeatism.

Armies are emanations of the nation, and nineteenth-century France produced the elevated army. France was then, and still is, a country of deep internal divisions, of disagreement concerning not only the functions but also the nature of government, of grievous national discord

---

integrated army shares the nation's basic values and accepts its position in the national division of labor. Gaetano Mosca's assertion that military subordination to civil authority in nineteenth-century Europe was a result of armies being "bureaucratized nobilities" and reflecting the ruling classes is really a reference to integrated armies. Gaetano Mosca, *The Ruling Class* (New York: McGraw Hill, 1939), pp. 222–43. The same is true of Professor Morris Janowitz's hypothesis of the "shift in officer recruitment" which is based on the twentieth-century phenomenon of officers being drawn from diverse social classes as the United States became more democratic. Morris Janowitz, *The Professional Soldier* (Glencoe: The Free Press, 1960), pp. 10–11. The citizen army concept, according to which every soldier is a civilian and every civilian is a soldier, is an effort to achieve a fully integrated army. Permeated with civilian values, standards, ideals, and thoughts, the civilianized army is offered as solving the problem of civilian control of the military. See Frederick M. Stern, *The Citizen Army* (New York: St. Martin's Press, 1957), and Maurice Mégret, "Fonction et integration politique de l'armée," in Tony Albord, *et al.*, *La Défense nationale* (Paris: Presses Universitaires de France, 1958), pp. 133–82.

instead of concord—and the army reflected these divisions. It did so not by reproducing in its midst the same rifts. Rather, it reflected the lack of a stable national base by forging its own foundation and folding in upon itself.

The elevated French army assumed an attitude of aloofness and withdrew from France, creating its own special, particular world. It attached to itself an exalted conception of its role as defender of the national patrimony and placed itself above political strife and politicians. The army became the ultimate guarantor of the nation. Its devotion was to something greater than ephemeral governments and temporal political difficulties: it was to the nation, to the fatherland.

It may appear that the elevated army was an ideal type for civilian control of the military, but such was not the case.[97] In the first place, the army created an artificial division between itself and the nation. But the army could not divorce itself completely from the nation because in spite of itself it was affected by the nation's political life.[98] Finally, in its separation and exalted conception of its role, the elevated army was easily converted into an alienated army.

Impelled by circumstances, the elevated army's feelings of separateness became the vehemence of alienation. The alienated army lost contact with the nation; it failed to understand—and be understood by—the nation.[99] The French army moved from resentment, to projection

[97] Creation of an elevated army seems to be the intention of Professor Samuel P. Huntington's objective civilian control model. Military men, according to Huntington, will be obedient servants of the state when they are motivated by and imbued with the ideals of their profession. Civilian control will be achieved "by professionalizing the military, by rendering them politically sterile and neutral." Samuel P. Huntington, *The Soldier and the State* (Cambridge: The Belknap Press, 1957), p. 84; see Part I.

[98] The danger of elevation is that "a standing army whose officers are permitted to remain aloof from the nation's economic and political life thus can become a law unto itself, ill disposed to listen to advice and criticism from civilians." Stern, *The Citizen Army*, p. 112. Paul H. Appelby has observed that "if a high degree of institutional autonomy should characterize the military establishment, the objective of popularly responsible civilian control would be lost." Appelby, "Civilian Control of a Department of National Defense," in Jerome G. Kerwin, ed., *Civil-Military Relationships in American Life* (Chicago: University of Chicago Press, 1948), p. 64.

[99] Fustel de Coulanges has warned "there is a necessary line between military institutions and political institutions. Agreement between them . . . assures stability; disagreement leads infallibly to revolution. If the army is not fashioned in the image of the state, then before long the army will fashion the state in its image." Quoted by Joseph Monteilhet, *Les institutions militaires de la France* (Paris: Felix Alcan, 1932), p. 113.

of its difficulties onto civilians, to political intervention. The state failing to provide stability, the army would do so; the state failing to subdue its enemies, both external and internal, the army would do so; the state failing to provide policy, the army would do so.

CHAPTER III

Composition of the Officer Corps

Il suffisait d'ouvrir les yeux pour voir arriver la guerre; je m'y préparais consciencieusement, comme à mon métier; vous moquerez-vous de moi si j'ajoute comme à une entrée en religion?—JEAN DE LARSAN.

OFFICERS CONSTITUTE a professional class with certain particular interests which force "every army to be 'in politics' in the larger sense," according to Alfred Vagts.[1] Since officers were certainly at the center of the French army's being "in politics" between 1958 and 1962, an examination of the officer corps as a social and professional group is in order. In regard to social background, the concern is whether the French officer corps was representative of the nation's class structure (in the sense that officers were drawn from the same class, or classes, which also provided the economic and political cadres) and therefore more likely to be representative of the nation, or whether recruitment was such that the officer corps was nonrepresentative of the nation's class structure and thereby more likely to be removed from the "pulse" of the country.

In general, officers have traditionally been recruited from the ruling classes, especially those officers in high command. But with levelings in society, the officer corps became more representative, as men from other than the upper classes increasingly found their way into the officer ranks. But in neither the nineteenth century nor the first half of the twentieth century was the French officer corps truly representative of

[1] Alfred Vagts, *A History of Militarism* (New York: W. W. Norton, 1937), p. 319. On the importance of the officer politically see Samuel P. Huntington, *The Soldier and the State* (Cambridge: The Belknap Press, 1957), p. 3; Katherine Chorley, *Armies and the Art of Revolution* (London: Faber and Faber, 1943), pp. 98–99; Michael Howard, ed., *Soldiers and Governments* (London: Eyre and Spottiswoode, 1957), p. 162.

France. While society was governed by the upper bourgeoisie in the nineteenth century, the officer corps was marked by the variety of its officers' social backgrounds. Raoul Girardet remarks that a distinguishing characteristic of the French army from 1815 to 1870, in relation to the army of the *ancien régime* and the European armies of the time, was the "very great diversity of its social structure, and the very clearly democratic character of the cadres' recruitment."[2] The twentieth-century French army has retained the "democratic character" of officer recruitment, even extended it. But it also has conserved a core of officers from the traditional, conservative families who predominate in the upper ranks, as their forebears did in earlier decades.

The permanent French army was created in 1445, consisting of fifteen companies of gendarmes with the "positions of command given to the highest personages of the Kingdom."[3] One of nobility's prerogatives was the privilege of military command, but under the *ancien régime* the noble's military activity was not that of the professional who made a career of the army; it was more in the nature of a service which intermittently attracted the aristocrat's attention. Some ten thousand families of the provincial nobility traditionally provided support to the army, with military service remaining the justification for the privileges they enjoyed. However, officers were drawn not only from the nobility during the *ancien régime* since two paths were available for commoners to become officers. One of these was followed by the bourgeois who could buy a commission; the second was open to the man who could work his way up from the ranks, the *officier de fortune*. Nonetheless, in the armies of the *ancien régime*, the men who entered the officers' ranks by these two paths remained in a minority, and in 1781 even these two paths were closed.

However, the Revolutionary period reopened the officer corps to commoners, and all Frenchmen who could prove they were worthy of command could attain command (hence, the Marshal's baton in the knapsack of every soldier). The army Napoleon led was

> that army in which a whole youth fired with ambition found a career, a refuge, the promise of adventure and opportunity for enthusiasm outside of revolutionary atrocities; an army for which the fusion of

---

[2] Raoul Girardet, *La Société militaire dans la France contemporaine* (Paris: Plon, 1953), p. 49.

[3] See *ibid.*, pp. 50–54. The intermittent service of the officer is shown by the fact that in 1787, of 36,000 officers apparently on pay status, only 13,000 were on active duty. Vagts, *A History of Militarism*, p. 61.

old regulars and companies of ardent volunteers achieved, after five years of varied campaigns, an incomparable quality.[4]

Among many other things, the concept of a military career open to all was bequeathed to France by the Revolutionary and Napoleonic periods. If the officer corps of the eighteenth century was not completely professional, its successor in the nineteenth century became so, and men dedicating their lives to the profession of warmaking henceforth led the nation's fighting forces.

The backbone of the French army after 1815 became the men who earned their officer's epaulets by working their way up from the ranks, the *officiers de fortune*, generally men from the lower classes of society. Considering the army an instrument of revolution and destroyer of the established order, the upper classes largely withdrew their support. Furthermore, the nobility still considered military service to be but a part of the noble life, not a life in itself. Finally, the army was held in low national esteem after Napoleon's fall, and apparently did not promise an attractive career.

Although the *officiers de fortune* were numerically dominant after 1815, they were clustered in the lower commissioned grades, and to retire as a captain was the ambition of such an officer. The hierarchies' upper reaches were reserved for the graduates of the great military schools, particularly Saint-Cyr. Although the academy was theoretically open to all, Saint-Cyr's high costs reduced the eligibles to those few sons of the bourgeoisie and the great families who decided upon a military career. In addition, many nobles who had fled during the Revolutionary period returned with the Restoration and were appointed to senior posts. However, the nobles began leaving the army with the coming to power of the citizen king, Louis Philippe, and would not return in any great numbers until the Second Empire. Under Louis Philippe the army remained in the doldrums, and the lure of money-making was greater than the lure of warmaking.[5]

[4] Lucien Romier, *A History of France* (London: Macmillan and Co., 1955), p. 348.

[5] The decline in the number of aristocrats entering Saint-Cyr (apparent before 1830 but accelerated thereafter), is revealed by the fact that in 1828 nearly half of the entrants to Saint-Cyr bore the particle *de* as part of their names. In 1833, the number of names with the *de* had dropped to one-fourth of the entrants; in 1843, it had dropped to one-fifth. Howard, *Soldiers and Governments*, p. 56. See also François Bédarida, "L'Armée et la République," *Revue Historique*, CCXXXII (July–September, 1964), 151, 160.

But Napoleon III restored the army's glory and promoted the military's development. A professional army had been evolving in France since 1815, nursed by low induction, long periods of service, and faith in the efficacy of small but highly trained forces. Amid Napoleon's great attention to ceremony and glory, the Second Empire culminated the drive toward a professional fighting machine. In the course of Napoleon III's reign, youths from the upper classes reappeared in greater numbers in the military schools, attracted by a strong authoritarian regime, regarding the army as the force of order, and now accepting it as a profession.[6]

With the birth of the Third Republic and its consolidation, the influx of the upper classes into the army increased, driven by the republicans' repeatedly purging the civil service and the judiciary from 1876 in order to remove nonrepublican elements. Regarded as undesirable in the nation's political or administrative life, the conservatives turned to the one avenue left open to them, the army. In still another manner, the republican regime assured that the traditional groups would increase numerically in the army when it established that half of each year's officers would come from Saint-Cyr or the Ecole Polytechnique, the latter school being the source of technical specialists. Some men of modest means entered these schools, but mainly the students came from the old aristocracy and the middle and high bourgeoisie. Speaking of the period up to around 1900, one student of the French army states that it was

> the dominant trend to put the officers into a caste ruled by the representatives of the traditionalist aristocracy, marked by the influence of the clergy and harboring a thorough contempt for republican institutions. Those officers who refused to conform all had the same story to report: for twenty-five years the climate in the Army had been hostile to everything that deviated from an all-embracing conservatism, that is, from monarchist sympathies or a monarchist tradition.[7]

[6] The return of the gentry to the army is evidenced in the following figures of entrants to Saint-Cyr from the Catholic schools, which attracted the upper classes and the wealthy; of 1,869 entrants to Saint-Cyr between 1847 and 1853, only 21 came from Catholic schools; of 1,887 entrants between 1863 and 1869, 526 were clerically educated. Howard, *Soldiers and Governments*, p. 59. Concerning the army in the period 1815–1870 see Girardet, *La Société militaire*, pp. 50–86; Joseph Monteilhet, *Les institutions militaires de la France* (Paris: Felix Alcan, 1932), pp. 1–64.

[7] Paul-Marie de la Gorce, *The French Army* (New York: George Braziller, 1963), p. 51.

In 1880 advancement from the ranks was all but shut off when it was decreed that henceforth officers could not be named from the non-commissioned grades without passing through one of three schools (Saint-Maixent for the infantry, Saumur for the cavalry, and Versaille for the artillery and engineers), where entrance was by competitive examination. Since the exams required some scholastic background, the lesser bourgeoisie came to predominate in these schools, bringing a new social level to the *officiers de fortune*, who formerly were mainly the sons of peasants and artisans.[8]

Between 1900 and 1911 the upper classes again refrained from sending their sons into the military profession as the army entered the crisis period described in the previous chapter. An indication of the reluctance to enter the army is seen in Saint-Cyr's enrollment, which dropped from 1,920 in 1897 to 982 in 1907.[9]

For a brief period just before 1914, the army regained its attractiveness, but following World War I, the military again lost its appeal. War-weary and pacifist Frenchmen all but forgot their army, except for the feeling that it was a tax burden.[10] A small, disregarded army was not a great career attraction, and the army's drawing power was slight until about 1936, when the international situation generated interest in defense and armies and resulted in increased applications to Saint-Cyr.

The elite of the French army officers are graduates of France's West Point, Saint-Cyr. Napoleon founded the academy in 1808 when he moved his military school from Fontainebleau to Saint-Cyr, formerly a school for daughters of the nobility. Napoleon also gave the school its motto: They learn that they may conquer. A "temple of tradition," the school was bombed out during World War II.[11] Since Saint-Cyr was uninhabitable at the end of the war, the academy was moved to a site in Brittany, where it became known as Saint-Cyr-Coëtquidan. Approximately eight hundred students study the military arts there, six hundred of these entering via examinations taken as civilians, with the remainder recruited by examination among young noncommissioned officers. In

[8] Monteilhet, *Les institutions militaires*, pp. 186–89; François Kuntz, *L'officier français dans la nation* (Paris: Charles-Lavauzelle et Cie., 1960), p. 67. In 1904, sergeants were given the right to occupy, without going through one of the schools, one-tenth of the vacancies for the rank of sublieutenant. Girardet, *La Société militaire*, p. 276.

[9] Girardet, *La Société militaire*, p. 274; see pp. 193–202, 238–78.

[10] Arpad Kovacs, "French Military Legislation in the Third Republic, 1871–1940," *Military Affairs*, XIII (Spring, 1949), 12.

[11] Jean Planchais, *L'Armée* (Paris: Buchet Chastel, 1959), p. 83.

September, 1961, the Minister of Armed Forces abolished the Inter-Service Military School with its two divisions (the Division Saint-Cyr for those who came directly from civilian life, and the Division of Troops for those who came from the ranks), and created in its stead two distinct schools. There is now the Special Military School of Saint-Cyr, open to civilians by competition, and the Military Inter-Service School for men from the noncommissioned ranks who desire to become officers. The location of the schools is the same, but the schools are separate.[12]

However, the graduates of Saint-Cyr are not the only French officers, since the Ecole Polytechnique has also provided commanders for the army, but in steadily decreasing numbers. In addition, there are the reservists (the short-term officers), and the men who have risen from the ranks. The losses in Indochina and Algeria took a heavy toll of young Saint-Cyrians, and a shortage of officers appeared in France.[13] Moreover, a lowering of the prestige of the officer in postwar France, the minimal pay and housing difficulties of officers, the troubles collectively known as the *malaise de l'armée*, contributed to the officer shortage. The number of applications for Saint-Cyr, which dropped from 587 in 1951 to 360 in 1954, bears witness to the diminished popularity of the army.[14]

Consequently, men who attained commissioned status through avenues other than Saint-Cyr or the Ecole Polytechnique entered the officer corps in increasing numbers. The influx from other sources of advancement to officer grade is revealed in the fact that in 1949 graduates of Saint-Cyr and the Ecole Polytechnique amounted to 81.6 percent of the French army officer corps; in 1958 alumni of these schools constituted only 47.7 percent of the officers in the French army. On the other hand, while in 1959 only 18.4 percent of officers were reservists or men who had advanced through the ranks, the proportion represented by these two groups had risen by 1958 to 52.3 percent of the army

[12] *Le Monde*, September 23, 1961, and November 7, 1961.

[13] In the war in Indochina, 2,005 French officers lost their lives. Jean-Raymond Tournoux, *Secrets d'état* (Paris: Plon, 1960), p. 93; it has been estimated that one out of every three Saint-Cyr graduates died in Indochina within two years of graduation. Blair Clark, "France's St. Cyr: 'Rise, Officers!'" *New York Times Magazine*, July 18, 1954, p. 8.

[14] Raoul Girardet, "Civil and Military Power in the Fourth Republic," in Samuel P. Huntington, ed., *Changing Patterns of Military Politics* (New York: The Free Press of Glencoe, 1962), p. 127. See also Raoul Girardet, *et al.*, *La Crise militaire française, 1945–1962* (Paris: Armand Colin, 1964), p. 34.

officers.[15] However, a heavy reliance upon the ranks and the non-commissioned officer schools to produce officers is nothing new in the French army. On the eve of the War of 1870, graduates of Saint-Cyr and the Ecole Polytechnique constituted but 40 percent of army officers; on the eve of World War I, 52.1 percent; and in 1938, 35.9 percent. Thus, the French army officer corps has long been characterized by diversity in recruitment and in social background.[16]

The broad range of backgrounds of army officers can be attributed not to changing French social structure, which has remained relatively immobile, but to military needs. It will be recalled that the lower classes had been admitted to the officer ranks even during the *ancien régime*, and with the exception of the period from 1781 to the Revolution, continued to be able to advance as *officiers de fortune*. Then the social level of *officiers de fortune* was raised from the peasant and artisan class to the petty bourgeoisie by laws passed early in the Third Republic requiring noncommissioned officers to pass through special schools to win a commission. Moreover, it was men of the latter class who entered the officer corps in great numbers after World War II. It may therefore be said that there has been no "shift in officer recruitment" in the French army, since the lower classes have long been present in officer grades in large numbers, and as a result of army needs, not as a result of the democratization of French society.[17]

[15] The graduates of the Ecole Polytechnique were 4.8 percent of the officer corps in 1949, and .32 percent of the officer corps in 1958. The Division Saint-Cyr graduates were 38.5 percent of the officer corps in 1949, and 22.8 percent of the officer corps in 1958. The Division of Troop graduates were 38.3 percent of the officer corps in 1949, and 24.6 percent of the officer corps in 1958. Reservists numbered 12.2 percent of the officer corps in 1949, and 17.5 percent of the officer corps in 1958. Officers who had advanced through the ranks were 5.4 percent of all officers in the army in 1949, and 35.8 percent of army officers in 1958. Capitaines T. et A., "Capitaines, ou bas-officiers? Essai sur la structure sociale de l'armée française," *La nouvelle critique*, No. 107 (June, 1959), 55.

[16] Girardet, *La Crise militaire française*, pp. 16–18; see also pp. 63–66.

[17] On the social composition of the French army officer corps see the report of an inquiry on ten thousand officers who had graduated from Saint-Cyr, conducted by the Military Sociology Committee (created by a group of professors of the Institute of Political Science in Paris and officers of the War College), Jacqueline Bernard, "L'origine sociale," *Le Monde*, December 23, 1960; *Le Monde*, December 29, 1960. See also Capitaines T. et A., "Essai sur la structure sociale," pp. 43–84; a study conducted by the Air Force Committee of Psychological Action and Instruction on cadets at French military academies, "Attitudes et motivations des candidats aux grandes écoles militaires," *Revue française de sociologie*, II (April–June, 1961), 133–51; Jean-Raymond Tournoux, "A Proletarian Army," *Reporter*, XXII (February

And as was true in earlier times, men who advanced from the ranks have remained in the lower commissioned grades. The military hierarchy has maintained its quality of being the preserve of the Saint-Cyrians. From 1949 to 1958 their proportion among superior officers remained unchanged at 65 percent; in 1960, 72 percent of the colonels, 56 percent of the lieutenant colonels, 46 percent of the majors, 25 percent of the captains, and 23 percent of the lieutenants were Saint-Cyr graduates.[18] Men who represent a wider social base are relegated to lower ranks of officership. Of 5,279 men listed as promoted from the ranks in the army's 1958 annual, 3,209 were serving in the grade of captain.[19] Only ninety-three men who had passed to officer's bars from the noncommissioned ranks had succeeded in penetrating the superior grades, representing only 1.5 percent of the total number of superior officers.

Judging from the foregoing, it may justly be said that "the grade of captain constitutes the Marshal's baton of almost the totality of officers from the ranks."[20] The situation is a deteriorating one for these officers because the percentage of the modern *officiers de fortune* who have advanced to superior positions has dropped from 3.5 percent in 1949 to 1.5 percent in 1958. Sixteen percent of a Saint-Cyr class will one day become generals, and 42 percent will advance to the grade of colonel. Fellow officers who are not graduates of Saint-Cyr can anticipate that only 3 percent of their number will ever wear generals' insignia, and only 15 percent that of a colonel. In addition the individual who is not a graduate of Saint-Cyr will find not only that his ultimate rank will be lower than his Saint-Cyr colleague, but also that promotions will come slower. For example, he can anticipate making captain at age thirty-three and major when forty-two years old. The Saint-Cyrian will attain these grades at an average age of twenty-nine and a half and thirty-eight and a half respectively:[21]

> Thus the sphere of high grades remains the guarded class, on the one hand of some sons of the high and middle bourgeoisie who choose in spite of everything the career of arms . . . on the other hand

18, 1960), 19–21; and a study based on information furnished by the commandant of Saint-Cyr concerning 4,400 cadets in the Division Saint-Cyr during the period 1945–1958, Girardet, *La Crise militaire française*, pp. 30–54; see also pp. 55–69.

[18] Tournoux, "A Proletarian Army," p. 19.

[19] Capitaines T. et A., "Essai sur la structure sociale," pp. 46–47.

[20] *Ibid.*, p. 62.

[21] Girardet, *La Crise militaire française*, p. 85; see pp. 79–84.

of officers "coming from everywhere" but individually giving desirable guarantees—"particularly qualified and chosen" to use an official phrase.[22]

Among the men of Saint-Cyr, the middle class and the provincial aristocracy continue to provide a solid core of aspiring officers. Sons of lesser civil servants and of proprietors of small businesses largely furnish the remainder of Saint-Cyrians. The slight representation of other occupational groups is seen in the figures produced by the Air Force Committee of Psychological Action and Instruction in their 1959 study of candidates at the military academies, which included the air force and navy schools as well as the army. The study revealed that only 5 percent of the candidates were sons of workers, 6 percent were sons of farmers, 5 percent were sons of clerks, and only 7 percent were sons of employees or artisans.[23]

Perhaps the most striking fact that emerged from this study and one conducted by the Military Sociology Committee was the steady progression of the sons and grandsons of military men entering the army. The proportion of military offspring at Saint-Cyr in the 1937–1939 period was 30 percent; in the 1945–1948 period the proportion of cadets at the Division Saint-Cyr whose fathers had been professional soldiers had risen to 33 percent, with this figure rising to 44 percent in the 1954–1958 period.[24] Almost one-third of these scions of military families were from two-generation military backgrounds, revealing the existence of a military tradition in their families.[25] In 1958, almost half of the candidates (44 percent) of the Division Saint-Cyr had military ancestors of at least one generation. The Division of Troops at Saint-Cyr indicated the same trend, with the percentage of military sons in the Division rising from 28 percent for the 1945–1948 period to 36.5 percent for the 1954–1958 period.[26] The French tradition of military families has continued and is growing.

Jean-Raymond Tournoux has written that the army officer corps has become proletarianized and has become close to the working class.[27]

---

[22] Capitaines T. et A., "Essai sur la structure sociale," p. 63.

[23] "Attitudes et motivations des candidats aux grandes écoles militaires," p. 135. See Girardet, *La Crise militaire française*, p. 41.

[24] *Le Monde*, December 28, 1960.

[25] See *ibid.*, and "Attitudes et motivations des candidats aux grandes écoles militaires," p. 135.

[26] *Le Monde*, December 28, 1960.

[27] Tournoux, "A Proletarian Army," p. 19.

This is a valid observation if one considers only one aspect of the question, that of the men entering the officer ranks by paths other than France's West Point. However, the accentuation of Saint-Cyr's traditional character presents another image, as Saint-Cyr continues to foster a society isolated from France.[28] Drawn largely from those classes that are "still embittered over being a ruling class no longer," the graduates of Saint-Cyr form a tightly knit caste.[29]

But what about the men who have become officers by other paths? They have come from different social levels than the Saint-Cyrians, and they are numerous in the officer corps. Perhaps they are closer to the nation, and could be said to be more "integrated" into the nation. However, this does not seem to be the case. French officers for decades have been drawn from basically the same social groups as in recent years. Actually, in social background the officer corps since 1815 has continually constituted a body removed from the more progressive classes of French life. The Saint-Cyrians of today are reminiscent of their nineteenth-century and early twentieth-century forebears in this respect. The former noncommissioned officers who have advanced to officer rank have also been drawn from certain elements of French society, coming especially from agricultural France, and increasingly in recent times from the petty bourgeoisie. They are from classes which represent "static" France, classes which have resisted change and which reflect one of France's basic divisions:

> The officers, as we have seen, came from very humble circumstances. The percentage of Saint-Cyr and Polytechnique graduates had shrunk considerably. And, conversely, promotions from the ranks and via the school for noncoms had become much more numerous than before the war. Thus the military milieu had been transformed. There were now families that had achieved upward social mobility by the presence of an officer in their midst. This milieu was, in the main, that of the agricultural or storekeeping petite bourgeoisie, and the families of noncoms now became the families of officers. This increased the isolation of the military in French society. For now the roots lay in classes that remained outside the immense economic transformations that had taken place in France in the previous fifteen years. . . . And indeed, in military circles today, as with certain groups of store-keepers, artisans and small farmers, there is the same rejection of modern economic transformations, the same fear of the risks of

[28] *Le Monde*, December 28, 1960; Jean Planchais, "The French Army: A Close-Up," *New York Times Magazine*, February 18, 1962, p. 16.
[29] Planchais, "The French Army," p. 16.

change, the same suspicion of all the revolutions of our day, which explain the immense success enjoyed, in 1956, by the Poujade movement.[30]

Since the end of World War II, the opportunity to be admitted to the officer class in France has been enhanced because of officer shortages created by war losses and a popular shying away from the military career. As a result, large numbers of men have been able to win officers' bars through the noncom schools and direct promotion from the ranks, but these same men are in general found in the lower levels of command. While the officer corps has remained open in this sense, admitting representatives of the lower classes, in another way it has become even more restrictive as Saint-Cyr has increasingly drawn cadets from its traditional recruitment sources, especially from military families.

In conclusion, we may say that the social composition of the modern French army officer corps has been such that officers have represented a special social grouping, composed of men generally removed, in terms of their background, from the mainstream of French life.

[30] De la Gorce, *The French Army*, p. 549.

CHAPTER IV

The Unity of the Army

La force publique est essentiellement obéissante. Nul corps armé ne peut délibérer.—LOI DE 14 SEPTEMBRE 1791.

UNITY IS an organizational necessity for an effective fighting force—thus the need for discipline in an army. But unity meant far more to the French officer after World War II than combat effectiveness. The French army was divided into two hostile camps in 1940, when its men were faced with the critical choice of following a condemned brigadier general to London, or a Marshal of France and his legally instituted government to Vichy. A livid scar was left on the officer corps by the crisis of conscience forced on the army by Charles de Gaulle.

Unity in the army became a fetish in the postwar world of France's officers, for the conviction was deep that a split such as the one experienced during World War II could not be permitted to recur. The call for unity, the fear of division, permeated the officer corps, with the result that the principle of unity became a tool of revolution, for wherever one part of the army went, according to the principle, the rest were sure to go. Several times an activist minority used the army's obsession with unity to attempt to rally others to their side. But the unity was an image. Men who varied greatly in background and experience, and who were divided into several schools of thought, feared disunity but remained divided.

Military discipline dictates that military men will act the same, not think the same, and armies find among their members men with diverse ideas. But the officers' differences are seldom expressed outside their own circles. Indeed, expressions of political opinion by French military men have been strictly regulated, to the extent that from 1872 to 1945 the soldier in France did not even have the right to vote. Even though he has won the right of suffrage, the officer's freedom to express his views on public matters remains limited. By a decree issued in 1933, officers on active duty must obtain the approval of the government before publishing any writings relative to "all questions implicating contemporary personalities, or of a nature to raise political or religious controversies."[1] Officers not on active duty may make no mention of their military grade without the approval of the government when writing on the above subjects. Failure to follow these regulations subjects the offender to both military and civilian disciplinary action.

But while publications can be controlled, thought and opinions are more difficult to restrain. Geographically, structurally, and mentally, the French army became divided after World War II, and all the exhortations to unity could not create a single-minded, unified entity.[2] The attitudes which will be discussed here were pieced together from various sources, and unfortunately, there is no way of precisely measuring their strength or the extent of their influence. The men who followed the rebellious generals in the April, 1961, putsch may have been driven by political conviction, by commitment to a French Algeria, by devotion to their leaders, by a general sense of bitterness growing since 1940, or by a complex intermeshing of these and other reasons.

But because strength and the extent of influence are immeasurable, a probing of attitudes is not rendered meaningless. It may reveal what some officers were thinking, and thus their feelings concerning certain problems and ways of solving them. It may indicate adherence to the regime or the existence of strands of thought which harbored hostility to the government. It may disclose altogether different concepts of government and ways to direct the nation's life. It may indicate, in short, whether the army was at one in thought with the nation it served, or whether it was determining its own solutions to problems and setting its own national goals. As shall be seen, the French army became an army searching for itself, for a doctrine, and for a voice. "And when the mute began to speak," reported the Paris-based David Schoenbrun, "it was not with one voice; it was with many voices, all discordant."[3]

---

[1] Article 29 of the decree of April 1, 1933. See *Le Monde*, September 18–19, 1960, and Prosper Weil, "Armée et fonction publique," in Tony Albord, *et al.*, *La Défense nationale* (Paris: Presses Universitaires de France, 1958), pp. 194–203.

[2] The danger of suspecting the army *en bloc* is raised by Jean Planchais. Since people may fail to see the various currents in the army, they may accuse all of the army and thereby offend the loyal officers. *Le Monde*, September 21, 1961.

[3] David Schoenbrun, "De Gaulle Faces an Anguished Army," *New York Times Magazine*, February 14, 1960, p. 13. The divisions in the army were apparently missed by Meisel as he seems content to lump the French officer corps under the

The army's many voices should not have been surprising given the French political environment and the fact that, "in sum, the whole spread of opinions in the nation are reflected in the army."[4]

Concerning the geographic factor, during the Algerian war, almost half the French army was sent to subdue the rebels. The remainder was divided between Germany, other parts of Africa, the Pacific, and France itself, where only fifty to sixty thousand troops were stationed. Thus the army was spatially divided, an important factor because many officers, serving overseas for long periods of time, in France only briefly and intermittently, lost contact with France. A study conducted by the Military Sociology Committee of the *Ecole supérieure de guerre* in 1959 disclosed that the average infantry officer had spent three-quarters of the years between 1946 and 1958 outside of France, spending more time in Africa than in his own country, with additional tours of duty in Germany and Asia.[5] For many officers, allegiances and loyalties went elsewhere than to the homeland, and for these nomads, *Algérie française* became more important than obedience to an unknown France.

Structurally, a difference in generations was perceptible in the French army officer corps, a deeper division than the usual divergence between young and old. Obedience became less an absolute for the young lieutenants and captains who fought a series of small encounters in the jungles of Indochina and the fields and mountains of Algeria, than for the older, higher-ranking officers schooled in more traditional modes of warfare. The battles waged molded the younger men into officers of great initiative, daring, and responsibility, more interested in results than staff studies. They also felt most strongly the humiliations and bitter reversals suffered by the army.

---

label of Fascist. James H. Meisel, *The Fall of the Republic* (Ann Arbor: The University of Michigan Press, 1962), pp. 3–5.

[4] Claude Dufresnoy, *Des officiers parlent* (Paris: Julliard, 1961), pp. 144–45. This book is a presentation of the opinions of some seventy officers on various questions. The officers were interviewed by Dufresnoy in 1959 and 1960, and they ranged in grade from sublieutenant to general. Almost all were serving at posts in Algeria.

[5] The average infantry officer spent 27 percent of the period 1946–1958 in France, 19 percent in Germany, 38.5 percent in Africa, 12.5 percent in Asia, and 3 percent in other overseas posts. The percentages for officers in other branches were approximately the same, with the exception of the average school staff officer who had spent an average of 39.5 percent of the period in France, and half as much time as the infantry officer in Africa. Raoul Girardet, *et al.*, *La Crise militaire française* (Paris: Armand Colin, 1964), p. 139.

They blamed their superior officers for being submissive to Paris and for worrying more about their own promotions than getting the needed materials and support necessary for victory. Learning new techniques of war from their adversaries in Indochina and applying them in Algeria, the subordinate officers thought their superiors lagged behind in appreciation of the new combat. They believed them to be professionally backward, thinking as they were in terms of World War II tactics, and became positive that the main qualifications for a general's stars had become docility to civilian authority and opportunism. They scorned the "unwieldiness and sclerosis of the military apparatus, and the conformism and routine into which many of their leaders had sunk." [6]

Antedating their sentiment was the longstanding division between the colonial army and the army of metropolitan France. From the time of Louis Napoleon, French overseas forces enjoyed greater prestige and glory than the continental army, since in the colonial areas empires were won and military honors were earned. A different spirit pervaded the colonial army, freer in its movements than the homeland army, less subordinate to civilian authority and less stringent in its application of government directives which came from faraway Paris. Augmenting the independent spirit of the colonial army were the difficulty of communications and an ignorance in Paris of colonial conditions. In the colonies, the line between civil and military authority was frequently weak, and officers often engaged in civil and administrative tasks. In Morocco, Tunisia, Algeria, and Madagascar, French officers had earlier engaged in nonmilitary duties, but never had they done so on the scale given them by Paris and Algiers after 1956. These functions, plus the traditional independence of the colonial army, helped to create another rift within the army, and between the army and the nation.

The cleavage between the professional army and the *contingent* (the draftees), is the last structural division to be mentioned. This division is found in all armies of the cadre-conscript type: the division between the professional and the amateur, between the military-oriented career officer and the civilian-oriented draftee. In a favorable situation, the difference is essentially one of career choice, with both the professional and the amateur sharing the basic values of the civilian world.

[6] Raoul Girardet, "Civil and Military Power in the Fourth Republic," in Samuel P. Huntington, ed., *Changing Patterns of Military Politics* (New York: The Free Press of Glencoe, 1962), pp. 126–27; see also Jean Planchais, "The French Army," *Atlas*, II (November, 1961), 335–38; *Le Monde*, March 19, 1958.

But in France, the professionals had created their own special world and the draftee became an intruder, his world and that of the professionals having little in common. What the draftee knew was the civilian world, not the professional's special caste society. That the division was important was demonstrated in the April, 1961, putsch, when men of the *contingent* refused to follow officers who were attacking the government. In his *Les Prétoriens*, Jean Lartéguy reveals the split between the professional and the amateur soldier and the relation of each to the nation. A lieutenant of the *contingent* tells Colonel Raspéguy, the pride and the commander of a famous paratroop division: "But we are four hundred thousand. It is we who are France, not you."[7]

Mentally, the French army officers were divided into traditionalists, technicians, and activists, the last mentioned being the most political elements of the army and among whom we find the progressives, the revolutionary war advocates, and the adherents of integral Catholicism. The traditionalists were those officers who were true to the tradition of obedience whether they approved of the orders they received or not. They were opposed to seeing the army become a political body, imposing its will on the nation, because to the traditionalist this was a reversal of roles. Discipline was for them the foundation of the relation between the army and the state it served, and an order from civilian masters was not a basis of discussion but a command to be executed. The *Grande Muette* was the army of the traditionalists.

The traditionalist's attitude was prevalent in the responses to questions relative to discipline posed to French officers by Claude Dufresnoy. A typical reply came from the captain who was asked in August, 1960, if he would accept negotiations with the Algerian rebels. "For me," answered the officer, "there is no problem, I obey the government. Yesterday, I obeyed M. Lacoste, today I obey General de Gaulle. I do not discuss the orders that I receive."[8] Even a major opposed to negotiations finally admitted that in his opinion the army would take the path of discipline. He first retorted that the army would revolt if the government undertook negotiations. But then, lowering his head, he amended, "It will obey."[9]

[7] Jean Lartéguy, *Les Prétoriens* (Paris: Les presses de la Cité, 1961), p. 46.

[8] Dufresnoy, *Des officiers parlent*, p. 136.

[9] *Ibid.*, p. 197. Of thirty-five officers who expressed themselves on the alternatives of discipline or revolt, twenty-seven affirmed the traditional position, with the remainder announcing they would actively resist the government if it entered negotiations with the FLN. See also Jean Planchais, "L'Armée, le régime, l'Algérie," *Le Monde*, March 11, 1960.

The second group, the technicians, were men who were more scientists and engineers than soldiers, not fitting into the usual stereotype of the career officer. Their problems were technical ones, and they were concerned with the less conventional types of warfare. They were "push-button" warriors and often seemed to have little in common with officers engaged in the more physical aspects of combat. In fact, the men who fought the close-contact wars of Indochina and Algeria felt a certain disdain toward the technicians, who were generally found in the rear echelons and in the staffs.[10]

It is the third category of officers, the activists (sometimes referred to as the ultras or militants), who were the politically ambitious elements of the French army in the last days of the Fourth Republic and the early years of the Fifth. Many of Dufresnoy's respondents referred to the activist group of the army, and all added that these men were a small minority among French officers. One lieutenant in September, 1959, estimated that if the government began negotiations with the FLN, four-tenths of the army would obey, simply content to see the war end and gladly follow the government's course. Another four-tenths would obey "because the army obeys the legal power." The remaining two-tenths would actively oppose the government's action, opined the lieutenant, and attempt to dictate a change of policy.[11] But even though the activists were few in number, they represented the politically dangerous officers.

In general, the activists wished to make the army their instrument of political action, imposing their desires on civil authorities and acting as a veto power over disliked government policies. Some of the activists were uninterested in political institutions and the political process as such, desiring only to ensure that the government, whatever it might be, keep Algeria French. Other officers, however, and these were apparently a minority of the activists, looked forward to a true national revolution, both political and social. In these circles was to be seen the historical attachment of the French army to the rightist viewpoint of a strong, authoritarian government. Activist officers, particularly those in the

[10] See Walter Kerr, "The French Army in Trouble," *Foreign Affairs*, XL (October, 1961), 89–90; John Terraine, "The Army in Modern France," *History Today*, XI (November, 1961), 742.

[11] Dufresnoy, *Des officiers parlent*, p. 34. Actually, this estimate of activists at two-tenths of the army seems to be high. It would have placed their number at around 6,600 officers, there being some 33,000 career army officers. Planchais has placed the number of activists at 2,000–3,000. Jean Planchais, "The French Army: A Close-Up," *New York Times Magazine*, February 18, 1962, p. 109.

psychological warfare bureaus, challenged republican ideas and concluded that a centralized government, free of control by political parties
and Parliament, would provide the best system of government to meet
the challenges facing France in the twentieth century.[12]

One strain of activists came to be labeled the "progressives" in their
approach to French political ills, and their doctrines have been called
both a kind of national socialism and a type of national communism.
But whatever the label, these officers envisaged an anticapitalist,
authoritarian government which would promote social and economic
reforms while adamantly opposing international communism. In the
progressives' hands, the army, long accused of conservatism, would
have become an instrument of social and economic change, benefiting
Moslems in Algeria, and workers and small businessmen in France.
Because of their vague programs, the progressive approach is difficult
to establish in detail, but it has been said that "some did not even
recoil from the idea of a national, Spartan, muscular, equalitarian and
patriotic Socialism, which would lure the working class away from the
Communist Party, and the Moslems from the F.L.N."[13]

Earlier it was mentioned that activists could be identified as progressives, revolutionary warfare advocates, and adherents of integral
Catholicism. These are not mutually exclusive groups, and conceivably
one man could become attached to all three. The chances that one
officer would be a believer in both revolutionary war and integral
Catholicism were very high.

The French officer who fought in Indochina and Algeria frequently
came to the conclusion that he and his comrades were being sacrificed
for nothing, struggling without policy or doctrine to guide and direct
their fight against an enemy fortified by communism. In the Catholic
church they found the ideology to oppose communism, and a refuge
and a doctrine were discovered as faith and state merged into integral
Catholicism, sometimes referred to as national Catholicism. According
to Madeleine Garrigou-Lagrange, writing in 1959, "in the name of God,
of Christian civilization and of the social doctrine of the Church, some

[12] Henri Alleg, a Communist arrested in Algiers in June, 1957, relates that while
being tortured by men of the 10th DP, he was told by one lieutenant: "What we are
doing here, we will do in France. . . . And your whore of a Republic, we will blow
it up into the air, too." Henri Alleg, *The Question* (New York: George Braziller,
1958, reprinted by Belmont Books), p. 32.

[13] Paul-Marie de la Gorce, *The French Army* (New York: George Braziller, 1963),
p. 479.

Catholics currently find themselves engaged in a temporal fight which takes on in their eyes the visage of a holy war."[14]

The moralistic, spiritualistic, humanistic church was pitted against materialistic, atheistic communism. Christianity was launched on a new crusade, and became a combatant in the world struggle. The rallying point for followers of integral Catholicism was order: social, economic, and political, best achieved by means of a conservative, authoritarian political system. Integral Catholicism's significance lies in the heavy political overtones which were inherent in this extreme right-wing movement and the fact that army officers, troubled by vacillating policies and colonial losses, were influenced by them. The intervention of the integral Catholic movement in politics was sanctioned by the rightist journal which pronounced "that the Church has the right to interest itself in politics as in all other matters, is a direct consequence of its sovereign majesty in the chapter of morals. . . ."[15]

Central promoters of the national Catholic movement were the Center of Superior Studies of Social Psychology of Georges Sauge, and the *Cité Catholique*. Sauge, a Communist at age sixteen but later converted by a Dominican, was convinced that the answer to communism was the Catholic church, the only body with a belief system capable of confronting Marxism-Leninism. Sauge, who was said to "exude from all his pores the satisfaction of being Georges Sauge," began his crusade in 1956.[16] His themes were patriotism and anticommunism, preached at meetings, in conferences, and in publications, in an effort at a "mass vaccination" against the Communist contagion.[17] Only a national

[14] Madeleine Garrigou-Lagrange, "Intégrisme et national-catholicisme," *Esprit*, November, 1959, p. 515. This article is a critical examination of the integral Catholic movement. See also Jacques Maître, "Le catholicisme d'extrême droite et la croisade anti-subversive," *Revue française de sociologie*, II (April–June, 1961), 106–17, a very good presentation of the ideological basis of the anti-Communist crusade of some army officers in France; Paul Gerin, *L'Algérie du 13 mai* (Paris: Gallimard, 1958), pp. 224–26; Jacques Fauvet and Jean Planchais, *La Fronde des généraux* (Paris: Arthaud, 1961), pp. 68–70.

[15] Quoted from *Verbe*, the organ of *Cité Catholique*, one of the organizations of the Catholic extreme Right, in Garrigou-Lagrange, "Intégrisme et national-catholicisme," p. 536.

[16] *Ibid.*, p. 523.

[17] For Sauge, anyone who was indifferent to communism was a transmission belt of communism. Charles de Gaulle was so considered by Sauge. Merry Bromberger, *et al.*, *Barricades et colonels* (Paris: Arthème Fayard, 1960), p. 76. Certain parallels

Christian reawakening, based upon God, country, and army, could save man and humanity, exhorted Sauge.

A more subtle, less gaudy organization was the *Cité Catholique*. Adopting the cell organization of its Communist foe, it created a network of some four hundred cells of from three to twenty members each, with a total membership which exceeded five thousand.[18] *Cité Catholique*'s concept of its role is seen in this extract from *Verbe*, its official journal:

> In struggling against the Algerian rebellion, we are conscious of being in the *avant-garde* of the fight against the world revolutionary movement, of fulfilling our duty as Frenchmen and as Christians, and of serving all humanity.[19]

The organization had its origins in 1946 when Jean Ousset (an anarchist converted to Catholicism) and his friend Jean Masson determined to become activists in the anti-Communist struggle, and in 1949, *Cité Catholique* was adopted as their movement's name. The *Cité Catholique* gained a large following, and cells made their appearance in the army, especially in psychological warfare circles. Although officers are forbidden to belong to organizations without the prior approval of the Minister of Armed Forces, the fact that these cells were secret facilitated their emergence. The first army cell was organized in 1957 by Captain de Cathelineau and by 1959 at least a hundred of them existed (accounting for less than 4 percent of the total *Cité Catholique* membership). Within these cells many officers "discovered with a joyful surprise their self-justification, learning that they are the 'crusaders' of modern times against the new crescent."[20]

From the harsh experiences endured in Indochina, the army concluded that capturing minds was more important in modern warfare than taking conventional military targets. Hence, a special psychological office was created in 1955 in the staff of the Tenth Military Region (Algeria). Its purpose was to raise the morale of friendly groups and sap the enemy's. At the end of 1956, Colonel Goussault took command of the office; his aides were Lieutenant Colonel Feaugas and Major

with rightist groups in the United States during the cold war come to mind when discussing the French extreme right.

[18] *Ibid.*, p. 77.

[19] Quoted from *Verbe*, January, 1959, by Garrigou-Lagrange, "Intégrisme et national-catholicisme," p. 521.

[20] Garrigou-Lagrange, "Intégrisme et national-catholicisme," p. 540. Captain de Cathelineau was killed later in 1957. De la Gorce, *The French Army*, p. 477.

Cogniet; all three were members of the *Cité Catholique*. The founder of *Cité Catholique*'s first army cell, Captain de Cathelineau, underlined the affinity of thought between the psychological service office and integral Catholicism:

> Psychological action in the army is the order of the day. It has at its disposal an official service at the Ministry of Armed Forces and its essential goal is to oppose to Marxist faith a national faith. Now, it has become evident that there is a serious basis to this national faith only in an authentic patriotism, taking root in the light of the doctrines of the Church. The *Cité Catholique* has no other goal than to beam this light. It is for the cadres of our army and of our youth the providential instrument which opens to our will all hopes.[21]

A national faith, founded on patriotism and the church, was the means to save France, promised the *Cité Catholique*. Order was considered to be more important than freedom of expression, which only strengthened the Communist enemy. Political liberalism would have to be supplanted by a strong and efficient government.

The doctrines of integral Catholicism were not those of the entire Catholic church, but were an exaggeration of certain aspects of the church turned to the uses of the extreme Right. The difference between the followers of integral Catholicism and the majority of the church's members was made manifest in two stories related by Simon's character, Jean de Larsan, in *Portrait d'un officier*. De Larsan tells of meeting a militant Catholic chaplain in Algeria who had found the war's stake in the battle between good and evil, the latter personified "by the monstrous coalition of Islam and Communism." Once reassured on the ends of the struggle, the chaplain told De Larsan, all means become justified; against those outside the law, no methods are illegitimate. "And if, by some scruple of pseudo-Christian sentimentality we fail to do our duty," the chaplain added, "it is then we who will be guilty—yes guilty before God for the blood of the innocents delivered to the malefactors whom we will have spared."[22] Reprisals, torture, and other methods of the "dirty war" had found their justification.

De Larsan met another priest in Algeria, outside a village which legionnaires had just destroyed in a pacification mission. Holding a small boy who had been beaten and whose father had been shot, the

[21] Quoted from *Verbe*, August–September, 1957, by Maître, "Le catholicisme d'extrême droite," p. 115.

[22] Pierre-Henri Simon, *Portrait d'un officier* (Paris: Editions du Seuil, 1958), p. 135.

priest sat on the ground with the boy, not trying to console him, but crying himself. When De Larsan asked him why, the priest replied: "I am so ashamed before this child."[23]

As to the question of activist penetration in the army, a leading commentator on the French army, Jean Planchais of *Le Monde*, answers: "Let us say immediately that the French army is not composed in its immense majority of 'lost soldiers' . . ." (the words used by De Gaulle to describe the men who entered the Secret Army Organization, *les soldats perdus*).[24] Perhaps the most that can be said is that although the number of activists was small, their influence was great. But since they were relatively few in number, the activists' success or failure depended upon the reaction of the mass of the army, and its reaction depended upon that of the nation.

Words such as "political army," or "army in politics," have been frequently used thus far, and will be again instead of referring only and specifically to the activists. This is not to confuse one part of the army with the whole, the political soldier with the apolitical, but is a matter of convenience, customary usage, and necessity. In the French army, the role of political leader was assumed by certain professional officers, but at the same time, as noted above, the reaction of the mass of the army affected the outcome of the activists' endeavors. Thus, to speak of the army in politics really is to refer to the relatively few politically ambitious officers, while simultaneously remembering that the entire army must be considered.

The split between the Gaullists and the anti-Gaullists was one more division in the army. The former had at its core the men who answered De Gaulle's call of June 18, 1940, and rallied to the General's Free French forces in London. Among the Gaullists, one also finds the members of the Resistance who were incorporated into the Regular army after the liberation, as well as the young officers who entered the army after the war and who adhered to Gaullism, not out of personal allegiance to De Gaulle, but out of acceptance of his policies. Those men who recalled De Gaulle's "unmilitary" action of 1940 and who chose to obey the legally constituted Pétain government comprised the anti-Gaullists. These and others also opposed him on policy grounds, especially his Algerian policy and his drive to create an independent French nuclear force.

[23] *Ibid.*, p. 136.

[24] Jean Planchais, "Les 'soldats perdus' et les autres," *Le Monde*, March 2, 1962.

Despite the numerous differences and divisions which existed in the army, the myth of the unity of the army remained intact and it became a convenient fiction for the activists, who used the passion for unity as a weapon in their assaults against the government in May, 1958, in January, 1960, and in April, 1961. Generally speaking, the strength of the activists was found in the units which had fought outside France for extended periods, especially in the paratroop units, the legionnaire units, and in the psychological service sections.

The airborne fighters that appeared in the army after World War II had become the elite troops of the French armed forces. Tough, well-trained, the "paras" developed into a legend during the Indochinese and Algerian conflicts. Like the already famous Foreign Legion, they constituted a body separate from the army and they gloried in their separateness. In Lartéguy's *Les Prétoriens*, Colonel Raspéguy observes: "We have created a sect of warriors apart from the army...."[25] A former colonel in the French army, Roger Trinquier, adds, "They [the "paras"] fought just for the regiment, for the honor of the regiment."[26] The paratroop recruiting posters attracted young men with the proud motto: "*Mon domaine la gloire, mon reve la bagarre.*"[27] Their camouflage uniforms, worn at all times—even in Paris—their proudly worn berets, extreme discipline, and their contempt for the "softer" elements of the army, contributed to the "paras" superman image, an image they did not contest. The "para" prayer expresses the Spartan attitude of these units and their devotion to duty:

> Give me, my God, what you still have
> Give me what no one asks for
> I do not ask for wealth
> Nor for success, nor even health
>
> People ask you so often, my God, for all that
> That you cannot have any left
> Give me, my God, what you still have
> Give me what people refuse to accept from you
>
> I want insecurity and disquietude
> I want turmoil and brawl

[25] Lartéguy, *Les Prétoriens*, p. 47.

[26] Roger Trinquier, *Le Coup d'état du 13 mai* (Paris: Editions l'Esprit Nouveau, 1962), p. 23.

[27] "My domain glory, my dream fighting." Pierre Leulliette, *St. Michael and the Dragon* (Boston: Houghton Mifflin Co., 1964), p. 2.

And if you should give them to me, my God
Once and for all
Let me be sure to have them always
For I will not always have the courage
To ask you for them.[28]

However, an attempt to explain political involvement by background proves inconclusive when applied to French army officers. Those who participated openly in attempts to overthrow the government were most often Saint-Cyr graduates, had served in Indochina and in Algeria, and had been in paratroop and/or Legion units. For example, of eighty-three officers tried in the aftermath of the April, 1961, putsch, thirty-eight had served in paratroop organizations and twenty-four in legionnaire units, several of the latter also being airborne troops.

But in surveying the men who remained loyal to the regime, judged so by the announcements of promotions and elevation to responsible posts after April, 1961, once more it is discovered that most were Saint-Cyrians, had served in Indochina and Algeria, and while the majority were not paratroop officers, several had careers in the colonial infantry. It should be mentioned that these officers were all general officers, thus older men, while the officers of the putsch trials were mostly younger officers. Perhaps the "loyal" officers, because of age considerations, had not been attracted to the new paratroop units which were formed after the war; hence the lack of "paras" in their midst.[29]

For a moment, let us look at a few of the men who made contrary choices when confronted with the problem of opposing the government or remaining loyal in 1961. General Jean Crépin earned his first star in 1952 at the age of forty-four and became the youngest general in the French army. A graduate of the Ecole Polytechnique, he served in China after his graduation. During World War II he was with the Free French as a commander of artillery under General Leclerc. Later he was sent to Indochina, ultimately taking part in truce negotiations with the Vietminh. After holding various staff positions, in 1959, Crépin was sent to Algeria and served on General Jacques Massu's staff, taking over Massu's job as Algiers area commander in January, 1960. Crépin,

[28] Quoted by Giles Perrault, *Les parachutistes* (Paris: Editions du Seuil, 1961), p. 157. This book is a study of military elites, concluding that they are politically dangerous.

[29] The generalizations on background are based on information compiled on eighty-three military men who overtly opposed the regime, and on fifty officers who remained faithful to the government.

a dyed-in-the-wool Gaullist, remained loyal to the government when others tried to lead the army against it.

An officer who decided to oppose the Fifth Republic was General Paul Gardy, a graduate of Saint-Cyr. Gardy entered the Foreign Legion after leaving Saint-Cyr and campaigned with the Legion in Syria and Morocco. He chose to remain in France with the armistice army when Pétain came to terms with the Germans in 1940. Among his other posts held after the war, Gardy was second-in-command of Sidi-Bel-Abbès, the Legion's headquarters. In 1959, General Gardy retired from the army, but kept his contacts with activist circles. In 1961 he joined in the April putsch.

Another officer who served with the Legion but who remained a loyalist was General Fernand Gambiez. Upon leaving Saint-Cyr, Gambiez chose the Legion and served in Morocco. When his time came to choose between London and Vichy, he selected the latter and the armistice army. After the war, he served in Indochina, Tunisia, and Algeria, and when forced to choose again, Gambiez remained loyal to the government.

Finally, let us mention General Paul Ducourneau, a Saint-Cyrian who escaped from France in 1942 and made his way to Africa. After the war, he joined an airborne unit and went to Indochina, then to Algeria in 1956 as the chief of Lacoste's special staff. When crowds attacked the Government General (the GG) building in Algiers on May 13, 1958, Ducourneau tried in vain to calm the milling mass. He later was named commander of the Twenty-fifth Paratroop Division, and subsequently made the commander of the Twenty-first Paratroop Division. Ducourneau remained among the faithful in 1961.

In the above few names, there are both loyal and disloyal Saint-Cyrians; one legionnaire takes one course, a second legionnaire follows another; Free French fighters divide, and armistice army men divide over the question of loyalty to the government; men who served in both Algeria and Indochina are found on both sides of the conflicting forces; a "para" chooses the government instead of rebellion. Concerning the matter of background and political involvement, a comment by Jean Planchais demonstrates the futility of searching for correlations between these factors. Planchais was maintaining that one could not speak of a Fascist or of a republican army, and what he had to say is apropos here: "There are quite simply men, who, when faced with the Algerian problem, react according to their temperament." [30]

[30] Planchais, "The French Army," p. 337. See John S. Ambler, *The French Army in Politics* (Columbus: Ohio State University Press, 1966), p. 357.

Then, too, aside from the men who clearly took sides in political controversies, there is the question of the uncertain and hesitating mass, the opportunists who refrained from joining sides until they could judge whom success would favor. It is the issue of officers reluctant to take a position since a career could have ended if they chose the wrong side, later facing either a court-martial or the more subtle methods of transfers and promotions slowed or stopped. There are, finally, the problems of time and circumstance.

But in their political activity, the dissident, activist officers depended upon the French army psychosis of unity to rally the army to their side. The many strands of thought and the differences in the army were apparently thought to be impotent behind the façade of unity. In order to avoid a clash of soldier against soldier, the dissidents thought the mass of officers would follow in rebellion rather than divide the army. The pronouncements of unity uttered by French army chiefs are countless. To take just one example, in the following declaration made by General André Demetz in 1960 the importance of unity to the army and to the nation are expressed:

> The unity of the army is also the supreme guarantor of national unity. Above local quarrels and partisan animosities, the soldier is responsible for the safeguarding of the national patrimony. No one can speak in its name who has not for his first care the protection of the body of the country. This unity, sealed in the tests and fraternity of combat experienced under the same uniform, we always find among our veterans. The army has counted almost everyone in its ranks. This is to say that at some point in the hours of doubt and of confusion, the army remains the national reality to which all refer.[31]

Demetz emphasizes in his words the importance of unity and also another influential concept: that of the army as the "supreme guarantor of national unity," the concept that has led many armies in many lands to rationalize their political interventions. Our attention must now go to this attitude, and then to that of the theory of revolutionary warfare, a theory which, as developed by certain French officers, placed the officer in a signal position: it became his duty, not to follow the nation, but to lead it.

[31] General Demetz, editorial in *L'Armée*, February 1, 1960, p. 7.

CHAPTER V

The Army Above the State

J'ai peut-être servi mon pays trop passionnément. Si j'avais été "un militaire qui fait sa carrière" je ne serais pas ici. Je preféré avoir été "un soldat qui fait son métier."—CAPTAIN ESTOUP, JULY, 1961.

WHEN THE ARMY entered the political swirl in France in 1958, it justified its action with a concept common to most armies which become deeply involved in political affairs. By the nature of their profession, military officers are imbued with nationalism, patriotism, devotion, and loyalty to the nation they have sworn to protect. In contrast to ephemeral governments, the nation they serve is a historical, current, and future reality. As a result, military men may come to consider themselves servants of the nation and not of transient political leaders. Such a feeling places the officers above the government in power in their higher loyalty to the nation. Politically, this may lead to difficulties, since the officers, as guardians of the national interest, may develop their own conceptions of that interest.

Other considerations serve to augment this prejudice. As an instrument of state, the military is supposed to be above politics and partisan strife. It is only a short step from this point to the conclusion that the armed forces are thus devoid of the petty cares and narrow interests of those concerned with less exalted tasks than national defense. Standing above self-interest, the defenders, with an Olympian calm, are able to discern what is really beneficial for the nation. When, therefore, the national interest is threatened by bumbling politicians, the military has not only the right but the duty to descend from its peculiar vantage point and indicate the proper course to be followed. Edwin Lieuwen has pointed out concerning Latin America:

> Whenever the armed forces assumed political power, whatever their motivations, they maintained they were doing so only because

79

the government had failed. Ostensibly they were motivated by only the purest of patriotic intentions. In their own eyes, grave national circumstances made intervention imperative. Indeed, ever since independence, the military had developed the firm conviction that it was their duty to step forward in times of internal crisis to save the nation from itself.[1]

General Douglas MacArthur also spoke of the military's "higher" loyalty:

> I find in existence a new and heretofore unknown and dangerous concept that the members of our armed forces owe primary allegiance and loyalty to those who temporarily exercise the authority of the executive branch of government, rather than to the country and its Constitution which they are sworn to defend.
>
> No proposition could be more dangerous. None could cast greater doubt upon the integrity of the armed forces.
>
> For its application would at once convert them from their traditional and constitutional role as the instrument for the defense of the Republic into something partaking of the nature of a pretorian guard, owing sole allegiance to the political master of the hour.[2]

Apparent in MacArthur's words is a division of loyalties, with the higher loyalty to the country rather than to those who personify it at the moment. The possible consequences of such thought have been outlined above, along with the rationale it can lend to politically ambitious armies.[3] When the term "national interest" is used by the military, it takes on an added luster which it does not have when found in the statements of other groups who attempt to justify their particular actions with its meaning. The resulting difference is due, of course, to the army's role as a national organization pledged to defend the nation.

[1] Edwin Lieuwen, *Arms and Politics in Latin America* (New York: Frederick A. Praeger, 1960), p. 124.

[2] From General Douglas MacArthur's address before the Massachusetts legislature in Boston, July 25, 1951; text of the speech in *New York Times*, July 26, 1951, p. 12.

[3] The problem of loyalty and allegiance with which we are dealing here is a conditional one for the military in respect to the government in being, since the absolute loyalty is to the country. On the other hand, there is also the problem of an army which serves with unconditional loyalty and obedience to a government. Does a soldier then have to obey his political superiors in all circumstances, or is there a point at which disobedience becomes the proper course of action?

The widespread use of lofty motives to justify military intervention in politics and a certain cynicism in regard to them is described in the following words:

> Establishment of a true democratic regime, struggle against corruption, free designation of the man who must govern the country: such are a few of the objectives which Colonel Peralta, who took power Sunday [March 31, 1963] in Guatemala, has already assigned his coup d'état. It is a language that one has already heard a certain number of times, and not only in Latin America.[4]

An army, because of its special prerogatives of unselfish devotion to the country and of being above petty and partisan politics, is in effect above those who wield the instruments of political power. If those in power abuse their privilege of ruling or do not rule in the country's best interests, then the army has both the obligation and the right to descend and restore order. It is a theory that the army is above the government of the moment.

Hereafter, I shall use the phraseology adopted by the French army, and instead of speaking of the army being above the government, I shall speak of the army above the state. The French officer makes a distinction between *patrie, nation,* and *état.* "*La patrie* has a primary reality to the nation, and more yet to the state. It is first in the ensemble of familiar things, tied to the natal soil, from which we received life and where we grew up . . . which fashioned us as a certain man, a man that one will never cease to be, even when life will have led us far away." As for the nation, "one has a *patrie,* one makes a *nation.* The *nation* is a community of men, it is a people." And last in the hierarchy is the state, *l'état,* "the public power enjoying total juridical autonomy."[5] Colonel Roger Trinquier explains:

> The state is, in fact, only a human institution, an instrument made by men in order to serve them. . . .
> If one loves the Fatherland [*patrie*], which is our land, or the Nation [*nation*], which is the people and our eternal and immutable

4 "Another Military Putsch," *Le Monde,* April 2, 1963. See also, on the problems encountered by serving the national interest rather than the current government, George A. Kelly, "Officers, Politics, Ideology," *Army,* XII (January, 1962), 31.

5 R. P. Y. Congar and Joseph Folliet, *Armée et vie nationale* (Lyons: Chronique sociale de France, 1962), pp. 10–14. See also René Rémond, *et al., L'Armée et la nation* (Paris: Arthème Fayard, 1960), pp. 19–31; and *Les valeurs fondamentales du patriotisme français* (Paris: George Lang, 1962), pp. 121–22.

values, one can neither love the State [*état*] nor be attached to it since it is only a continually changing instrument.[6]

Consequently, "it seems natural and legitimate to the army consciously to take the part of the nation against a state. . . . "[7]

In his interviews with French officers, Claude Dufresnoy found the army united on only one point: the belief that it was the repository "of the superior interests of the country. . . ."[8] Accepting the idea of serving the nation instead of the government of the moment was easy for the French officer. His ancestor officers of the nineteenth century frequently served regimes with which they felt little kinship, but their consciences were eased when they pledged themselves to the nation, which stood above the ruler of the moment. Thus, the nineteenth-century officers' idea of the army above the state was conceived in relation to political abstention.

The Third Republic accentuated the concept as governments came and went, and the officer found his constant in *la patrie*, the fatherland, and it became the object of his loyalty, not the Republic and the shifting sands of its governments.[9] Officers came to believe that civilians were indifferent to the fatherland and concerned themselves with only the mundane, immediate concerns of daily life.[10] The army thereby became the sole repository of the values of *la patrie*, of national greatness, and the common denominator to which the nation could appeal when in difficulty.

Traditionally apolitical, the army was placed in an advantageous position to become a national arbiter, since it could stress its role of being above politics and "legitimately pretend to have a just notion of the 'superior interests of the country.'"[11] Indeed, the army's political

[6] Roger Trinquier, *Le Coup d'état du 13 mai* (Paris: Editions l'Esprit Nouveau, 1962), p. 15.

[7] François Kuntz, *L'officier français dans la nation* (Paris: Charles-Lavauzelle et Cie., 1960), p. 179.

[8] Claude Dufresnoy, *Des officiers parlent* (Paris: Julliard, 1961), p. viii.

[9] This attitude was well expressed by General Galliffet when, as Minister of War, he stated in an order of the day following Dreyfus' pardon by President Emile Loubet in 1899, "Vive l'Armée, which belongs to no party, but to France alone." Quoted by Guy Chapman, *The Dreyfus Case* (New York: Reynal and Co., 1955), p. 304.

[10] General Valluy, "Armée française 1961," *La Revue des deux mondes*, XII (June 15, 1961), 586–87.

[11] Captain André Souyris, "L'action psychologique dans les forces armées," *Revue militaire d'information*, No. 298 (October, 1958), 38.

tasks are much simplified in comparison with those of other national groups who must take into consideration special interests and their political positions and followings. "The army has only one worry here: the national interest. It is an enormous advantage," General Raoul Salan informed a reporter in 1958.[12]

The concept enticingly invites the army, as the repository of national greatness, to take the part of the nation against the state when the latter becomes destructive and capricious in the exercise of its temporary power.[13] The army, the only true representative of the national community, remaining free of the material pursuits of the civilians, staunchly stands as the sole refuge of ideals and values. In periods of crisis, it falls to the army to intervene "as a pressing duty," because of its unique advantages and its pure concern for the good of the country.[14] Colonel Trinquier declares that the army's "first mission is not the defense of the state, but the defense of the nation, that is to say, the protection of our countrymen."[15]

Not only does the army have the duty of playing the role of national savior when necessary, but it has also been crowned national leader: "The army has become the nation's best guide. . . . It must remain closely united around its leaders, imbued with the vision of the great task of renewing France, a task which has fallen to it."[16] Assuring stability and national continuity in the highest interest of the country, the army is not a menace to civil order but its safeguard.[17]

[12] Reported from an interview with General Raoul Salan, *Le Monde*, June 11, 1958.

[13] See a letter from Raoul Girardet defending the right of the army to continue a war it thinks just and legitimate, in the face of a contrary general will. Girardet prefers "soldiers who fight to ones who retreat." *Le Monde*, December 12–13, 1961; see also Kuntz, *L'officier français*, pp. 178–79.

[14] René Bertrand-Serret, "L'Armée et le régime," *Ecrits de Paris*, July–August, 1959, pp. 63 and 79.

[15] Trinquier, *Le Coup d'état*, p. 16.

[16] General André Zeller, order #1 on being reappointed De Gaulle's army Chief of Staff, *Le Monde*, July 4, 1958.

[17] General Paul Ely, "L'armée dans la nation," *Revue militaire d'information*, No. 297 (August–September, 1958), 181–82. The army is also essential as a "common denominator" in the battle against communism, according to one French colonel. In an ideological war the French, separated into numerous currents, find it difficult to find a unifying coalition. Hence, the true French soul, the common conscience of France, must be found. The officers of the military establishment are the best qualified for the quest by their sense of man, their dignity, their meditations on their campaigns. The structure of the army, its intellectual discipline, and its schools make

The political role incumbent upon the army is clearly expressed in the words of a young officer who wrote in October, 1958:

> Politics is fundamentally the affair of the Prince. . . . In order to assist him in his duties, the Prince disposes (apart from his functionaries, simple emanations of himself, inevitable multiplication essential to a modern state) of three corps having their personal ethic and whose role depasses [*sic*] in grandeur the human expression of their activity. These are the Magistracy, guardian of the law; the Police, protector of individuals; the Army, rampart of the collectivity. And of the three the most exacting for its members, who are expected to give their all because it is the defender of the most general interest, the one whose calling is therefore essentially political, is the Army.[18]

Thus the army adopted a political theory granting to itself the function of national political overseer. If necessary, this overseer could exercise its prerogatives by actual seizure of power in uncommon circumstances, but in normal times it would be present as a permanent veto power above the state. The obedience of the army became conditional obedience, effective to the extent that the state's actions conformed to the national interest as defined by the army. The army acted to seize power in 1958 and 1961; in 1960 it remained inactive in a confrontation between Paris and Algiers, hoping to play the role of arbiter. For much of the remainder of the time between 1958 and 1961, the army attempted to play the role of veto power, establishing limits beyond which the state was not to pass, particularly in regard to Algerian policy and to the formation of a leftist government in France.[19]

The theory of the army above the state places an army above the law and endows it with a political wisdom apparently not available to those whose profession is politics. As Marcel Pacaut, a faculty member at

---

it a powerful tool to reach all milieus and avoid mistakes. "The army is without doubt the most solid framework which is available to oppose this conquest of minds and of hearts, a counterattack led in the name of French traditions and imperatives." Colonel de Metz, "Du role nationale de l'officier," *Revue de Défense nationale*, August–September, 1958, pp. 1334–36.

[18] Quoted by Roy C. Macridis and Bernard E. Brown, *The De Gaulle Republic* (Homewood, Illinois: The Dorsey Press, 1960), p. 109.

[19] Jean-Marie Domenach, "The French Army in Politics," *Foreign Affairs*, XXXIX (January, 1961), 192–93. Domenach's phrase for the army's veto power is "permanent blackmail."

Lyons University, asked: "By what divine grace were they ultimate arbiters? Who has given them prescience and infallibility?"[20] Ultimately, the following question must be faced: Is the army the master of the state, or is it a servant of the state? One of the foundations of civil control is that the military is an instrument, a basis an army denies when it ascribes to itself the right to judge and to make its obedience conditional. A second foundation of civil control is that, in a democracy, the military does not have, nor has any special group, the right to dictate to the remainder of the nation. A decision reached through the democratic processes of the nation is the final word of the nation, not one dictated by a special group of the state, no matter how exalted its conception of its national functions and no matter how well rationalized by the advocates of intervention.

It could be added that the French army, as we have seen, has not been devoid of internal divisions and differences. The army's ability to discern a proper course free of conflicting cares is thus dealt a damaging blow. And so is the assumption of infallibility and the ability to recognize the real "national interest" as groups within the army fight among themselves over what the real "national interest" might be. Finally, as George A. Kelly has pointed out, "the difficulty here is, of course, that nations are made for men and not vice-versa, even if the men should be unworthy of the construction, and that men take orders necessarily from their superiors, not from some abstract and deified notion of an ideal political solution."[21]

Armies everywhere have cast their eyes above the governments they ostensibly serve in order to find the source of their political motivations and to justify them. The French army readily accepted the notion of being aloof from political controversy, for it had placed itself above governments since the nineteenth century. Formerly, however, the idea was a way to avoid political controversy by being above and untouched by petty politics. Thereby, an officer could serve any government—no matter how swiftly governments changed—since his allegiance was to the *patrie*, which was unchanging. But under the Fourth Republic, the concept of the army above the state was elaborated into an enticing theory to justify political intervention. Having already considered itself

[20] From a letter by Marcel Pacaut, professor at the Faculty of Letters and Human Sciences at Lyons, in *Le Monde*, January 10, 1959; see also a letter from Pierre-Henri Simon, "Du role politique de l'armée," *Le Monde*, January 29, 1959.

[21] Kelly, "Officers, Politics, Ideology," p. 33.

for years as a special body of the nation, the French army easily assimilated the notion of having a particularly incisive knowledge of the nation and therefore of its real interests.

The idea of the army above the state was transformed from a rationalization of political abstention into a theory dictating political action by the army when the nation was internally in peril—a circumstance to be determined by the army. The nation would be defended by its guardians, as a nation should be when it is in danger. By its political intervention, the army would be performing its function of protector of the national interests; the weapons of defense would be different, not the cause for action.

CHAPTER VI

The Theory of Revolutionary War

Il est temps que l'Armée cesse d'être "la grande muette." Le moment est venu pour le monde libre, s'il ne veut pas mourir de mort violente, d'appliquer certaines méthodes de son adversaire.
— GENERAL LIONEL-MAX CHASSIN.

THE FRENCH ARMY found itself beaten in Indochina by an enemy which should not have been the victor according to the rules of conventional warfare. However, the adversary had not used conventional warfare to defeat the French but had relied upon unorthodox techniques of combat. Studying and analyzing its defeat, the French army found that the victor had been, not an army, but a people who had warred against it in what the French referred to as revolutionary war (*la guerre révolutionnaire*). The French discovered that the primary target in such combat was the minds of the peoples among whom the battle was fought. It was a war of ideas and emotions, not of armed columns or massed military strength, and it was waged by an insidious enemy who gnawed from within, weakening and destroying the government in much the same way a termite causes ruin in a house.

Another principle the officers drew from their experiences in Indochina was that revolutionary war was permanent, and consequently the words "civilian" and "military," "war" and "peace," had lost their meaning. Waged everywhere in an undeclared state, the conflict demanded that all energies of the nation be concentrated on the adversary's defeat. And the real enemy was not the Vietminh in Indochina nor the National Liberation Front in Algeria. Behind them, supporting them, exploiting difficulties wherever possible, lurked the real and ever present foe—international communism.[1]

[1] The importance to the army of the Indochinese experience is met again and again. For only one of many possible examples: "There, [in Indochina] began for

87

Under whatever guise or appeal communism might have appeared—nationalism, independence, liberation—the goal of the movement remained constant: to overthrow the established powers and to institute another regime, this to be accomplished through a harmonization of political, economic, social, psychological, and military actions. The aim was to destroy the will to resist of both the enemy army and the civilian population, "not thanks to an army of the classic type, but thanks to the participation of a population conquered physically and morally by procedures at one and the same time destructive and constructive."[2]

Revolutionary war was total war, not confined to armies meeting on a battlefield but extended to the minds of men far from the range of gunfire. The theory was succinctly defined by Paul Gerin as follows:

> Revolutionary war is a doctrine of war elaborated by Marxist-Leninist theoreticians, and applied by diverse revolutionary movements in order to seize power by progressively securing the physical and psychological control of the population, with the aid of particular techniques relying on a mystique and following a determined process.[3]

The essentials of revolutionary war are here: its Communist inspiration; its goal of seizing power; the methods of control to be exercised on the population; the reliance on special techniques and a "mystique" to achieve its ends.

But revolutionary war was not an invention of the Communists, and as the above quotation indicates, they only "elaborated" upon it. In his study of the subject, Colonel Gabriel Bonnet agrees with the writer of Ecclesiastes that "there is no new thing under the sun . . ." and traces revolutionary war back to the ancient Chinese. Whenever you have partisans plus psychological warfare, asserts Bonnet, you have revolutionary war.[4] The combination appears in numerous conflicts, widely separated in time and space. For example, it is seen in the Spanish struggle against Napoleon I, in Arabia with T. E. Lawrence, in the Irish

---

me and my comrades the discovery of the war in the crowd, with which I believe many among us are impregnated." Testimony of Colonel Jean Gardes, one of the accused at the Barricades Trials, *Le Monde*, November 10, 1960.

2 Michel Déon, *L'Armée d'Algérie et la pacification* (Paris: Plon, 1959), p. 16.

3 Paul Gerin, *L'Algérie du 13 mai* (Paris: Gallimard, 1958), p. 123.

4 Colonel Gabriel Bonnet, *Les guerres insurrectionnelles et révolutionnaires* (Paris: Payot, 1958), p. 60.

Rebellion, and after World War II, in Yugoslavia, Greece, China, Indo-china, Algeria, South Vietnam, and in numerous other countries.

Although the Communists are often credited with developing revolutionary war, Lawrence of Arabia in a few pages set down the principles of subversive struggles. Where can one find a better description of a revolutionary army than in the following words?

> ... but suppose we were ... an influence, an idea, a thing intangible, invulnerable, without front or back, drifting about like a gas. ... We might be a vapor, blowing where we listed. Our kingdom's lay in each man's mind; and as we wanted nothing material to live on, so we might offer nothing material to the killing.[5]

Analyzing its defeat, the French army found in revolutionary war the vaporous foe that had eluded it in the strange conflict unsuccessfully waged in Indochina, a conflict in which an enemy seldom seen had defeated crack French units. The enemy was solidified, taking body and substance in the Communist conspiracy, which had launched a permanent, universal, revolutionary struggle for the conquest of men's minds and the world. Behind nationalist struggles in Indochina and Algeria were the Communists, the real opponents. If checked in one part of the world, they would strike elsewhere, sometimes openly, more often in a subversive attack to undermine a nation. The universality of the enemy permitted veterans of Indochina to call their new enemies in Algeria "Viets," the name of the old foe in Indochina, for they were, as they saw it, facing the same opponent although in a different land.[6]

Since the army faced the enemy everywhere, no retreats could be made anywhere; to do so would mean an advance of communism. Negotiation was considered but another means of surrender because one could not treat with the Communist conspiracy. Even in the most nationalistic movements the Communist specter was discerned, and it

---

[5] T. E. Lawrence, *Seven Pillars of Wisdom* (Garden City: Doubleday, Doran, and Co., 1935), p. 192; see pp. 193–96.

[6] Jean-Jacques Servan-Schreiber, *Lieutenant in Algeria* (New York: Alfred A. Knopf, 1957), p. 65. On the universality of revolutionary war see the following: Major Jacques Hogard, "Guerre révolutionnaire ou révolution dans l'art de guerre," *Revue de Défense nationale*, December, 1956, pp. 1498 and 1508–11; (cited hereafter as RDN); Hogard, "Cette guerre de notre temps," RDN, August–September, 1958, p. 1316; Claude Delmas, *La guerre révolutionnaire* (Paris: Presses Universitaires de France, 1959), pp. 27–35; Colonel Charles Lacheroy, "La guerre révolutionnaire," in Tony Albord, *et al.*, *La Défense nationale* (Paris: Presses Universitaires de France, 1958), p. 322.

was remembered that Lenin had called for an alliance between the proletariat of the advanced countries and the peoples of the under-developed areas in order to break the imperialistic yoke. The alliances were to be consummated even if it meant temporary cooperation with bourgeois forces.[7] "Nationalism," therefore, "according to a dictum that became almost a password, was the antechamber of communism," observes Paul-Marie de la Gorce.[8]

Having fought colonial wars for some years, the French army, the only army which had continuously engaged the omnipresent Communist enemy since the end of World War II, concluded it was the free world's defender and savior. General Maxime Weygand, for example, wondered about those "friendly" nations who wished to see the French leave Algeria. "Do they not see," asked the General, "that for several years France is the only country in the West which sheds its blood and exhausts its resources for the very reasons that the Atlantic pact was consecrated? Have they forgotten that for Lenin, it was by Africa that Europe would succumb?"[9] Furthermore, many officers had considered communism a major danger since the early days of Bolshevik rule in Russia. The government's acceptance of the theory of revolutionary war made the army's opposition official, while the free world alliances endorsed the universality of conflict and the common danger.[10]

[7] See V. I. Lenin, "Preliminary Draft of Theses on the National and Colonial Questions" (June 5, 1920), reprinted in Alvin Z. Rubinstein, *The Foreign Policy of the Soviet Union* (New York: Random House, 1960), pp. 358–60.

[8] Paul-Marie de la Gorce, *The French Army* (New York: George Braziller, 1963), p. 433.

[9] *Le Monde*, March 6, 1958.

[10] On French army opposition to communism in the interwar period see De la Gorce, *The French Army*, pp. 142, 243, 360, 403; Saul K. Padover, "France in Defeat: Causes and Consequences," *World Politics*, II (April, 1950), 312–13. The French army's belief in their status as defenders of the free world is seen in remarks such as the following: Major Rioval, testifying before the High Military Tribunal for his role in the April, 1961, putsch, said: "If I am before you today it is because I believe Algeria and the Sahara were the advanced bastion of the free world and that it was proper to defend them quite as much as Berlin. . . ." Maurice Cottaz, ed., *Les Procès du putsch d'Alger et du complot de Paris* (Paris: Nouvelles Editions Latines, 1962), p. 181; a colonel of the fifth bureau, the section charged with psychological warfare, expressed his fears of the Communist conspiracy to Claude Dufresnoy, warning that "subversive war is everywhere, you cannot imagine its power." The colonel saw no alternatives to a French Algeria; if not, "Communist infiltration and communism in all North Africa within five years. Look at the map," he instructed Dufresnoy. "You see North Africa facing Europe? It is the last rampart in the Mediterranean against communism." Claude Dufresnoy, *Des officiers parlent* (Paris: Julliard, 1961), pp. 24–27.

Recognizing the "true" enemy was the first step in the construction of a counterrevolutionary force. Next was the consideration of his methods, methods which had enabled the Vietminh to defeat the materially superior French forces. A war that sought not conventional military objectives, but the conquest of men's minds as well as their bodies was discovered. The army learned of the new warfare's totality by considering the principles of the "war in the crowd" (*guerre dans la foule*), which revealed that the war was fought in the midst of a people, socially, economically, psychologically, and militarily. In order to destroy rebel forces, the army concluded, their bases of support must be captured and converted to the benefit of the forces of order. These bases of support were the populations in the country at stake.

To win the *guerre dans la foule*, announced the students of revolutionary war, the army would have to adopt weapons which affected the mind—the psychological pressures of persuasion, suggestion, intimidation, agitation—any and all methods which could sway the morale and feelings of the masses. The attempts to win over populations were reduced to a series of techniques, and success was understood to be only a question of adopting proper methods.

The techniques of revolutionary war were found to proceed through five stages. First, agitation and propaganda are instituted to form networks which diffuse the ideology and exploit existing difficulties in the area chosen to construct a base of support. A more elaborate organization is then established to provide support and sources of information. Next, armed bands begin terrorist activities and guerilla operations. If these efforts are successful in loosening the government's hold on the locality, a "free zone," a base of support, is gained which is given a provisional government and a legal appearance. The fifth and last phase, a general offensive, more political and psychological than military, is later launched throughout the country. However, the fifth phase frequently is unnecessary since the government may have broken by the time the last stage is reached. Also, the stages are not a fixed progression, but are flexible and can be applied as circumstances dictate. Advancement to a higher stage, skipping one, or retreating to a lower one depends upon the strength and conviction of the forces of order.

The base of support is a recurrent phrase in revolutionary war writings, and indicates an area in which the population is firmly "enrolled" and which serves as a "spot of oil" which spreads to enlarge the territory under control. To win a base of support, both destructive and constructive methods are used. The destructive aspects of revolutionary war include the methods of dislocation, intimidation, demoralization, intoxication of the neutrals, and, finally, the elimination of the unyielding. The first method, dislocation, makes use of strikes, riots, and terrorism (both specific and random assassinations) to create a breach between the population and the established order. Next comes intimidation—an attempt to reinforce the gains made by dislocation. Monstrous meetings are now held, sabotage is undertaken, the techniques of guerilla warfare are introduced, and terrorism is continued.

Demoralization is now engaged, and the attempt is made to depreciate the successes of the adversary, to inflate his failures, and to instill doubts concerning his good faith, administration, and justice. Those individuals who have so far remained neutral are the target of the next effort, intoxication, and they are swamped under a flood of justifications. If this effort is not completely successful, then the final destructive stage is entered, and those who have not been won to the cause by the earlier destructive means are eliminated.

Constructive and destructive methods are simultaneously applied, reinforcing one another. A base must be organized, a task accomplished by the constructive method of selecting activists to join and support the movement. The activists then establish revolutionary nets, the beginning of the framework which will soon control the sector's population. Through the use of slogans adapted to the situation ("independence," for example), the masses become an organized, animated group.

Finally, the population is totally regulated by means of parallel hierarchies, a dualistic technique of controlling the people. One hierarchy is territorially based (building, block, district), with power at each level lodged in a committee which in turn is narrowly subordinated to the committee above. The second hierarchy is based on the population, organized according to group characteristics, by age, profession, religion, etc. Each hierarchy is organizationally independent of the other, but each spies on the other, each is controlled by the "party," and each exists to assure the body-and-soul control of the population. The objective of these methods is to win the "war in the crowd." By destroying the enemy's social and governmental foundations and building one's own, bases of support are multiplied. As the "spot of oil" spreads, additional zones are "liberated," and "conquest on the surface will succeed conquest in depth." [11]

[11] Ximenès, "Essai sur la guerre révolutionnaire," *Revue militaire d'information*, No. 281 (February–March, 1957), 14; (cited hereafter as RMI). The main theoreticians of revolutionary war were Colonel Lacheroy, "La guerre révolutionnaire," pp. 307–33; Hogard, "Guerre révolutionnaire ou révolution dans l'art de guerre,"

By discovering these techniques and methods, the students of revolutionary war located the battleground where they were applied: in and among the masses who were to be "won." Success on the battleground was not measured in lives taken, they learned, but in souls saved. Having become familiar with the techniques and methods of the enemy, the theorists of revolutionary war were prepared to develop their counterstrategy. The tactics of revolutionary war were adopted and modified for use as a defense against the overthrow of established regimes by international communism. Mao Tse-tung had written, "the army must be in the people as a fish in the water." Therefore, in view of the new warfare's methods, it became the army's obligation to become immersed into the populations and win them over to France. As one French officer asserted: "I knew, after Indo-China, that the stake of a revolutionary war is the conquest of man." [12] Since revolutionary war was essentially psychological and since the army intended to meet the enemy on his chosen terrain, the army had to be prepared to wage the struggle.

The first Center for the Instruction of Psychological War was established in Paris in February, 1955, when the Morale and Information Section was renamed the Psychological and Morale Section. The following month, psychological warfare offices opened in Algeria, but these were not officially consecrated until 1957, when the creation of the fifth bureaus authoritatively recognized their existence. Attached to regional and command staffs, the fifth bureaus were to build confidence and morale in the army and in the nation.[13]

In April, 1956, the then Minister of National Defense, Bourgès-Maunoury, had instituted at the Ministry the Psychological Action and Information Service, which became the fifth section of the national

pp. 1497–1513; Hogard, "Cette guerre de notre temps," pp. 1304–19; Captain André Souyris, "L'action psychologique dans les forces armées," *RMI*, No. 298 (October, 1958), 34–45; and Souyris, "Réalité et aspects de la guerre psychologique," *RMI*, No. 302 (February, 1959), 7–28; see also A Group of Officers, "La guerre du Vietminh," *RMI*, No. 281 (February–March, 1957), 25–41; Captain de Arbonneau, "Réflexions sur les formes non spécifiquement militaires," *RMI*, No. 328 (June, 1961), 6–17. For a detailed description of the techniques of revolutionary war directed against an established regime see Hogard, "Guerre révolutionnaire et pacification," *RMI*, No. 280 (January, 1957), 7–24; and Ximenès, "Essai," pp. 11–22.

[12] Captain Georges Oudinot in Cottaz, *Les Procès du putsch d'Alger*, p. 130. See also Lacheroy, "La guerre révolutionnaire," pp. 311–12; Roger Trinquier, *La guerre moderne* (Paris: La Table Ronde, 1961), pp. 47–48; Ximenès, "Essai," pp. 19–20.

[13] *Le Monde*, February 12, 1960.

defense staff. Also in 1956, the first units of what came to be called the Seventh Arm had been constituted in Algeria. These were three companies, each assigned to an army corps in Algeria, which were to be engaged in initiating the "war in the crowd." [14] Meanwhile, students in military schools were exposed to revolutionary war doctrines when General Jean Lecompte introduced into the War College curriculum the required reading of the works of Mao Tse-tung.[15] Chairs of psychological action were created at Saint-Cyr and other high-level military schools, and on May 11, 1958, a special school of revolutionary war was opened at Philippeville.[16]

Supported in the highest echelons, the theories of revolutionary war gained wide circulation in the French army, and the men assigned to the psychological warfare offices set themselves to their task of construction and destruction. Not finding a coherent policy or ideology in the government's directives, the fifth bureaus' officers became concerned with ends as well as methods. Consequently, it was determined that the struggle was to be waged in the name of anticommunism, of East *versus* West, and of Christianity against atheism, the last assimilated from and shared with integral Catholicism.

From their Indochinese experiences, the psychological warfare experts had drawn the conclusion that ideas were but a means to move masses as desired. According to the officers of the fifth bureaus, the Communists had used the myth of nationalism in Indochina to win the people and they were doing the same in Algeria. However, the mystique of nationalism was nothing but a mask behind which the Communists maneuvered, the masks merely being fitted to the masses to be won. Therefore, one advocate of revolutionary war could say: "If the nationalist idea does not exist, they will create it." [17] Another psychological warfare officer could then add: "There is only one danger: communism. Against a fanaticism it is necessary to deploy another fanaticism. In order to defeat an ideology, it is necessary to fight it with

[14] *Ibid.*, August 23, 1958; Jean-Raymond Tournoux, *Secrets d'état* (Paris: Plon, 1960), p. 125.

[15] Jean Planchais, "The French Army: Not by Force Alone," *Reporter*, XVII (November 28, 1957), 36.

[16] Paul Ribeaud, *Barricades pour un drapeau* (Paris: La Table Ronde, 1960), pp. 11–18. The school was suppressed within two years. See Peter Paret, *French Revolutionary Warfare from Indochina to Algeria* (New York: Frederick A. Praeger, 1964), p. 55.

[17] Testimony of Colonel Joseph Broizat, Alain de Sérigny, *Un Procès* (Paris: La Table Ronde, 1961), p. 31.

another ideology."[18] What the ideology might be mattered little, since reflexes, conditioned by the techniques of control, would lead the masses to accept it. Summed up, the problem was simply to "take the brain as a bucket . . . empty it of bad ideas, fill it with good ones."[19]

In order to oppose the mystique of nationalism, behind which the Communists were hiding, the revolutionary war officers in Algeria adopted the theme of European and Moslem integration. Many French officers, particularly those in progressive circles, accepted the idea of integration as a valid solution to the Algerian problem. Having little use for the *colons* (Europeans of Algeria), these officers ardently desired social and economic elevation and equal citizenship privileges for the Moslem. However, for the activists of psychological warfare in particular, integration was essentially a tool in the contest with the Communists' entry, nationalism. It was nothing more than the contents to pour into the "buckets" of the Algerian masses.

The Algerian war became a two-front war. The attempt to destroy the rebels continued, but the struggle for the minds of the masses was also engaged. While the SAS men who went to work among the Moslems were apparently honest in their efforts, most of the officers who operated behind them in the psychological warfare offices at the staff headquarters continued to think of their work and that of the SAS as machinations in the cold war. To build a road or to destroy it, to kill a man or to convert him, were different tactics of the same struggle. The army had the difficult task of making friends with the Moslem and winning him to the support of France, while concurrently attempting to destroy Moslems.

As a result, pacification was given two accepted but different definitions: it meant "to restore the peace" by aiding and helping the Moslems, proving the French were their friends; but it also meant "to break the rebellion," which involved pursuing and destroying the FLN and its supporters.[20] Among the Moslems, the army's efforts "to restore the peace," became overshadowed by its attempts "to break the rebellion," for the hand that destroyed left a deeper impression than the helping hand.

[18] Dufresnoy, *Des officiers parlent*, p. 8.

[19] A captain of a fifth bureau, March, 1959, quoted by Pierre Boudot, *L'Algérie mal enchaînée* (Paris: Gallimard, 1961), p. 107. See also Lacheroy, "La guerre révolutionnaire," pp. 316–22.

[20] Jean-Michel Darboise, *et al.*, *Officiers en Algérie* (Paris: François Maspero, 1960), p. 9.

The predicament into which the policy of pacification put both the Moslem and the soldier is revealed in the experience of an SAS captain who took a small party to an Algerian village which had been recently terrorized by the rebels. As the Frenchmen approached, the villagers fled, ignoring the shouts of the SAS officer to halt. However, the flight ended when the captain shot one of the running men. Standing around the fallen Moslem, the villagers listened to the captain:

> Once more I have come to you and you run away. One of you has just been shot for nothing; I know that he is one of the rare ones among you who has never helped the *fellagas* [the rebels]. If you continue to obey the orders of the rebels, my paratroops will shoot you all, one after the other [to break the rebellion?].
>
> Yet, I came as a friend and I had hoped that the Doctor, instead of being busy with a wounded man, would have been able to see to your ills [restore the peace?].[21]

In their pacification campaign, the officers and men of the French army, especially in the psychological service sections and the SAS, entered new fields and were given new functions.[22] For these men, the division of labor between soldier and civilian ceased to exist. The assumption of administrative and other civilian tasks could not but broaden the political perspectives of military men so involved. The army's experience in civil fields, its revolutionary war theory, and its mental and physical separation from France combined to politicize the army.

Total war demands total engagement. It is a commonplace that modern war requires the admittance of military leaders to higher councils of government; however, the theorists of revolutionary war carried the issue much further than merely being heard in government circles. In the doctrines of revolutionary war, the traditional officer of the apolitical *Grande Muette* found his opposite in the officers who proclaimed that the civilian and military domains, carefully separated in earlier times, were now inextricably intertwined. Modern conditions, it was asserted, actually compelled officers to involve themselves in politi-

[21] Related in Jean-Yves Alquier, *Nous avons pacifié Tazalt* (Paris: Robert Laffont, 1957), pp. 40–41.

[22] Technically, the SAS men were representatives of the *sous-prefects* with the task of coordinating local social and economic development. See *Le Monde*, September 5, 1959 and September 16, 1959. In practice, the SAS was an arm of the psychological service sections.

cal affairs. According to General Pierre Boyer de Latour, a firm believer in pacification techniques and the theories of revolutionary war, "in subversive war, it is obvious that the political fact is more important than the military fact." It follows that "the army was then obliged to become politically involved to win."[23] "Revolutionary war," adds Colonel Bonnet, "seeks a political victory rather than a victory of arms. Besides, the latter is only a consequence of the former. The two are inseparable."[24]

That some officers had concluded that the civil-military fields were now not only joined, but that the army should assume a predominant political role, is manifest in the remark purportedly made to Albert-Paul Lentin by an unidentified high-ranking paratroop officer: "Our idea is that of a political army, at the head of the nation. Whether one call it psychological, subversive, or revolutionary, the wars of today are political."[25] As Jean Planchais warned, "from psychological action to political action the border . . . is narrow."[26]

The French army officers who became devotees of revolutionary war were a minority, but they were indeed an active minority. Their ideas spread across France and appeared in books, newspapers, and military journals, particularly in 1957–1958 when revolutionary war theory was at its peak. In 1959, revolutionary war advocacy began to diminish, as the methods and the activities of the most committed became controversial. Finally, in 1960, following the Week of the Barricades, the fifth bureaus were suppressed by government order. But even though the title fifth bureau disappeared, the work of maintaining contact with the Moslems was merely decentralized and distributed to other staff agencies. Not until after the abortive April putsch of 1961 did these agencies lose their recently acquired functions.[27]

To judge the exact extent of the influence of revolutionary war theory

[23] Pierre Boyer de Latour, *Le martyre de l'armée française* (Paris: Les presses du Mail, 1961), p. 15.

[24] Bonnet, *Les guerres insurrectionnelles*, p. 62.

[25] Albert-Paul Lentin, *L'Algérie des colonels* (Paris: Petite bibliothèque républicaine, 1958), p. 48. Lentin is an obvious opponent of the "paras" and the "colonels," whom he claims to be Fascist.

[26] Jean Planchais, *Le Monde*, August 23, 1958.

[27] See *Le Monde*, February 12, 1960; especially the article by Alain Jacob, *Le Monde*, March 31, 1960; *Le Monde*, May 6, 1960. In 1960, the Office of Studies and Liaison had been created and attached to one staff, and a new Human Problems Section attached to another. These new offices were suppressed in 1961. *Le Monde*, May 5, 1961.

on the army is as impossible as measuring the influence of any idea on a man's actions. But it may be said that among the men most opposed to a liberal Algerian policy were individuals who had absorbed most fully the principles of the war for minds.[28] Even for those who did not completely come under its sway, revolutionary war theory provided a beguiling justification for their reluctance to accept government policies, especially the Fifth Republic's Algerian policy. Revolutionary war theory opened the way to and justified a questioning of national and international policy, and sanctioned political involvement.

The influence of the theory can also be perceived in the operations of the Secret Army Organization (OAS), to which many of its most ardent supporters fled after the failure to overturn the Fifth Republic in April, 1961. The use of propaganda, selective and nonselective terrorism, and the attempts to demoralize and intimidate the French people had the mark of psychological warfare techniques. Moreover, the OAS established information networks in France, created "shock groups" (OAS gunmen) and proclaimed a provisional government, all on the lines of revolutionary war methods.[29]

In France and in the army, the theory of revolutionary war was widespread, but relatively few really accepted it in all its ramifications. The Communist enemy, the dangers of subversive war, the perils of living in an era of total war were ably pointed out by the Lacheroys and Hogards. But it was the conclusions drawn by these and other men which gave the theory its uniqueness.

Remembering the army's doldrums during the interwar years, French army officers were determined to learn from their Indochinese loss, hoping to be one war ahead next time instead of one behind. When

[28] For example, Colonel Lacheroy, one of the main theoreticians of revolutionary war, and Colonel Jean Gardes, who directed the fifth bureau in Algiers in 1959, were both sentenced to death *in absentia* for their roles in the abortive April putsch. Cottaz, *Les Procès du putsch d'Alger*, pp. 97–98. Lacheroy fled to Spain after the putsch and was arrested by the Spanish authorities. After being held for a time on the island of Palma he was released on July 24, 1962, and given freedom to reside in Spain, but having to report to the police twice a week. *Le Monde*, July 25, 1962.

[29] The OAS was the army of the National Resistance Council; see *Le Monde*, August 24, 1962. On the OAS organization see the series by Alain Jacob, *Le Monde*, November 15–17, and November 19–20, 1961. See also Benjamin Welles in the *New York Times*, March 19, 1962, p. 1:5; March 20, 1962, p. 15:1; March 21, 1962, p. 7:1. For further information refer to *Le Procès d'Edmond Jouhaud* (Paris: Editions Albin Michel, 1962), pp. 79–120, 270–87; Paul H. Meisel, *The Fall of the Republic* (Ann Arbor: The University of Michigan Press, 1962), pp. 202–53; George A. Kelly, *Lost Soldiers* (Cambridge: The M.I.T. Press, 1965), pp. 330–58.

their theories were criticized, the officers who promoted them answered that they were the De Gaulles of the 1950's, and De Gaulle himself was now a backward-looking Pétain. Their reference was to the 1930's when De Gaulle had been the advocate of mobile mechanized forces and had been opposed by Pétain and other defenders of the static warfare tactics of World War I vintage. For a time, the French seemed to be awed by the revolutionary war theorists, but the nation finally refused to accept their dogmatic assumptions, and after 1960 the theory of revolutionary war entered a decline from which it has not recovered.

In their desire to defend Western traditions, the revolutionary war officers did not pale before abandoning these traditions in order to defend them. However, many Frenchmen, including many French officers, were appalled at the methods of the fifth bureaus. Colonel Joseph Broizat, a fifth bureau officer, had described the theory of revolutionary war during the Barricades Trials. In a letter to *Le Monde*, J. M. Théolleyre said of the colonel: "He is one of those who rejoin the Middle Ages in their conception of good and evil, convinced of being one of the knights of good. But for this fight he does not hesitate to choose the methods of the adversary."[30] Broizat replied that he admitted his *intransigeance*, but that his conception of good and evil stemmed from the Bolshevik victory of 1917, not the Middle Ages. As to accepting the methods of the enemy, he asked that *some* be substituted for *the*, concluding that exceptional situations require exceptional arrangements.[31] In revolutionary war, "all means are good means," Colonel Bonnet informs us.[32]

In order to combat communism, the activists of psychological action were led to dream of revamping the nation, of structuring it in

[30] J. M. Théolleyre, *Le Monde*, January 15–16, 1961.

[31] Colonel Broizat, *Le Monde*, January 20, 1961.

[32] Bonnet, *Les guerres insurrectionnelles*, p. 62. Torture became a justifiable method of combat in the doctrines of revolutionary war. A terrorist is a soldier of subversive war and must run the risks of a soldier. The ordinary combatant fights on the battlefield, with the risks of such a milieu. The terrorist must run the risks of his field of battle with the knowledge that when he is captured he will not be treated as an ordinary criminal or prisoner of war, since he fits neither category. He will not be punished for crimes committed. As in all war, the goal is to defeat the enemy and since the prisoner may possess information concerning that enemy he will be questioned to avoid future attacks. If he answers quickly there is no difficulty; if not, "specialists" may be called in for the interrogation. The terrorist soldier must then, as the soldier in open combat, be prepared to face suffering and even death at the hands of his enemies. Trinquier, *La guerre moderne*, pp. 38–39. See Jean Planchais, *Le Monde*, October 30, 1958.

accordance with their interpretation of national strengths and weaknesses, and their analysis of the demands imposed by the enemy, which was an internal threat as well as external. In pursuing the goal of being an army in the nation, like a fish in the water, they went to the point of wishing "to choose the dimensions, the lighting and the temperature of the acquarium."[33] The result could well have been a France that had ceased to be France.

The reasons for the decline of revolutionary war theory are found in the excesses of the psychological action officers and in the weaknesses inherent in the theory itself. Enemies were found everywhere, all dissenters became Communists, and the Communists were everywhere since the enemy was everywhere. In the eyes of fifth bureau officers, the Algerian war assumed an importance in the cold war that it did not warrant, and they became blinded to the Algerian peoples' legitimate aspirations. But in its belief in the unlimited possibilities of manipulating people, in its disbelief in the validity of ideas, in believing that minds are little else than buckets, to be emptied and filled at will, revolutionary war had within itself its greatest flaws.

The French army was not and could not be a part of the Moslem population. Victory by the Vietminh was not based on a manufactured nationalism, nor was Algerian nationalism a fabrication. The successful insurrections in Indochina and Algeria were not products of proper methods, but were due to the fact that the content of the revolutionaries' promises reflected the aspirations of the people for independence. In their study of Mao Tse-tung, French officers overlooked an essential part of his teachings: Mao's insistence that revolutionary war must be adapted to time and circumstance.[34] His experiences were of a Chinese army among Chinese. The French army remained a French army among Moslems, no matter what methods were used, no matter what mystique it manufactured. The movements of nationalism were too strong for the French army to halt. The greatest conquest of the revolutionary war theorists was over themselves. They became intoxicated with their own creation, and became the victims of that creation.

[33] Gerin, *L'Algérie du 13 mai*, p. 143. See Maurice Duverger, *La Cinquième République* (Paris: Presses Universitaires de France, 1960), p. 261.

[34] See Anne Freemantle, ed., *Mao Tse-tung: An Anthology of His Writings* (New York: The New American Library, 1962), pp. 74–76; Walter Darnell Jacobs, "Mao Tse-tung as a Guerrilla: A Second Look," *Military Review*, XXXVII (February, 1958), 26–30.

Charles de Gaulle's judgment of revolutionary war? "All that is invented by the army to struggle against the will of the nation."[35]

As a consequence of the theories of revolutionary war, political activity by the army was understood by some officers to be a necessary aspect of national defense. In addition, officers of the French army generally shared the notion of the army as the ultimate guarantor of the nation, a body free of partisan biases, interested only in the "real" interests of the nation. These "real" interests had been imperiled, thought many members of the French army, by the political bunglers of the *système*. It was therefore necessary for the army to become a guide through the involved and tangled labyrinth of French political life. Standing above the maze, the army could distinguish the proper path. In May, 1958, the army assumed its role as guide.

[35] Quoted by Tournoux, *Secrets d'état*, p. 437. George A. Kelly observes that "with a certain Algerian solution achieved, the torch of subversive war has seemingly been passed to the next runner." Consequently, "the 'years of meditation' have begun for America." Kelly, *Lost Soldiers*, pp. 365–66.

CHAPTER VII

The King-Makers

La "grande muette" a parlé elle a été entendue parce qu'elle inspirait confidence au pays.—GENERAL RAOUL SALAN.

THE Sakhiet-Sidi-Youssef bombing on February 8, 1958, resulted in a deterioration of Franco-Tunisian relations. In order to ameliorate conditions, the United States offered its good offices to the two nations, and veteran diplomat Robert Murphy was assigned to lead a mission with instructions to assuage French-Tunisian animosity. The question of the American efforts led to the fall of the Félix Gaillard government, the refusal of confidence taking place amid a wave of anti-Americanism, xenophobia, and indignation over American "interference" in French affairs.[1]

After both Georges Bidault and René Pleven had failed to form a new government, Pierre Pflimlin on May 10 agreed to make the attempt. Pflimlin's efforts were closely followed in Algeria, because he was suspected of being liberal on the Algerian question. Devotees of *Algérie française* feared that a Pflimlin government would mean the abandonment of Algeria to the National Liberation Front (FLN).

In a speech at Strasbourg on April 17, Pflimlin had stated that his position on Algeria could be summed up in the formula: neither abandonment nor adventure. Pflimlin favors negotiations with the rebels, concluded many of his listeners. Furthermore, in the *Nouvel Alsacien* of April 23, Pflimlin had written that it was necessary to engage in conversations with FLN representatives and ascertain the terms of a cease-fire. On May 2, he repeated the theme of the necessity

[1] *Le Monde*, April 17, 1958. See *Le Monde*, May 9, 1958; Roy C. Macridis and Bernard E. Brown, *The De Gaulle Republic* (Homewood, Illinois: The Dorsey Press, 1960), pp. 57–60.

for negotiations leading to a cease-fire.[2] The suspicions regarding Pflimlin were magnified when Jacques Soustelle, a firm advocate of a French Algeria and a former Algerian Governor General, let it be known that he had a copy of a secret note sent by the prospective Premier to the presidents of several parliamentary groups. Soustelle alleged that in the "secret note" Pflimlin had announced his intention of initiating conversations with the FLN through the good offices of Tunisia and Morocco.[3]

In Gaullist circles in France, among the civilian ultras in Algeria, among the high command and the colonels in the army, the conviction was shared that the time had come for action. The exact number of plots aimed at bringing down the Fourth Republic prior to May 13 is unknown, their number having been advanced in figures ranging from thirteen to thirty-one. Basically, however, those conspiring against the Republic can be divided into two groups of activists: the Gaullists, and those whose plans for a national rebirth revolved around the creation of a Committee of Public Safety to replace the moribund Fourth Republic. Particularly strong in the latter group were the Algerian ultras and a circle of army officers, most of the latter colonels. For convenience' sake, the second group will be referred to as the activists and the former as the Gaullists (recognizing, of course, that the Gaullists were also activists). The Algiers high command was concerned with the national crisis, but available evidence indicates that the officers at the top of the military hierarchy in Algiers in May, 1958, were not directly involved in any of the conspiracies against the regime.

A straight chronological account of the events preceding May 13 would lead to confusion because of the number of individuals active in different places and in different ways in those hectic days preceding the assault against the Republic. Instead, let us look first at the activists, then at the Gaullists, and finally at the actions of the Algiers high command. We will then be better prepared to follow the events of May 13 and those which led to De Gaulle's investiture as Premier of France.

The outlines of the activists' plot can be traced to 1957 and to the secret society of the *Cagoule* and to the powerful veterans' group, the

---

[2] See Alain de Sérigny, *La Révolution de 13 mai* (Paris: Plon, 1958), pp. 21–24. On April 24, Pflimlin wrote: "We refuse . . . to be locked in the dilemma of toughness or surrender. We believe there exists a third policy: talks with the representatives of those whom we fight." Quoted by Joseph Kraft, *The Struggle for Algeria* (Garden City: Doubleday and Co., 1961), p. 172.

[3] De Sérigny, *La Révolution*, p. 24.

Veterans of Indochina and the French Union. Taking form in 1957, the conspiracy between these two organizations (the *Cagoule* was headed by retired General Paul Cherrière, the veterans group by General Lionel-Max Chassin, who was on active duty), envisaged Algiers as the spearhead of an attack on the Republic.

Having concluded that the incumbent regime was incapable of solving France's problems, Cherrière and Chassin planned a coup d'état which was to begin in Algiers. An insurrection in that turbulent city would demonstrate the weakness of Paris, and the army would have to choose between Paris and Algiers. "Do not worry," Cherrière assured Chassin, "Salan will march with us." [4] Cherrière, with Raoul Salan and the army behind him (Salan was the commander of all French forces in Algeria), then was to appear on the balcony of the Government General building (the seat of government in Algiers, commonly referred to as the GG), and declare himself the head of a Committee of Public Safety (CPS).

Trouble in France was expected from the Communists; to restore order, troops would be sent from Algeria and mainland units under General Roger Miquel would join the movement. Miquel, who commanded the paratroops in France, had told Chassin, "If grave events are produced, you can count on me. I do not concern myself with politics, but I do concern myself with the defense of the nation." [5] With France at his command, Cherrière would then enter Paris to establish a political-military directory. As it turned out, the outline was closely followed in May, 1958, but with a change in the names of the leading characters.

As the crisis brought about by the fall of the Gaillard government daily worsened, the activists became more active. Robert Martel, head of the seventeen-thousand-member *Union française nord-africaine*, the Algiers Poujadist leader, a mystic and a member of *Cité Catholique*; Dr. Bernard Lefevre, a Poujadist, antidemocrat, and admirer of Salazar's regime in Portugal; Pierre Lagaillarde, former officer in the French army, and now the Student Union's fiery and ambitious president; the mysterious Dr. René Kovacs, leader of the Resistance Organization of French Algeria, and implicated in the bazooka affair; Joseph Ortiz, a Poujadist, also involved in the bazooka affair, and connected with many

---

[4] Jean-Raymond Tournoux, *Secrets d'état* (Paris: Plon, 1960), p. 188. There is no evidence, however, that Salan was a party to the scheme.

[5] *Ibid.*, p. 186. General Miquel would later play an important role in the events of May, 1958.

Far Right organizations in Algiers, spokesman for the cause of *Algérie française* from behind the counter of his bar—these and other conspirators gathered frequently to discuss the course of events. Realizing their schemes had little chance for success without the army's backing, the activists solicited army support, and officers were present at several of their meetings.

While the activists were making preparations, so were the Gaullists. Prominent names in this group include then Senator Michel Debré, Léon Delbecque, Jacques Soustelle, Jacques Chaban-Delmas, Roger Frey, Oliver Guichard, and General André Petit. Chaban-Delmas, Minister of National Defense in the Gaillard government, had sent Delbecque to Algiers to establish communications outside the formal channels, the so-called antenna. The Minister of National Defense, a man who had enjoyed a spectacular career (at twenty-nine he was a general in the Resistance, at thirty-one he was elected to the National Assembly, later he was elected Mayor of Bordeaux and at thirty-seven held his first government portfolio), was, while holding the office of prime defender of the government, plotting against it. Delbecque became the counselor to the powerful instrument of mass action in Algiers, the Union for the Safety and the Resurrection of French Algeria (USRAF), and created the Algiers Vigilance Committee, which included most of the patriotic and veterans groups in Algiers and was led by Gaullist sympathizers.

On May 10, a busy plotters' day, a meeting of leading Gaullists was held in Paris. Convinced that the situation was desperate and that the return of De Gaulle was imperative, General Petit (the aide of Chief of Staff General Paul Ely) was present at this meeting, which also included Frey, Guichard, Debré, and Delbecque, the last named having returned from Algiers with Alain de Sérigny, the influential editor of *L'Echo d'Algérie*. Not yet admitted into the plotters' circle of Gaullists, Sérigny waited for Delbecque for half an hour while the latter conferred with his Gaullist friends. When he returned to the car, he said to Sérigny, a firm partisan of *Algérie française*: "We have the green light for the 13th."[6]

Also on the tenth, the Algiers Vigilance Committee issued a proclamation calling for a demonstration and a strike to take place on May 13, the day Pflimlin was to seek investiture as premier. Although no connection has been firmly established between the Paris meeting and the issuance of the proclamation, it would seem safe to assume that the

[6] *Ibid.*, p. 260.

order for the demonstration came soon after the "green light" was given. Meeting in Paris the same day, May 10, the Veterans Action Committee (CANAC), founded in 1957 by nineteen veterans' associations agreeing to work together for the cause of *Algérie française*, also picked the thirteenth for action, calling for a mass demonstration in both Paris and Algiers, as a tribute to three captured French soldiers who had been executed by the FLN. The Algiers demonstration was set to take place at the *Monument aux morts* (Memorial to the Dead) and high military officials were to attend. Thus the people of Algiers were called upon by CANAC to demonstrate on May 13 as a tribute to the three executed men, and by the Algiers Vigilance Committee to protest the investiture of Pflimlin.

The activists, aware of what was in store and the designs of the Gaullists, determined that they too would act on the thirteenth, but before the Gaullists, stealing the revolution. At a meeting in Algiers on the tenth, Lefevre, Martel, and Lagaillarde discussed the coming uprising. As these activists spoke of their plans, Colonel Robert Thomazo (the aide of the Algiers district commander, General Paul Allard), who was also present, warned them: "The army will not follow you. . . . You are headed for a catastrophe." [7]

On the other side of the Mediterranean, General Petit again met Delbecque and Debré, who was to become De Gaulle's first Premier under the Fifth Republic, on May 12 in Paris. It was decided that the General and Delbecque would return to Algiers the next day, Petit to contact the military leaders in Algiers and Delbecque to handle the civilian elements. Their task was to rally their listeners to De Gaulle who would, assured Debré, follow a French Algeria policy and institute a strong presidential system. [8] Jacques Soustelle, scholar, strong Gaullist, and ardent partisan of *Algérie française*, aptly described by Professor James H. Meisel as "that man with the burning heart and the cool brain," was to accompany Petit to Algiers the next day. [9] However, on the thirteenth, Petit left without Soustelle, who had decided to remain in Paris for the Pflimlin investiture debate. Delbecque had preceded Petit to Algiers, and was disappointed to discover that Soustelle

[7] *Ibid.*, p. 269.

[8] *Ibid.*, p. 273. See the testimony of Léon Delbecque in Maurice Cottaz, ed., *Les Procès du putsch d'Alger et du complot de Paris* (Paris: Nouvelles Editions Latines, 1962), pp. 30–31.

[9] James H. Meisel, *The Fall of the Republic* (Ann Arbor: The University of Michigan Press, 1962), p. 58.

had not arrived with the General. Soustelle was to have been the political head of the Gaullist movement in Algiers, where he enjoyed great popularity from his days as Governor General in 1955.

When Petit left Paris, he also took with him instructions from General Ely (who was not involved in the Gaullist plot and who was unaware of the plans involving Soustelle's accompanying Petit): "Preserve the unity of the army. Repeat to Salan," ordered Ely, "that whatever happens, the military hierarchy must be respected, unity saved." [10] Ely's admonition to Petit that the army must be kept unified and disciplined was a call for order. Ironically, these words would be used to take the army into revolution, as it was argued that the entire army had to follow the lead of the Algiers officers in order to safeguard the army's unity.

The call to action had been given for the thirteenth. What of the high command, the men who were responsible for the army's actions? The army which they led, especially in Algeria, was an uneasy one. In 1957, Robert Lacoste, the Resident Minister, had alerted Paris that "the army is not completely reliable." [11] In March, 1958, the following could be read in a nonofficial military journal: "Let us say it clearly; if the nation were to disinterest itself in the Algerian war as it disinterested itself in the Indo-Chinese war, the army would not be able to support alone the weight of the struggle without grave risks for our institutions themselves." [12]

That the army was concerned with political matters and Pflimlin's attempt to form a government is without question. The colonels' concern was manifested in their activist contacts. But the high command reflected their concern, not by entering into conspiratorial activity (with the exception of Petit), but by making their grievances directly known to French political leaders. They did not conspire, they advised. But one may wonder at the degree of military propriety in their remarks.

May 13 is the day usually associated with the overt entrance of the army into French political life. The official entrance was actually four days earlier. Generals Salan, Edmond Jouhaud, and Paul Allard (respectively, the military Commander in Chief in Algeria, commander of the Fifth Aerial District, and the commander of the Tenth Military

[10] Tournoux, *Secrets d'état*, p. 273.

[11] Related by Robert Lacoste at the July 6, 1958, National Information Conference of the Socialist Party, *Le Monde*, July 22, 1958.

[12] Quoted from the *Message des forces armées*, March, 1958, in Jacques Dusquesne, *L'Algérie ou la guerre des mythes* (Paris: Desclée de Brouwer, 1958), p. 56.

District), on May 9 sent a message to President René Coty, transmitted through the Chief of Staff of National Defense, General Ely. Signed by Salan, the generals' message informed Coty that the only settlement of the rebellion the army would accept would be a cease-fire in which the rebels laid down their arms, and with a wide amnesty, returned to a "renovated French-Moslem community."[13] Only a government firmly attached to the maintenance of the French flag in Algeria could dispel the anguish felt by the army in the face of prospective negotiations. Finally came the warning:

> The army in Algeria is troubled by its responsibilities. . . . The entire French Army would be outraged by the abandonment of the national heritage. It would be impossible to predict its reaction of despair.[14]

Generals Salan, Jouhaud, and Allard had become alarmed over the ministerial crisis; they were concerned about the European population of Algeria, and they felt the army's uneasiness and its fears of another abandonment. According to General Allard, they therefore decided to send the message expressing their anxiety, and addressed it to the President of the Republic since he was the highest authority of the state. Others in Paris were concerned only with "current affairs."[15] Apparently, the generals felt that the President, like themselves, was above the petty concerns of daily events and in a position to discern the "real" national interest. Salan has said that "it was my duty to alert the Chief of State on the drama of a new abandonment."[16] But it may be seriously questioned whether it was an "alert" or the outline of the policy desired by the army, deviation from which would bring a

[13] *L'Année politique 1958* (Paris: Presses Universitaires de France, 1959), pp. 529–30. One writer includes General Massu (commander of the 10th DP) in the group of generals who sent the telegram to President Coty. See Paul-Marie de la Gorce, *The French Army* (New York: George Braziller, 1963), p. 464. General Salan, during his trial, testified that General André Dulac was present when the telegram was written, but made no mention of Massu. (Dulac was the chief of Salan's staff.) *Le Procès de Raoul Salan* (Paris: Editions Albin Michel, 1962), p. 78. However, General Allard averred that while Salan was writing the telegram, Jouhaud was to Salan's right, and he, Allard, was at Salan's left. "All three of us participated in the writing of the telegram. . . ." Allard made no mention of any other officers being present. *Ibid.*, pp. 187–88. See also *Le Procès d'Edmond Jouhaud* (Paris: Editions Albin Michel, 1962), pp. 195–96.

[14] *L'Année politique 1958*, pp. 529–30.

[15] Testimony of General Allard, *Le Procès Salan*, p. 187. See also *Le Procès Jouhaud*, pp. 95–96.

[16] *Le Procès Salan*, p. 78.

"reaction of despair." Henri Azeau, speaking of the message, calls it the army's pronunciamento.[17]

On May 12, Salan telephoned the secretary general of CANAC in Paris, told him that the army would no longer consent to policies of abandonment, and asked for the support of the veterans' associations of CANAC (which represented more than a million French veterans).[18] Salan had an additional opportunity to make his views known that day. Obviously concerned with the army's reaction to his proposals and stand, Pflimlin sent a special envoy to Algiers to meet with army leaders on the twelfth. The messenger, M. Peyra, took with him to the meeting at the GG the text of the investiture speech which Pflimlin planned to read to the National Assembly the next day. Attending the Algiers meeting, besides Peyra, were Generals Salan, Jouhaud, and Allard, and Admiral Philippe-Marie Auboyneau.

Pflimlin's envoy was informed by Salan that the article which had appeared in the *Nouvel Alsacien* had created an explosive situation. The General added that "the intentions of the future premier in regard to Algeria are impossible to accept here. I add that the only guarantor of *Algérie française* for us is General de Gaulle."[19] When Peyra read Pflimlin's speech, serious objections were raised by the military listeners when they heard that following an increased military effort, negotiations would be opened with the FLN through the good offices of Tunisia and Morocco. The generals declared that they would be unable to risk further lives if negotiations were to be the outcome.[20]

In the course of the conversation at this noon meeting in Algiers on May 12, Salan told Peyra that "in order to avoid disorder, I suggest that M. Pflimlin withdraw."[21] Certainly a strong presumption of political advising by a military figure. Meanwhile, in Paris, General Ely conferred with Pflimlin and warned him of the perils of being too explicit concerning a cease-fire. "You go too far. . . . We are in an explosive situation. . . . Take care. . . ."[22]

Although General Salan and his entourage were expressing their harsh political sentiments, the high command was not directly responsible for what happened on May 13 at the Memorial to the Dead and at

[17] Henri Azeau, *Révolte militaire* (Paris: Plon, 1961), pp. 24–25.
[18] Tournoux, *Secrets d'état*, pp. 257–58.
[19] *Le Procès Salan*, p. 78.
[20] See the testimony of General Allard, *ibid.*, p. 188; and De Sérigny, *La révolution*, p. 44.
[21] *Le Procès Salan*, p. 78.
[22] Tournoux, *Secrets d'état*, pp. 247–48.

the Forum, and the insurrection seems to have taken the high command by surprise. In fact, General Salan was not trusted by the activists and had the reputation of being a "republican" general, and the "seller" of Indochina. He had been the target of a bazooka attack in 1957, the attempt on his life coming not from the FLN but from the European activists.[23] Salan, an air force officer, remains an enigmatic figure, a man called by his subordinates the Mandarin, a reflection of his affinity for the Orient (he spent ten years in Indochina). Colder than General Maurice Challe, also an air force officer, he never enjoyed the popularity with his men which Challe later earned when he succeeded Salan in Algeria. Although both were airmen, they gained great familiarity and contact with the army and its officers during their tenure as Inter-Service Commander in Algeria, a post more concerned with ground warfare than air combat.

But if the high command did not have a hand in the actual preparation of the revolt, its attitude must at least have encouraged conspiratorial subordinates in their endeavors. In any case, when the generals were presented with the situation created by the activists on the thirteenth, they accepted it and took control of it. The weight of the Algiers high command, and thus of the army of Algeria, was added to the attack against the Republic on May 13 and the following days. "In brief," explain two students of the event, "the uprising of May 13 was prepared by the Gaullists and activists, facilitated by the psychological services of the army, accepted by the generals, and finally taken over by the Gaullists."[24] Paul-Marie de la Gorce sums up the situation:

> In Algeria and France alike, it was the young officers who led the assault against the government and the regime, thus collaborating in the plans of action of the political factions. At the summit of the hierarchy, the generals pointed to the activities in which they

[23] The mysterious Dr. Kovacs and nineteen others were arrested in *l'affaire de bazooka*. Charges and stories of a plot that included Soustelle and Debré were put forth by Kovacs, but the affair was never fully exposed nor the stories verified. The bazooka attack was nonetheless intended to remove personalities thought to be insufficiently "resolved to defend the ideal of a French Algeria." *Le Monde*, August 15–16, 1958. On the bazooka affair see Merry and Serge Bromberger, *Les 13 complots du 13 mai* (Paris: Arthème Fayard, 1959), pp. 95–104; *Le Procès Salan*, pp. 230–35, 276–80, 420–31. No judicial action was taken until De Gaulle assumed power. Then, in October, 1958, five of Salan's would-be assassins received sentences of five to ten years imprisonment. The sixth, Dr. Kovacs, was sentenced to death *in absentia*. See *Le Monde*, October 17, 1958; *Le Monde*, October 26–27, 1958.

[24] Macridis and Brown, *The De Gaulle Republic*, p. 63.

themselves had no part, in order to exert the maximum pressure on the government.[25]

A crowd of one hundred thousand filled the square in front of the Memorial to the Dead in Algiers on May 13. Slogans were chanted, songs were sung, and warnings were made by the Vigilance Committee concerning the fate of French Algeria if Pflimlin were made premier. Late in the afternoon, Generals Salan and Massu appeared and laid wreaths at the Memorial. When the ceremony ended at a little past six in the evening, the generals left, thinking the day's activities had run their course. But even as the wreaths were being placed by the generals, members of the *Association générale des élèves des lycées et collèges d'Algérie* (an organization composed of younger students than Lagaillarde's *Association générale des étudiants Algériens*), were headed for the Forum, the vast area in front of the GG. The younger students had decided to take the revolution out of the hands of Delbecque and the older Algerian ultras. Lagaillarde's shouts soon brought others to the Forum, however. At first held back by the men of the Republican Security Companies (CRS), the mob entered the GG after the CRS was ordered to withdraw and was replaced by paratroops, who allowed their ranks to be breached.

Once inside the building, the insurgents sacked offices and destroyed dossiers and documents while paratroops watched. Some important police and security files were protected by the troops, but many conveniently disappeared, such as the file on the bazooka case, which included, among the suspects, some members of the soon-to-be-proclaimed Committee of Public Safety.[26]

Paratroop General Massu arrived on the scene at 7:30 P.M., and Salan shortly thereafter. Salan attempted to address the crowd, but was shouted down. Lagaillarde and other ultras urged Massu, a popular

[25] De la Gorce, *The French Army*, p. 469.

[26] The events of May 13, hastily sketched here, are given an hour-by-hour accounting in Bromberger, *Les 13 complots*, pp. 165–202. Also of great value is Tournoux, *Secrets d'état*, pp. 260–90. Three books devoted to eye-witness accounts are De Sérigny, *La Révolution*, Paul Gerin, *L'Algérie du 13 mai* (Paris: Gallimard, 1958), and Roger Trinquier, *Le Coup d'état du 13 mai* (Paris: Editions l'Esprit Nouveau, 1962). For accounts in English, see Macridis and Brown, *The De Gaulle Republic*, pp. 62–81; Phillip Williams and Martin Harrison, *De Gaulle's Republic* (New York: Longmans, Green, and Co., 1961), pp. 51–64; Meisel, *The Fall of the Republic*, pp. 15–49; and especially Phillip Williams, "How the Fourth Republic Died: Sources for the Revolution of May 1958," *French Historical Studies*, III (Spring, 1963), 1–43.

hero since the winning of the battle of Algiers, to head a Committee of Public Safety. A little before nine o'clock he agreed, later explaining his action by saying that given only a few seconds to reflect, he had decided to enter the committee with the hope of controlling its actions.[27] When Massu offered his explanation of his action during a press conference on the fifteenth, a reporter asked him when the CPS would give up its functions. Massu replied that it would do so as soon as a new minister for Algeria arrived in Algiers. "I wish," continued Massu, "to avoid bloodshed. I am not an insubordinate general. The Algerians are determined to maintain their pressure. They will go to the end. One can no longer fool them. It is necessary that the homeland know it."[28]

Massu later reiterated that he joined the CPS to keep the demonstration under control. "I do not care to hold power, not for an instant. When the crowd acted on May 13, and one took account of the forces which were in movement, it was necessary to jump on the locomotive in order to keep an eye on it and see that it went in the right direction. But I am a soldier and wish only to return to my troops."[29]

At 9:10 P.M. on May 13, Massu announced the creation of a CPS which included himself, three other army officers, and eleven civilians, four of whom were Moslems.[30] Colonel Roger Trinquier, on the scene

[27] Massu in a May 15 press conference, *Le Monde*, May 16, 1958.

[28] *Le Monde*, May 16, 1958. When the outburst came on May 13, Generals Cherrière and Chassin were unable to play any important part. Not until the end of the day of May 13 did these two gentlemen even learn what had taken place in Algiers. Cherrière, when he heard the news, announced: "I leave without delay." However, he discovered that all flights from France had been forbidden; he finally was able to make his way to Algiers, but not until the nineteenth. By then, the Gaullists had the situation in hand and Cherrière became a De Gaulle supporter. Cherrière later said that his plan had been successful, but De Gaulle had been the one to profit by it. Chassin had left Paris on the thirteenth, and gone to the Loire region where he formed a *maquis* of twelve men. He would later declare: "I am the only Frenchman who dared to cross the Rubicon." Tournoux, *Secrets d'état*, p. 328. On the evening of the thirteenth, the police arrived at Chassin's apartment only to find that the General had departed. Shortly after the police's arrival, the doorbell rang. A policeman opened the door to Major Puga of the general staff. When questioned, the major explained that he had come to see his mistress. "Mrs. Chassin?" asked one of the officers. "No, I have mistaken the floor!" Major Puga spent the next fifteen days in the Santé Prison. Bromberger, *Les 13 complots*, p. 211.

[29] *Le Monde*, June 17, 1958.

[30] Besides Massu, the CPS included: Colonel Ducasse, Chief of Staff of the 10th DP; Colonel Trinquier, commander of the Third Regiment of Colonial Paratroops; Colonel Thomazo, of General Allard's staff; and the civilians Lagaillarde, Del-

when Massu decided to form and join the CPS, relates the confusion of the situation and the hasty manner in which a list of members was drawn up. For example, as Massu was on his way to the microphone to announce his decision, Colonel Thomazo stopped him and said, "Add me." Thomazo's name was accordingly added.[31]

The committee was heavily ultra and it appeared the European settlers had taken the revolution away from Delbecque and destroyed his plans for a De Gaulle restoration. The extremists initiated the storming of the GG, and the CPS was weighted in their favor. From the balcony of the GG, Massu read to the crowd below a copy of a telegram he had sent to President Coty:

> Inform you creation of civil and military committee of public safety in Algiers, under my Presidency, me General Massu, because of gravity of situation and absolute necessity to maintain order, and to avoid bloodshed. Situation requires creation in Paris of a government of public safety, the only government capable of keeping Algeria an integral part of the homeland.[32]

Massu then assured his audience that the army shared the sentiments of the people, but warned that the cause of *Algérie française* would best be served by order and discipline. Just a few minutes later (9:35 P.M.), Salan received a wire from outgoing Premier Felix Gaillard, entrusting him with the power "to take all measures necessary for the maintenance of order, protection of goods and persons until new orders."[33]

The news of the events in Algiers resulted in the investiture of Pflimlin during the night of May 13–14. Without the demonstration which had been designed to prevent his taking power, he probably would not have been elected to office. But the news of the revolt galvanized the Assembly, and Pflimlin was invested by a comfortable margin.

The new Cabinet met at 5:25 A.M. and the new Minister of National Defense, Pierre de Chevigné, is reputed to have said that he would put the army back in its place. De Chevigné, a former officer himself, said he would do so by arresting five generals guilty of insurrection and breaking ten colonels. Then the revolt would be over.[34] Pflimlin, however,

becque, Martel, Montigny, Baufier, Moreau Paracchini, Mahdi, Berkani, Chikh, and Madhani (the last four named were Moslems). *Le Monde*, May 15, 1958.

[31] Trinquier, *Le Coup d'état*, p. 102.

[32] *Le Monde*, May 15, 1958.

[33] Cited in De Sérigny, *La Révolution*, p. 70; see Bromberger, *Les 13 complots*, p. 193.

[34] Bromberger, *Les 13 complots*, p. 215.

thought it wiser to cover the army's action in Algiers and give the government's confidence to Salan. General Salan was in a delicate position according to the new Premier, and his playing a double game was understandable. The path of a return to legality for the generals had to remain open. The army had remained a force of order, or rather, said Pflimlin, the army "canalizes disorder."[35]

Pflimlin recognized that the army had engaged in irregular activity, but he hoped to rally the army back to the central power in Paris. For when Parisians and Algerians awoke on May 14, there were two governments contesting for power: the government in Paris, headed by Premier Pflimlin, and the Algiers Committee of Public Safety. President Coty at six-thirty that morning broadcast an appeal to the army to obey the legal government:

> Guardian of the national unity, I call to your patriotism and your good sense not to add to the trials of your country that of a division of the French in the face of the enemy.
>
> Head of the armies by virtue of article 33 of the Constitution [The President of the Republic . . . shall have the title of Commander in Chief of the Armed Forces]. I give you the order to continue to do your duty, under the authority of the government of the French Republic.[36]

A follow-up radio announcement was made by Pflimlin in which he acknowledged that the army's intervention in Algiers was under conditions not yet clearly defined. But "I am convinced," he told his listeners, "that our army, true to its traditions of loyalty, will answer the call which was addressed to it by the President of the Republic. It is inconceivable that our soldiers would turn against the law and against national unity: this would be the greatest of misfortunes for the country."[37]

At noon on the fourteenth, Pflimlin called General Salan and told him that he counted on him to maintain order and unity in his command. Pflimlin then confirmed the powers which Gaillard had earlier given Salan. The army must not depart from legality, said Pflimlin. "I do not depart from legality," replied Salan;[38] and he then announced in a communiqué to the people under his jurisdiction that he had assumed full civil and military powers in order to assure order.

[35] Tournoux, *Secrets d'état*, p. 290.
[36] *Le Monde*, May 15, 1958.
[37] *Le Monde*, May 16, 1958.
[38] Tournoux, *Secrets d'état*, p. 295.

General Raoul Salan

General Edmond Jouhaud

General Henri Zeller

General Jacques Massu

Courtesy of the French Embassy Press and Information Division

Entrance to the Academy of Saint-Cyr at Coetquidan.

Courtesy of the French Embassy Press and Information Division

A Foreign Legion patrol leaving Fort Flatters for information about
FLN movements in the region.

French and Vietnamese combat patrol, February, 1954.

Dien Bien Phu, March, 1954.

Courtesy of the French Embassy Press and Information Division

An underground command post at Dien Bien Phu.

Official portrait of President de
Gaulle in his military uniform,
1959.

De Gaulle delivering his New
Year's message to the nation
on television, December 31,
1962.

The path of legality had been kept open by Paris through Gaillard's and Pflimlin's conferral of powers, but actually no one really knew, at this point, whether the army was part of the revolution, controlling it, or obedient to Paris. Earlier in the day, after the news of Pflimlin's investiture reached Algiers, Massu had read an inflammatory proclamation of the CPS. Calling the new government a government of abandonment, Massu proclaimed, "In any event the Committee of Public Safety which I represent continues to assure liaison between the population and the army, *and assumes power until the final victory. . . .*" [39]

Then, later the same day, came Salan's communiqué announcing his assumption of civil and military powers and urging the people of Algiers to return to their occupations and to order. Salan made it clear that authority was in his hands, and not in any newly formed organizations attempting to usurp power, when he referred to "the Committee of Public Safety, constituted under the pressure of events to affirm the will of the Franco-Moslem populations *and the high command which transmits orders to it.*" [40] It appeared that Salan was affirming hierarchy and legality and depriving the CPS of authority, contrary to what Massu seemed to have in mind.

In Paris, the government had decided to vest its confidence in the army and indeed it had no choice. The only hope for Paris to regain control in Algiers was to regain control of the army. Therefore, it was made to appear that Salan had been acting for the government since the thirteenth and not against it. Had not Salan been entrusted with full authority by the government? The army had simply been obeying its superior in Algiers, Salan, who was the government's representative. [41]

But mutual suspicion reigned between Algiers and Paris. The army feared that the government's endowing the military with authority in Algiers was but a tactic to quiet officers who would be arrested once calm was restored. And, of course, there was the longstanding military distrust of politicians under any conditions. Paris, for its part, was not sure what role the army had played on May 13 and what role it intended

[39] Quoted by De Sérigny, *La Révolution*, p. 76; Bromberger, *Les 13 complots*, pp. 219–20; (italics mine).

[40] *Le Monde*, May 15, 1958; (italics mine).

[41] An official communiqué of May 15 announced that "the government charges General Salan, superior commander of troops, to maintain order in Algiers and to assure the protection of property and of persons. General Salan has effectively assumed this mission dating from May 14." *Le Monde*, May 15, 1958; see Jacques Fauvet's column on army actions "legalized" by Paris, *Le Monde*, May 16, 1958.

to play in forthcoming days. Furthermore, suspicions were nourished when Paris was reinforced by gendarmes, extreme rightists in Paris were arrested, and air travel between Algeria and France was cut off.

But in Algiers, Salan found himself in an unusually powerful position. The government, which was not sure of him, had conferred full powers on him. The European insurgents had no confidence in him, but could not do without him since he controlled the army, the key to their success, and he had already made public his position that the CPS would take orders from him and not vice versa. And the activists, who had upset the Gaullist timetable, had cried "the army to power" to win army support away from Delbecque and his Gaullist promoters.

Yet Delbecque too had to court Salan. Soustelle had not been able to come to Algiers (he would arrive on the seventeenth), and Delbecque now had to look to the civil-military commander for support in his attempt to bring De Gaulle to power. Salan was thus the target of appeals from all sides on the thirteenth and fourteenth, each side promoting its designs and giving ominous warnings concerning the other groups. As for Salan on these days, he remained an enigma, reports Roger Trinquier, listening to all, joining with none.[42]

The decisive moment seems to have come on the morning of the fifteenth when Salan made a telephone call to intimates in Paris. Salan asked them their estimate of the situation and announced that things could not go on in their present state in Algiers. The Parisians' answer was that De Gaulle alone was capable of preventing a civil war, and they believed that the General was ready "to assume his responsibilities."[43]

Forty-five minutes later, Salan spoke from the GG: "With the army which you love, which loves you, guided by the generals who gather round me, Jouhaud, Allard, Massu, who have saved you from the *fellagas* [rebels], we will win because we have deserved it."[44] Salan concluded his short address with "*Vive la France! Vive l'Algérie française!*" He then half-turned, but was motioned back to the microphone by Delbecque. Salan then proclaimed the words which signaled that Pflimlin had failed to rally the army and save the Fourth Republic: "*Vive de Gaulle!*"[45]

[42] Trinquier, *Le Coup d'état*, p. 119.
[43] Tournoux, *Secrets d'état*, p. 298.
[44] *Le Monde*, May 16, 1958.
[45] Tournoux, *Secrets d'état*, p. 299.

Salan at 12:15 P.M. again telephoned his Paris "brain-trust." "*Eh bien*," said Salan, "I cried: *Vive de Gaulle*. Are you happy?"[46] Those desiring the return of General de Gaulle to power were certainly happy: "For the handful of devoted Gaullists it was the decisive moment. In his concern for his own precarious position their enemy Salan had reopened the way to the solution which ... had seemed blocked."[47]

De Gaulle had maintained a loud silence since the 1951 failure of his Rally of the French People (RPF) to earn enough votes to return him to power. As the May crisis intensified, De Gaulle remained silent. Gaullists were, of course, working for him, but none claimed that they did so at his bidding and no one was authorized to speak for him. But that De Gaulle was aware of the efforts in his behalf, and of other movements against the Republic, seems without question. Professor Meisel opines that De Gaulle "was very well informed about all plans and plots, about those centering around his figure and about the others too."[48] David Schoenbrun "does not doubt for a moment that de Gaulle was in complete control of the Gaullists at all times. It could not —should not—have been otherwise."[49] The Sage of Colombey was surely privy to most plots, and overseer of one. It is difficult to believe that men as close to De Gaulle as Debré and Chaban-Delmas would have followed their intricate course without his consent and guiding hand. The General had been waiting for the proper moment to speak and to act. Far too intelligent to trust in chance, De Gaulle realized that luck is a matter of opportunity and preparation coinciding. He and the Gaullists had been preparing, and now opportunity was near.

De Gaulle's name had been heard in France more and more in the winter and spring of 1958 and calls for his return had begun to appear from many and varied sources. These and the situation of the army undoubtedly influenced him, and the prospect of returning to public office must have appeared much less remote than it had for several years. On May 5, President Coty had written a letter to De Gaulle

[46] *Ibid.* Tournoux identifies Salan's Paris contacts as Captain Agostini, Colonels Juille and Nery, and Alexander Sanguinetti, but provides no additional information on these men.

[47] Williams and Harrison, *De Gaulle's Republic*, p. 59.

[48] Meisel, *Fall of the Republic*, p. 29.

[49] David Schoenbrun, *The Three Lives of Charles de Gaulle* (New York: Atheneum, 1966), p. 234.

asking the conditions under which he envisaged a return to power. The General's reply, which came the next day, laid down conditions that would not then have been accepted by the National Assembly.[50]

A second communication came to De Gaulle on May 12, this one from General Ely, who wrote: "The army . . . is cut off from the nation. It is menaced with subversion. It is open, in case a government of abandonment is formed, to secession from the homeland. *Your high authority must intervene to save the country, the national unity, and that of the French forces.*"[51] At a press conference on the afternoon of the fifteenth, De Gaulle announced: "I am ready to assume the powers of the Republic."[52] De Gaulle's very name stood for patriotism and determination, and although few French army officers were Gaullists, most would rally to him since they thought Charles de Gaulle would never consent to further abandonment of French national territory.

On the same day that Salan was crying "*Vive de Gaulle!*" from the balcony of the GG in Algiers, another general in Paris was speaking De Gaulle's name also. Guy Mollet, newly made vice-president of Pflimlin's Cabinet, was visited by General Maurice Challe. Challe, who was at that time on the general staff, told Mollet of the army's despair and its resolution to refuse to accept a government of abandonment. The Pflimlin government, Challe said, was not viable and if a government of "national union" were not instituted, only De Gaulle would be able to set affairs in order.

When Mollet told the General that he had stepped beyond the boundaries of his military functions, the General agreed, accepted the responsibility for having done so, and requested that the Premier be informed of their conversation. Later in the day Mollet passed on Challe's words in a Cabinet meeting. De Chevigné, the Minister of Defense, was dismayed. He already suspected General Ely of plotting and now he became convinced that the entire Paris high command was involved in a conspiracy. General André Martin, Challe's aide, was

[50] De Gaulle's conditions: The President of the Republic must write a letter to De Gaulle asking him to constitute a government without requiring the General to come to the President's residence for the traditional previous talks; no visits to see the presidents of the two chambers; no consultations with party chiefs; the composition of De Gaulle's Cabinet would not be discussed by the parties; the General would not have to appear before the Assembly for the vote of investiture. Bromberger, *Les 13 complots*, p. 18.

[51] *Ibid.*, p. 153; (italics mine).

[52] *Le Monde*, May 17, 1958.

therefore also suspected. That night Challe was "escorted" to Brest, and Martin to Metz.[53]

Suddenly, on May 16, Salan issued an order of the day which appeared to mark his return to obedience and faithfulness to the government. "I will keep you on the path of honor," his men read, "of loyalty, and of fidelity to the institutions which the country has given itself."[54] Reacting to the order, Pflimlin told the Council of the Republic the same day that "a declaration made in Algiers . . . confirms my hope that General Salan intends to defend not only France, but also the regular institutions of the Republic."[55]

But the next day, May 17, Salan's and the army's course in regard to the government became clear—a race to the Rubicon. Jacques Soustelle, who had been under close observation by Paris police, escaped France in the trunk of a car and made his way to Algiers. The meeting of Salan and Soustelle was at first far from cordial, since each feared for his own leadership in the face of the other. Salan, who seems to have been hoping for Pflimlin to step aside and thus make possible the formation of a CPS in Paris, apparently now decided that such was not to be the course of events. Therefore, he and Soustelle joined forces and the army became committed to the return of De Gaulle. The revolution was now on a Gaullist course. The hopes of the army for some accommodation with Paris were over, for in joining with Soustelle and Delbecque the army became part of the *De Gaulle au pouvoir* (De Gaulle to power) movement.

The same day General Ely resigned his post as Chief of Staff, having failed to convince Pflimlin of the necessity to form a CPS. After the refusal of two others to replace Ely, General Henri Lorrillot assumed the vacated post, immediately wiring Salan to assure him that he undertook the functions of chief of staff only to bring maximum support to the army in Algeria.[56] By resigning his post, General Ely, the "conscience of the army," expressed his disapproval of the government and regained his moral authority over the army, authority he had been in the process of losing. Without any official position, Ely remained in

[53] See Tournoux, *Secrets d'état*, pp. 300–301; Jacques Fauvet and Jean Planchais, *La Fronde des généraux* (Paris: Arthaud, 1961), pp. 48–49; *Le Monde*, May 18–19, 1958.

[54] *Le Monde*, May 17, 1958.

[55] *Journal officiel, Débats parlémentaires*, May 16, 1958, p. 878.

[56] De Sérigny, *La Révolution*, p. 139.

contact with the army, entertaining a stream of officers who came to see him. Fearing for the army's unity, Ely devoted himself to preserving that unity.

Pflimlin still attempted to keep the appearance of concord between the Paris government and Algiers' military rulers. Dreading most a military coup, the ministers' concern was not so much to keep De Gaulle out of power as to prevent Algiers from giving France military rule. Amicable relations between Paris and Algiers were the government's only delaying tactic until the situation could somehow be resolved. Despite the fact it was apparent that the army had turned on the government, Pflimlin on May 19 advised the National Assembly that the army, caught in a difficult situation, had acted in republican loyalty and in the best interests of France and Algeria. De Chevigné agreed with the Premier's analysis and extended the government's confidence to the army stationed in France.[57]

Also on the nineteenth, De Gaulle held another press conference, informing his listeners in his usual grand style that he might again be of use to France. "Useful, how? Well, if the people so desire, as in the previous great crisis, at the head of the government of the French Republic."[58] But his assumption of power, specified De Gaulle, would be through the Republic's regular and legal procedures of delegating authority.

Meanwhile, Pflimlin continued expressing his confidence in the army. On May 21, the Premier told the deputies that in the eyes of the government the commanders in Algiers had fulfilled their duties. Furthermore, Pflimlin went on to say, Salan had never behaved in any manner which might have shed doubt on his loyalty to the Republic's institutions. The National Assembly then passed a resolution expressing its gratitude to the army for services rendered to the Republic.[59]

[57] *Le Monde*, May 22, 1958. August Pinton, speaking to the Council of the Republic a few days earlier, expressed another opinion of the army's actions: "There have been, to be sure, many conspiracies against the Republic. But it is the first time since the 18 Brumaire that a conspiracy has been associated with clear acts of military insubordination. The coup d'état of December 2 [1851] did not originate with the army, which on that day simply obeyed the orders of the President of the Republic. For the first time in 160 years we are confronted with the threat of military authorities turning against the civilian ones." *Journal officiel, Débats parlémentaires*, May 16, 1958, p. 875.

[58] *L'Année politique 1958*, pp. 534–35.

[59] See *Journal officiel, Débats parlémentaires*, May 20, 1958, p. 2390; May 21, 1958, p. 897.

While the government was expressing its gratitude, its military chiefs in Algiers were also making statements. Speaking to a crowd gathered at the Forum, Salan thanked it for "these good words, 'Army to Power'" and then promised: "Together we will march up the Champs Elysées, and the people of France will cover us with flowers."[60] General Massu then stepped to the microphone, and indicating Salan as the "Boss" in Algiers, said that he would remain such until their goals were achieved—the constitution of a government of public safety in Paris.[61]

Two days later, on the twenty-third, a Committee of Public Safety for all Algeria was proclaimed, with Massu named one of two presidents. The goal of the committee was expressed as the establishment of a CPS in Paris, with De Gaulle at its head.[62] Speaking the same day in Oran, Massu stated that the homeland's liberation was awaited. Salan then added: "Your cries of hope must rise toward France, and they will know that we are determined to maintain a French Algeria toward and against all."[63]

If the cries of Oran were not heard in Paris, the taking over of Corsica on the twenty-fourth certainly was. With the aid of activists and paratroops stationed on the island, the prefecture of Ajaccio was taken over and a Committee of Public Safety was formed. A detachment of 160 Republican Security Company troops sent from Nice to restore order were, according to some informants, disarmed by the paratroops, and according to others, offered to aid the insurgents. The spectacle of the crowds—eight to ten thousand persons—supporting the "paras" in Ajaccio may have influenced the CRS in the latter course of action.[64]

With the taking of Corsica, the government was directly challenged and there was now only defeat for the army if Pflimlin survived, or victory if De Gaulle emerged at the head of a new government. The army, in taking Corsica, demonstrated that "liberation" was on the way to the mainland. It could have been excused for its actions in Algeria on the grounds of its fear of Algerian abandonment, or by virtue of the special powers given to Salan. But Corsica offered no such

[60] *Le Monde*, May 23, 1958.

[61] *Ibid.*

[62] *Le Monde*, May 24, 1958; also *Le Monde*, May 25–26, 1958, which gives the complete text of the announced CPS goals.

[63] *Le Monde*, May 24, 1958.

[64] On the Corsican operation see Bromberger, *Les 13 complots*, pp. 339–54; Tournoux, *Secrets d'état*, pp. 332–37.

excuses; Corsica was a blatant warning to Paris. Pflimlin could not counterattack, fearing the creation of a totally intolerable situation, for if he ordered mainland troops to move against Corsica, he did not know whether they would obey, or if the army's unity would keep military units from firing on one another. Pflimlin faced the unhappy prospect of having no army or of sending civilians to fight the army if the unity of the army remained intact.

The day after the establishment of the CPS on Corsica, Maurice Schuman (Minister of Foreign Affairs) received a call from Oliver Guichard, one of De Gaulle's intimates. Corsica, said Guichard, was a warning and demonstrated the emptiness of the government's power. Guichard stated that De Gaulle, in whose name he was speaking and acting, was the only person who could prevent a civil war. "You well understand his position! The General does not wish to arrive at the Elysée in a paratroop helicopter. He means to save the Republic by legally taking command of a Republican government."[65]

General Massu estimated on May 24 that the government in Paris had very few days left in office. The days of the Cabinet were numbered, he told a correspondent, and added that within a week "we will obtain the changes necessary to save not only Algeria, but also France."[66] After the taking of Corsica, it was obvious De Gaulle was going to return to power, for only his return could prevent the army from invading France itself, a plight recognized by Coty and the most ordinary citizen. Unable to defend Corsica, the government was likewise unable to defend itself; it was without protection. The question was how and when the General would take over.

De Gaulle and Pflimlin met secretly on May 26, but failed to agree on the question of transferring power. De Gaulle desired that Pflimlin should resign, following which De Gaulle would assume the powers of the Republic. Pflimlin told De Gaulle that the Assembly looked unfavorably on him but that if the General would condemn the Corsican action and military preparations for the invasion of the mainland, his chances of investiture would improve. De Gaulle refused, saying he had no authority to issue a condemnation and would do so only when he was in power. The men parted without having come to any accord except that they might meet again.

Yet the next day De Gaulle publicly stated that he had initiated the procedures to form a new government. Pflimlin was aghast and the

[65] Tournoux, *Secrets d'état*, pp. 360–61.
[66] *Le Monde*, May 25–26, 1958.

National Assembly astounded, for neither had any knowledge of such procedures being in course. Nonetheless, Pflimlin resigned on the twenty-eighth after meeting with his Cabinet and discussing the inevitability of civil war if De Gaulle did not assume the leadership of France.

President Coty on the twenty-eighth asked André Le Troquer, president of the National Assembly, and Gaston Monnerville, president of the Council of the Republic, to meet with De Gaulle and determine the procedures for the General's investiture. When the men met at Saint Cloud on the west side of Paris, a stormy session ensued. De Gaulle's conditions for a return to power, which he avowed would never be by the favor of a military putsch, included the same proposals as in his earlier reply to Coty: no visits to the presidents of the chambers, no consultations with the parties, and no attendance at the investiture debate. After hearing De Gaulle's conditions, Le Troquer snapped, "You have the soul of a dictator! You like personal power too much!" De Gaulle replied, "I restored the Republic, M. Le Troquer." [67]

De Gaulle then added two more conditions—full powers for at least one year and the adjournment of Parliament. "Do not ask me to betray the constitution," Le Troquer retorted. [68] More words, anger, and finally they parted after finding no common grounds for De Gaulle's return to power. The next morning, President Coty decided to call publicly for a De Gaulle government. In his message, read by Le Troquer the afternoon of the twenty-ninth, Coty offered the Assembly two choices: accept De Gaulle with the powers he asked for, or he, President Coty, would resign from office and retire to Le Havre. [69]

Charles de Gaulle answered Coty's summons to form a government, and went to see the President at the Elysée Palace. Coty asked De Gaulle's concurrence on two points: first, the Parliament would adjourn itself for only six months; second, De Gaulle would have to honor the National Assembly by appearing before it. De Gaulle agreed to both conditions. On June 1, 1958, after a brief appearance at the Palais Bourbon, he was invested as premier by a vote of 329 to 224. He had won his investiture legally, within the framework of the Fourth Republic Constitution he had come to destroy. He had been haunted

[67] On the meeting, see Tournoux, *Secrets d'état*, pp. 382–84; Bromberger, *Les 13 complots*, pp. 389–415, and André Le Troquer, *La parole est à André Le Troquer* (Paris: La Table Ronde, 1962), pp. 190–95.

[68] Tournoux, *Secrets d'état*, p. 383.

[69] The text of the message is reprinted in *Le Monde*, May 30, 1958.

too long by the questions concerning his legitimacy as leader of the Free French during World War II to attempt any but a legal seizure of power. And he could subsequently maintain that he had gained power by constitutional means, not by a military putsch.

At his investiture, De Gaulle appeared relaxed, and waved and nodded to acquaintances in the chamber. On the day of his return to power in France, De Gaulle, "once the [investiture] session began . . . further surprised and pleased his audience by frankly entering into the banter, the shrugs, and the grimaces of French parliamentary debate." [70] The following day, an enabling bill was before the Assembly which provided for giving De Gaulle full power for six months, adjourning the Assembly, and permitting him to rewrite the constitution. "De Gaulle dropped in unexpectedly. He was the perfect politician," writes one of De Gaulle's biographers, "charming them all." [71] The bill passed and was subsequently called by De Gaulle's entourage "Operation Seduction." The deputies voted themselves out of power, but legality was maintained as power was constitutionally passed on to a new government.

De Gaulle's authority was legitimate and emanated from investiture by the representatives of the Fourth Republic. Later he would say:

> The army in France has no political force. It is, of course, always for order and *la Patrie*. It is also always against weak governments.
> But that does not suffice for the army to wish to be the state. No revolution in French history was ever made by the army. The eighteenth century revolution was made by the bourgeoisie. The people made Bonaparte. Not even Pétain was made by the army—that was Parliament. And de Gaulle was not made by the army. [72]

His power was drawn from the nation's institutions, not from the army, an important difference when the army began making demands. De Gaulle would be the servant of France, not the army's puppet, even though the army's role was of paramount importance in De Gaulle's investiture. Of the event that started De Gaulle on the path back to the premiership, De Gaulle has purportedly asserted: "May 13th was an act of illegality; I will never consider myself as its heir." [73] But even

---

[70] Nicolas Wahl, *The Fifth Republic* (New York: Random House, 1959), p. 38.

[71] Alden Hatch, *The De Gaulle Nobody Knows* (New York: Hawthorn Books, 1960), p. 235.

[72] Quoted by Cyrus Leo Sulzberger, *The Test: De Gaulle and Algeria* (New York: Harcourt, Brace, and World, 1962), p. 100.

[73] Claude Paillat, *Deuxième dossier secret de l'Algérie* (Paris: Le Livre Contemporain, 1962), p. 26.

though De Gaulle could maintain that he had become head of France by legal means, surely the army's shadow weighed heavily in the days prior to June 1, 1958.

As early as May 12, Colonel André Gribius, commander of an armored unit at Rambouillet, just outside Paris, had been contacted by Delbecque. The colonel was asked whether Delbecque could depend on him and his tanks if, in a few hours or days, grave events occurred in France resulting in the birth of a Fifth Republic. Gribius replied in the affirmative on the condition that De Gaulle would be restored to power. Colonel Gribius was assured of that result. "Then, M. Delbecque, you can count on me. . . ."[74]

After May 13, plans for possible military action against the Republic were initiated by General Massu, counseled by Delbecque. On the seventeenth or eighteenth, Massu sent two officers to France, Major Vitasse (a confidant of General Massu), and Captain Lamouliatte (a confidant of Delbecque), who contacted General Miquel in Toulouse the evening of their arrival.[75] The area under Miquel's command in southwest France had attracted many North African repatriates who could be relied upon if necessary to help end the abandonment of North Africa. Furthermore, the area had been a center of resistance under the occupation and many of its inhabitants were skilled in the use of arms. But most important, Toulouse was the "para" capital with paratroop training centers in the area.

General Miquel was not originally a Gaullist, but he had come to the conclusion that the Algerian war was going to lead to a popular front which the Communists would eventually dominate with a coup de Prague the inevitable result. He became a Gaullist when he saw a movement underway which would bring a strong man to power and prevent what Miquel feared was in store for France. He was an obvious choice to lead a military movement in France since he controlled the paratroops, the "shock troops" of France's army.

When Vitasse and Lamouliatte met Miquel, they showed him their orders signed by Salan, Jouhaud, and Massu, stipulating that they were to prepare the path in France for De Gaulle's return to power. Miquel was asked to take command of the military insurrectionary movement in France. Miquel answered "yes," and the conversation, which lasted four hours, went on to cover questions of troops, police, transportation, etc. The forces at Miquel's disposal numbered 4,000 paratroops

[74] Tournoux, *Secrets d'état*, pp. 265–66.

[75] Tournoux gives May 17 for this action, *ibid.*, p. 373; May 18 is the date given by the Brombergers, *Les 13 complots*, pp. 305–14.

(1,500 coming from Algiers, led by Massu, and 2,500 in training at Pau), the Second Armored Group under Gribius, some North African units stationed in France which would add another 3,000–4,000 men, plus the men of the CRS which Minister of Interior Jules Moch was at that time conveniently calling to Paris. He was assembling the troops who were to participate in the overthrow of the regime he was trying to protect.

In addition, the greater number of Paris' twenty-thousand-man police force were counted on to join the movement, and the Paris police had already formed a secret CPS under Jean Dides. Reservists were to be recruited and uniformed, particularly the veterans of Indochina and former paratroops. In sum, the forces to be raised totaled fifty to sixty thousand men. Following their meeting with Miquel, the two officers from Algiers went to Lyons and Paris to spread word of Algiers' determination and to gain the adherence of units outlined in the plan.

On May 23, after a short trip to Algiers, Vitasse returned to Toulouse and informed Miquel that all was ready. It was then decided that the operation could be given a code name. Someone suggested " Grenade." "Too violent," another protested. "A little psychological action should be used," said another. "Let us call it—Resurrection!"[76] So christened, Operation Resurrection called for a landing of paratroops from Algiers at Villacoublay and Le Bourget (airfields just north and west of Paris) which would be previously secured by Gribius' tank units; the "paras" would then proceed to occupy Paris before dawn, aided by the CRS, the Paris police, and volunteer commandos. Committees of Public Safety would be formed at each city hall, and when the situation was in hand, General Salan would arrive by special plane from Algiers, taking civil and military command of France until De Gaulle assumed power.

Generals Miquel and Massu would go by helicopter to Colombey-les-deux-Eglises to present France to De Gaulle. The entire operation, optimistically promised the planners, was to be accomplished without firing a shot.[77] The goals of Operation Resurrection, as explained to Miquel, did not constitute an attempt at a military putsch in the sense of the army taking power for itself. What the army was doing was intervening by exercising strong pressures to bring about the legal investiture of De Gaulle.

[76] Related in Tournoux, *Secrets d'état*, p. 376.

[77] For a synopsis of the plan see *ibid.*, pp. 377–80; Bromberger, *Les 13 complots*, pp. 378–79.

The army was aware of De Gaulle's desire to come to power only by legal means and procedures, and Salan was reluctant, in view of De Gaulle's attitude, to give the signal for Operation Resurrection to be unleashed. Therefore, Delbecque conferred with Massu and Soustelle and the Corsican operation was decided upon as a compromise between remaining in Algiers and an invasion of the mainland. It would place the Assembly in the position of having to choose between the army's stepping across the Mediterranean—which would mean chaos and perhaps civil war—and De Gaulle's returning to power. Salan agreed to the Corsican operation and the result was exactly as anticipated. The Assembly chose De Gaulle.

Among the government's leaders, only Guy Mollet and Jules Moch seemed to have had any inkling of what the army had prepared, but they apparently kept the information to themselves in order not to destroy the remaining morale of the other ministers. National Defense Minister De Chevigné refused as late as the twenty-seventh to accept the military threat as a reality. "The generals are too intelligent . . . to throw themselves into such a folly," declared the former Spahis colonel.[78] Yet it has been alleged that some fifty officers of all grades were meeting twice a day as a staff working for the investiture of De Gaulle.[79]

Early on the twenty-seventh, De Gaulle received information from General Grout de Beaufort (who was to be in command of Paris for Operation Resurrection) that the generals in Algeria were prepared to launch Operation Resurrection on the night of May 28. The night before, as we have seen, De Gaulle had met with Pflimlin on the question of the transfer of power. Now, when De Gaulle learned that the invasion was definitely set for the twenty-eighth, he perceived that the only way to stop the move was for him to announce he was carrying out the steps leading to investiture. Therefore, on the twenty-seventh, in order to forestall the generals in Algeria, De Gaulle made the announcement that he had undertaken the necessary preliminary steps to power. Pflimlin, who did not have the same information, was taken aback by the move since he and De Gaulle had separated in a difference of opinion. Actually, De Gaulle had acted to prevent the invasion of France by the French army.[80]

---

[78] Bromberger, *Les 13 complots*, p. 381.

[79] Pierre Lagaillarde, *On a triché avec l'honneur* (Paris: La Table Ronde, 1960), pp. 43–44.

[80] See the statements by Jules Moch at the July, 1958, National Information Congress of the Socialist Party; Moch claims that only De Gaulle's declaration kept

When De Gaulle declared he had initiated the procedures to form a government, he also sent a wire to Salan forbidding all operations against the public order. The wire was sent through official channels and when General Lorrillot saw it, he is said to have thought: "De Gaulle blocks the landing. And by the official path yet. *Il est formidable!*"[81] That afternoon Miquel received a coded message from Algiers: "Action foreseen is not envisaged for the moment."[82]

General André Dulac, in answer to a telegram from De Gaulle, in company with Major Mouchonnet, Colonel de la Borderie, and Colonel de Fanchenal, arrived at Colombey-les-deux-Eglises as Salan's representative on May 28 in order to apprise De Gaulle of the situation. Dulac was asked by De Gaulle about the projected paratroop attack on Paris, and Dulac told him what he knew of the plan. De Gaulle expressed his regret that such an operation had even to be considered and then, Dulac has testified, he was given the following instructions: "You will say to Salan that what he has done and what he will do, is for the good of France."[83] Like many of De Gaulle's statements, this had an oracular quality into which many things could be read.

Another account of the meeting is that De Gaulle instructed Dulac to inform Salan that he, De Gaulle, would be pleased if Salan came with the "first wave."[84] Salan, after all, had been given legal powers by Pflimlin and Gaillard, and a shred of legality was still attached to Salan, an important consideration for one wishing to take power legitimately. When Dulac returned to Algiers, he is said to have repeated De Gaulle's words to Salan, Jouhaud, Massu, Allard, and Soustelle: "Since, in these conditions, they do not want De Gaulle, make it necessary."[85] The sanction of Operation Resurrection by General de Gaulle.

The same day that De Gaulle was entertaining Dulac and his companions, President Coty was informed by General de Beaufort that the army landing in France, blocked on the twenty-seventh by De Gaulle, had been re-scheduled for May 30. The last day the operation could be

---

order. *Le Monde*, July 8, 1958; also an article relating a conversation with Moch on June 18, 1958, R. H. S. Crossman, "De Gaulle Against the Colonels," *New Statesman*, LV (June 28, 1958), 826; and Bromberger, *Les 13 complots*, pp. 385–87.

[81] Bromberger, *Les 13 complots*, p. 386.

[82] *Ibid.*

[83] From the testimony of General André Dulac, *Le Procès Salan*, p. 376.

[84] Paillat, *Deuxième dossier*, p. 26.

[85] *Ibid.*, p. 25.

stopped was the following day, May 29. By then, to avoid civil war, De Gaulle would have to be definitely on the path to power. Coty immediately called De Gaulle, who agreed to come to Paris for conversations.

That night De Gaulle met Le Troquer and Monnerville in a session which ended in reciprocal anger. The two presidents of the assemblies met with Coty at 1:00 A.M. on May 29, and Coty said a year later, recalling that hectic night, that at 2:00 A.M. he still did not know what to do. Not until eight o'clock the next morning did he decide; then he wrote his message, or rather ultimatum, to Parliament announcing his retirement if De Gaulle were not invested with full powers. Said Coty to some men who were with him, "I have no other solution."[86] The order for the execution of Operation Resurrection never came; De Gaulle assumed power through legal investiture. The army's design of acting as a pressure group had succeeded—its choice for the head of France was in command of the nation.

Had De Gaulle been used by the army—or had the army been used by De Gaulle, who had maintained that he would take power only through legal procedures and not by a military putsch? There is some reason to wonder whether, although De Gaulle preferred to take power legally, the military would be called upon if necessary to ensure his return to the leadership of France by forcing the National Assembly to "legally" invest him as Premier.

On the twenty-seventh De Gaulle forestalled the army's invasion of the mainland and the next day, in his meeting with Dulac, apparently gave his approval to Operation Resurrection. Later, probably as a consequence of his inconclusive meeting with Le Troquer and Monnerville on the night of the twenty-eighth, De Gaulle decided that more than approval of Operation Resurrection had become necessary, that the time for decisive use of the army had arrived. During Jouhaud's trial in April, 1962, a telegram was read which indicates Operation Resurrection received the "go sign" from De Gaulle on the twenty-ninth. Feeling that the road to investiture under his conditions was impossible, De Gaulle must have come to the conclusion that more "pressure" was essential.

May 29, 1958: addressee: to the attention of General Jouhaud: Confirmation interrupted telephone conversation—Stop—Tell Commanding General and General Massu that General de Gaulle

---

[86] Tournoux, *Secrets d'état*, p. 383.

completely agrees—Stop—We await your echeloned arrival beginning from 2:30, May 30, 1958—Stop—Everything ready here—Stop—No change can intervene—Stop. . . .

> Signed: Grandfather
> (alias of Vitasse).[87]

The motors of the aircraft which were to bring the paratroops to Paris were warming up, dramatically stated Jouhaud's defense counsel, when the wire arrived which read: "General de Gaulle received by President Coty. Stop the operation."[88] The army's pressure and actions had led the nation to the brink of civil war, pressures and actions that seem to have been manipulated by the new Premier to his own ends.

Few Frenchmen mourned the passing of the Fourth Republic, and the army's attitude, and the nation's, too, is summed up in the words of the anonymous officer who said: "No casualties, fortunately . . . except the Republic, and that's not serious."[89] The army had tested and found effective its political power. Used or user, it could say that it had destroyed one government and had been instrumental in the establishment of another. General Miquel, the metropolitan leader of Operation Resurrection, in a campaign speech on November 24, 1958, told his listeners: "As of May 14, in accord with General Salan, I was chief of a clandestine resistance movement for the whole of France. It is therefore I who carried De Gaulle to power."[90]

According to many observers and military participants, the army acted on May 13 only to "canalize" the insurrection and maintain order. General Massu told De Gaulle on June 4 that "to see that the patriotic movement did not degenerate into a riot and perhaps end in bloodshed, I judged it my duty to participate in it. . . ."[91] Speaking of May 13, General Salan maintained later that he had purified the movement and kept it from excesses. Also, added Salan, the army's action kept the movement out of the hands of particular interests. The call for De Gaulle on May 15 was an appeal to the only man who could save France and maintain unity.[92]

[87] *Le Procès Jouhaud*, p. 302.

[88] *Ibid.*, p. 303.

[89] Quoted by Williams and Harrison, *De Gaulle's Republic*, p. 55.

[90] *Le Monde*, December 6, 1958.

[91] Quoted by De Sérigny, *La Révolution*, p. 137.

[92] Salan press conference, *Le Monde*, October 27, 1960.

The army, according to this viewpoint, limited the revolt, moderated it, and oriented it in the nation's best interests, playing the role of arbiter and preventing civil war. A schism between France and Algeria had been prevented by the army and the solidarity of France had been preserved. Present in both France and Algeria, the army was the element of national unity which carried the nation through a time of crisis, acting in disinterestedness and on behalf of the nation.

François Mitterand (president of the Democratic and Socialist Union of the Resistance) answered the army's apologists as he declared: "When they repeat everywhere that the army dammed up, canalized, the revolt, I am one of those who say: this is not true. The riot was able to succeed only because the army desired that it succeed."[93] Speaking to the National Assembly on June 1, Mitterand lamented that in September, 1944, De Gaulle had appeared before the parliamentarians with two companions, "honor and fatherland. Today they are *coup de force and sedition*."[94]

It cannot be denied that on May 13, and increasingly in the following days, the French army left its traditional apolitical role and exerted its weight to influence, nay, direct the political destiny of France. In 1851 the army had followed the orders of the civilian commander in chief. In 1958 it ignored the incumbent civilian chiefs, drove them out of office, and imposed the successor. De Gaulle, who had always desired to rule free of and above parties and special groups, entered office confronting what had become the strongest pressure group in France. After May 13, when France faced an important political issue, the question raised by Frenchmen was: "What will the army do?"[95] And the army correctly felt that De Gaulle was in power because it had put him there. Little wonder that De Gaulle insisted upon legal, legitimate investiture. He could undoubtedly foresee that the army would expect payment of political debts and that he would need a sound basis to forestall settlement and give him some freedom of action.

Just after taking office, De Gaulle confronted Léon Delbecque, who brought news from Algeria that there was unrest in army circles because De Gaulle was taking men of the system into his government, for example Pflimlin. De Gaulle cut short the man who had played an

[93] Speech of Mitterand to the National Foundation of Political Science, June 26, 1958, *Le Monde*, July 8–9, 1958.

[94] Quoted by Le Troquer, *La parole*, p. 201.

[95] Jean Planchais, "The French Army: A Close-up," *New York Times Magazine*, February 18, 1962, p. 16.

important part in returning him to power: "I am the arbiter!"[96] Delbecque nonetheless added that there could be incidents as a result of this problem during De Gaulle's forthcoming visit to Algiers. De Gaulle then expressed his opinion of the army's role in his government:

> *Eh Bien!* You will convert the recalcitrants before my arrival. As to the army, it must obey. It will obey, because it is disciplined. It wanted de Gaulle. It has de Gaulle.[97]

He turned out to be a different De Gaulle from the one the army anticipated.

[96] Tournoux, *Secrets d'état*, p. 402.
[97] *Ibid.*

CHAPTER VIII

La Grande Bavarde

Dans un pays où les militaires feraient la loi, on ne peut guère douter que les ressorts du pouvoir, tendus à l'excès, finiraient par se briser ... il convient que la politique ne se mêle point a l'armée. ...
— CHARLES DE GAULLE.

WHILE DE GAULLE'S vote of confidence was still echoing in the halls of the Palais Bourbon, the new Premier was on his way to Algeria. De Gaulle arrived in Algiers on June 4 and spoke from the Government General building the next day,[1] telling the crowd below him everything and nothing as he started his speech by saying, with Delphian grandeur, "I have understood you." Premier de Gaulle then went on to praise the army as "coherent, eager, and disciplined, under the orders of its chiefs. ... I render it [the army] homage," De Gaulle continued, "I express my confidence in it. I count on it for today and tomorrow."[2] The next day, June 6, De Gaulle again praised the army: "I salute you and your flags," read his order of the day, and he again expressed his confidence in the army, "complete and resolute."[3]

From the visiting Premier, Salan received a letter conferring on him the functions of Algeria's Delegate General. The army had been extolled by De Gaulle, but in his orders to Salan, the army's relation to De Gaulle was succinctly but clearly expressed. "You will communicate directly with me," ordered De Gaulle, "to whom you are subordinated. ..."[4] The Committees of Public Safety also had their role in Algeria made explicit. The committees "can not, evidently, in any situation,

---

[1] General Ely returned as Chief of the General Staff the same day, June 4, 1958. *Le Monde*, June 5, 1958.

[2] *Le Monde*, June 6, 1958.

[3] *Le Monde*, June 8–9, 1958.

[4] *Ibid.*

encroach upon the functions of the regular authorities,"[5] said De Gaulle, adding that their proper role was to unify public opinion, and to act as intermediaries between the European and Moslem communities.

In the course of his Algerian trip, De Gaulle clearly indicated his concept of the army's subordinate role, expressed his confidence in the army, commended it, and endowed it with vast legal powers to control Algerian affairs, a move which led many officers to believe that the army's new vocation was recognized and confirmed. The army's integration theme was encouraged in De Gaulle's Algiers speech, in which he attested that there was only one category of inhabitants in Algeria, all French, and all possessing the same rights and duties. Fear of abandonment, the army's crucial fear, was eased when De Gaulle at Mostaganem let escape the words, " *Vive l'Algérie française.*"[6] In vain the army would wait to hear these words again from their Chief.

Three days after his June 7 return from Algeria, De Gaulle received a motion from the Algerian CPS, requesting that municipal elections should be delayed until after the referendum which would be held when De Gaulle's constitution was completed. In addition, the CPS urged that political parties in Algeria be suppressed. De Gaulle's reaction was to admonish Salan for transmitting the CPS request and to warn the committee that it had no other role than to express personal opinions. It was not to tell the government what to do.[7]

From July 1 to July 3, De Gaulle was again in Algeria, a trip ostensibly taken to study the "military situation."[8] He talked with many military men, particularly those engaged in work with the Moslems. He strengthened his ties with the army, listened to the officers' problems, and told them they had a twofold task: securing peace, and helping the Moslems lead a better life. Commenting on the General's trip, Jean Planchais noted that the army was no longer an apolitical, passively obedient army, and that it was prepared to exercise a veto on Algerian policies with which it did not agree. De Gaulle must have become aware of such attitudes and been impressed with them in his conversations with the officers of Algeria.[9]

[5] *Ibid.*
[6] *Ibid.*
[7] *Le Monde*, June 12, 1958.
[8] See *Le Monde*, July 4, 1958.
[9] *Le Monde*, July 1, 1958; *Le Monde*, July 2, 1958.

But as a result of his second tour of Algeria, the Premier was understood to have won the loyalty of the army, even of the paratroops. Planchais' judgment was that "the most important result of General de Gaulle's tour has been to end in an almost total rallying of the army."[10] It was noted that there were a few activists who were not yet satisfied with De Gaulle's actions and statements, and who had pressed for more assurance of his devotion to *Algérie française*. However, these were considered few in number and weak in effect.

But even with the army's "rallying," it was sensed that the army was not yet a completely trustworthy body. Activists were voicing their dissatisfaction and the realization of the army's veto power weighed over decisions taken concerning Algeria. The army's task and role as an essential instrument to lead the nation in the proper directions was expressed by General André Zeller on July 4, 1958, when he assumed the post of army Chief of Staff. "True to its traditions and conscious of its mission," the General counseled, "it [the army] has become for the nation the best of guides."[11] The army had a mission of national renovation, and to assure its successful completion Zeller asked for discipline and unity. By one of her highest army personalities, France was told to look to the army for guidance. The opportunity for the army to act as a guide, at least in Algeria, was afforded by the campaign for the adoption of the De Gaulle constitution.

Even though the ballot was to be cast as a simple "yes" or "no," when the voters went to the polls to vote on the constitution that had been drafted during the summer of 1958, several factors had to be taken into consideration, enumerated by Professors Macridis and Brown as follows:

> Although the overt purpose of the referendum was the approval or disapproval of the constitution, many other issues were implicitly put before the electorate. At the risk of oversimplifying the French political scene, the issues may be summed up as follows: the conditions surrounding de Gaulle's return to power; the Algerian conflict, which involved two possible solutions—integration, as advocated by Jacques Soustelle, and various liberal schemes ranging from "ceasefire, elections, negotiations," as advanced earlier by Guy Mollet, to negotiations with the rebels; a liberal policy for the French Union based upon a recognition of the right for independence,

10 *Le Monde*, July 5, 1958.
11 *Le Monde*, July 4, 1958.

as outlined by de Gaulle during his tour of Africa in August, 1958; the composition of de Gaulle's government and the delegation of full powers to it for a period of four months.[12]

In August, 1958, a *New York Times* correspondent wrote that two months after De Gaulle's return to power, the threat of a military coup and civil war was still discussed in Paris as a real possibility. As September 28, the day of the referendum, approached, the feeling spread that all of the arguments pro and con on the constitution were dwarfed by the consideration that the constitution had to be accepted or France would again face chaos. The nation experienced the same sense of urgency in September, 1958, as the National Assembly had on June 1. De Gaulle stood as "the last barrier between the Republic and those in Algeria and France who wished to do it in."[13] If the constitution were rejected, and with it all that its acceptance implied, De Gaulle, it was feared, would return to private life. The field would then be open for the army to impose its will on the nation and this time there would be no one for France to call on to prevent a military takeover.

While the army was a sinister shadow over the referendum in metropolitan France, in Algeria it was an active participant in the campaign. For the army, a "yes" vote was a vote for integration and continued French presence in Algeria. It was a vote for De Gaulle and for a government capable of taking firm measures against the rebels in Algeria and the "soft" elements in France, bringing to an end a long series of humiliating retreats.

To assure a heavy affirmative vote, the army waged a full-scale electoral campaign in Algeria. In June, a staff note explained the basic conditions for the campaign. It asserted that the success of the referendum was vital to France, for its defeat would mean endangering the national renovation which had been undertaken in May, 1958. The wielder of civil and military powers in Algeria, the army, had to undertake an extensive propaganda program to ensure a massive "oui."

To this end, the staff instructed that a vast psychological action campaign should be put into motion. The military at all echelons was called upon to prepare the Moslem population for correct voting in September. The Gaullist myth was to be fostered and spread. Suggested techniques included posting pictures of De Gaulle everywhere, widely using the

---

[12] Roy C. Macridis and Bernard E. Brown, *The De Gaulle Republic* (Homewood, Illinois: The Dorsey Press, 1960), p. 210.

[13] Henry Giniger, *New York Times*, August 3, 1958, p. 13:1.

Cross of Lorraine as the myth's symbol, and continually speaking of De Gaulle at psychological action meetings, taking as themes, "the General is henceforth the Head of France," "the General is peace," and "you are all French, you are all sons of General de Gaulle." This was not, the note advised, a limiting list, but only in the nature of a few suggestions.[14]

The army's position in the referendum was clearly set forth by General Massu in a radio Algiers broadcast on August 3:

> Yet the "system" was not such or such a man, it was a mode of government. A change of government does not consist of replacing some men by others, but in modifying the structures. In order to overthrow it [the system] it is essentially necessary to win the referendum.[15]

Two days later Salan added in another broadcast that all persons in Algeria were to remain united and disciplined "behind the chief whom we have called," and work together to realize the goal of a greater France, consisting of European France and Algerian France.[16]

A strong and disciplined France, able to keep Algeria French, was the army's goal. If the Moslems would express their accord with this position, it would prove that the army's integration efforts had been successful. A massive "yes" would then be a blow against the rebels of the FLN, who were chanting independence, and against the "soft" elements in France calling for another betrayal of national territory. It would be a vote of confidence in France and the French army. The necessity to win near unanimous victory was affirmed in an order from General Salan:

> All cadres must seek to obtain the maximum number of votes approving the text of the constitution presented by General de Gaulle. It is the duty of everyone to furnish all the necessary explanations . . . in order that the new constitution be approved by a large margin.[17]

[14] Note 1247/ZSA/5 from the staff of the South Algerian Zone, 20th Infantry Division, dated June 27, 1958, signed by General Henri de Pouilly; *Le Monde*, July 13, 1958.

[15] *Le Monde*, August 6, 1958.

[16] *Le Monde*, August 7, 1958.

[17] Order of General Salan, 1532/EM10/5/PPS dated July 12, 1958; *Le Monde*, September 25, 1958. That there were elements in the army still bound to the traditions of apoliticism was made evident in a letter sent by Captain André Masson, on active duty in Algiers, through channels to General Salan concerning Salan's order of

Meetings held in Algiers under the auspices of the army's psychological service sections officially opened the battle for the "yes" in Algeria on September 7. At these meetings and subsequent ones held throughout Algeria, the listeners heard lectures on the virtues of the new constitution and praises of De Gaulle. Those who lived far from meeting places were carried to the gatherings in military trucks. Posters, radio broadcasts, loudspeakers, and other media were the army's weapons in the campaign to win the referendum. An observer of the situation reported that only organizations which advocated a "yes" vote were allowed to campaign in Algeria, the constitution's opponents being denied press and radio space by Salan's and Massu's censorship. The referendum was obviously not to be a free contest, but an imposed decision.[18]

Voting took place in Algeria on September 26, 27, and 28. The polling places were protected by the army, and so were the routes to the polls, with rebel units pinned down to keep them from carrying out threats of reprisals against Moslems who voted. For those who had no way to get to the polls, the army provided transportation. Technically, the balloting was free, and the Hoppenot commission, headed by Henri-Etienne Hoppenot, set up to control the elections in Algeria, labored to control official intervention and interference with the voters.[19] Yet the

---

July 12. The captain said he could not accept the order in silence. The acceptance or nonacceptance of the constitution would have to be a free choice, to be made by individual judgment, wrote the captain. The captain added that perhaps his view differed from Salan's. "Your powers of command cannot oblige me to an opinion that I do not have, and still less oblige me to propagandize an opinion which you determine." *Le Monde*, September 25, 1958. Another captain had earlier sent a letter expressing his devotion to the laws of the Republic, a letter that had curious repercussions on the captain. On May 20, 1958, Captain Léon Howard had sent a letter to the President of the Republic expressing his wish to struggle for the laws of the Republic and expressing his contrary attitude toward the position of his military superiors in Algeria. A week later the captain was given thirty days confinement for having violated channels in writing directly to Coty. On June 5, Captain Howard received a letter of thanks from the President. The captain was thus thanked by Paris for the act which had earned him a reprisal in Algiers. See *Le Monde*, September 11, 1958.

18 Gaston Défferre, *Le Monde*, September 11, 1958.

19 In each polling place Hoppenot had the following sign displayed: "No one can be forced to vote or be prevented from doing so. Free access to polling places must be guaranteed." *Le Monde*, September 17, 1958. The Central Control Commission of the Referendum in Algeria, which Hoppenot headed, was charged to watch over the liberty of the vote, to ensure that no voter was prevented from voting or forced to vote, and that each voter would be free to vote "yes" or "no" in secret. *Le Monde*, September 13, 1958.

Moslem voters were caught in a dilemma, and only in the remotest sense could the referendum in Algeria be called a free vote. Thinking of going to the polls, the Moslem voter had to consider the FLN, prepared to murder those who disobeyed its order to refrain from voting; also he was well aware that he stood in the shadow of the French army, which had made its position clear as to how the Moslem should vote in the unilateral propaganda campaign. While the actual casting of the ballots was honest, the army's pressures in the preceding days stripped away any sense of freedom the Moslems might have had in the election.

In Algeria, 80 percent of the eligible population voted, 96 percent voting "oui," an overwhelming success for the De Gaulle constitution —and the army.[20] Three consequences emerged from the referendum vote: first, the Moslems, caught between the pressures of the army and the FLN, were not able to make a really free choice. Those who had maintained that a free vote was impossible in Algeria after four years of war and in the presence of the warring forces had their fears confirmed, a lesson not lost on De Gaulle.[21] Second, other factors may be considered when explaining the massive affirmative answer in Algeria, but certainly the military's efforts to influence that result cannot be denied. As a consequence of the heavy returns approving the army's position, the army was convinced that its political strength had again been demonstrated. And the vote for "oui," according to the army, signified a vote for integration and *Algérie française*. Deviation from these goals would be interpreted in the future as a betrayal of the referendum, as the army had understood it.[22]

The third result of the elections of September 28 was the army's increased resolve to maintain its position in Algeria. By voting "oui," insisted the army, the Moslems proved that they desired integration and French presence. In campaigning for these principles, more promises and vows of remaining in Algeria had been made by French soldiers and officers, with the result that the fear of abandonment and betrayal was

[20] The results of the referendum: In France, 17,668,790 voted "yes"; 4,624,511 voted "no." In Algeria, 3,357,763 voted "yes"; 118,631 voted "no." In Algeria, 896,961 eligible voters failed to appear at the polls. *L'Année politique 1958* (Paris: Presses Universitaires de France, 1959), p. 591. *Le Monde* reported 80.9 percent of those eligible voted, of whom 96.6 percent voted "yes," and only 3.4 percent voted "no." *Le Monde*, September 30, 1958. On the referendum and the army see Joseph Kraft, *The Struggle for Algeria* (Garden City: Doubleday and Co., 1961), pp. 225–26.

[21] Phillip Williams and Martin Harrison, *De Gaulle's Republic* (New York: Longmans, Green, and Co., 1961), p. 94.

[22] See André Euloge and Antoine Moulinier, *L'Envers des barricades* (Paris: Plon, 1960), pp. 47–48.

etched even deeper into their minds and hearts. A move away from integration and French presence would mean betraying the confidence of those who had believed and voted "yes." General Faure told of being asked many times in the Kabylia region in the days before the referendum if he would give his word as a French officer that the French army would stay in Algeria. "I gave them my word," said the General, "that France would never abandon Algeria." He would then be asked if he spoke in the name of De Gaulle. Faure had always answered "yes." [23]

The result of the referendum in France, where the vote was heavily in favor of the constitution, also had its effect on the army as a political force. The affirmative response in Algeria was interpreted by the army as a vote for integration and army presence, but the heavy "yes" vote in France indicated that the nation was behind De Gaulle. Perhaps the same could be said for Algeria, but there it is impossible to say what the vote would have been without the stark reality of the army's pressure.

An extensive propaganda campaign was, of course, carried out in France to assure victory for De Gaulle. It was essential that the people of France register their assent to his constitution (and thereby to him) by a sizeable margin, if any taint of illegitimacy in his coming to power was to be exorcised. The army's propaganda activities on the mainland were negligible, if existent at all, and the victory in France was clearly a Gaullist victory. His power could now be interpreted as founded on the free votes of the French people and not on paratroop bayonets, giving De Gaulle the legitimate basis to begin his maneuvers against the men who had put him in office. Philippe Herreman wrote from Algiers that the Europeans there were also wondering whether the mainland's acceptance of De Gaulle would not make him "free of the paternity of the men of May 13 and the colonels." [24] De Gaulle now had a counterbalance to the army in his proven national civilian support.

During the first week of October, the triumphant De Gaulle returned to Algeria and on October 3 presented his Constantine Plan, a five-year program which envisaged far-reaching social, economic, and financial measures for Algeria. Many officers who believed in the necessity of bettering conditions for all Algerians looked upon the plan with great favor. [25] When De Gaulle returned to France on October 4, he left a

[23] *Le Monde*, September 28–29, 1958.

[24] *Le Monde*, October 1, 1958.

[25] See *Le Monde*, October 5–6, 1958, for the text of the speech; also *L'Année politique 1958*, p. 561.

letter for Salan thanking him for the army's efforts in the referendum and asking for the earliest possible complete pacification of Algeria.[26] The army thereby received the gratitude of its Commander in Chief and a military mission dear to its heart.

On October 9, De Gaulle made his first move to constrain the political activities of his army. General Salan, on that fall day, received instructions from De Gaulle for the military members of the CPSs to withdraw from such organizations. Salan, it is said, held the orders for forty-eight hours "without daring to render them public."[27] Finally, on October 13, General Massu addressed the CPS of Algeria-Sahara: "Gentlemen, in execution of an order from the Head of the Government, we quit the Committee of Public Safety."[28] Massu and other military members of the committee then marched out of the room, leaving behind the astounded civilians. Obediently, the military withdrew from committees all over Algeria. Many observers took the army's following of De Gaulle's order as evidence that the army was returning to its tradition of political neutrality and discipline. The army, wrote Philippe Herreman from Algiers, "in the manner it has obeyed the order of the Head of the Government, proves that it has returned to the tradition of discipline."[29] A sanguine and premature judgment, as soon would become all too apparent.

But for the present, the separation of civil and military power in Algeria had begun; the army obeyed, although its Algerian chief had hesitated to give the executing order for the officers to leave the CPSs. To do other than obey De Gaulle would have been to challenge the man whom the army had put in office and for whom the army had waged a victorious campaign in Algeria the previous month. Moreover, it was obvious the nation now had a leader. "The Premier spoke in the tone of command. The army obeyed," noted *Le Monde*.[30]

When the army left the CPSs, the united front of civilians and military men was broken, at least officially. As many activists as before were in the army, but their attempts to aid the ultras would no longer have the semiofficial status of civil-military decisions reached within a CPS which included both civilians and officers. The order was a

[26] *Le Monde*, October 5–6, 1958.

[27] Euloge and Moulinier, *L'Envers des barricades*, p. 50.

[28] *Le Monde*, October 15, 1958; Euloge and Moulinier give the date of Massu's departure as October 14, *L'Envers des barricades*, p. 50.

[29] *Le Monde*, October 16, 1958.

[30] *Le Monde*, October 18, 1958.

separation order, a command for the army to remove itself from political organizations.[31] De Gaulle's instructions also demanded that the legislative elections, scheduled to take place on November 13, be completely free. Salan was told that on election day Algeria would elect its deputies, two-thirds of whom would be Moslems, to the French Parliament.

During the electoral campaign all opinions were to be expressed, even those voicing demands for Algerian independence. All candidates were to be able to campaign without constraint, and military authorities were assigned the task of assuring the diverse parties their rights. The purpose of the free election was to permit the selection of an Algerian political elite which would fill a void that an election of "official" or "approved" candidates would leave empty. The existence of the void, created by an absence of true Moslem leaders, was what had opened the way to rebellion in the first place, the note continued. The freedom of the elections was therefore essential:

> The superior interest of the country demands that the election should take place in conditions of liberty and absolute sincerity and that lists of representatives of all tendencies—I say of all tendencies—should be able to solicit, competitively and on equal footing, the votes of the electorate.[32]

Hoppenot's Central Control Commission was again to oversee the elections in Algeria, with restrictive measures against any party or candidate to be taken by the authorities only after the commission had approved the action. An indication of the army's reaction and subsequent behavior is revealed in a note drafted by Colonel Marzloff, a sector commander, who told his men that the army was not to intervene in the choice of candidates or establishment of lists. But since the FLN could be expected to carry the fight onto the electoral field and introduce candidates of its choice, continued the colonel (actually, the FLN boycotted the campaign), the army would have to watch candidates very closely, and he asked to be informed of all candidates and the party they represented. The nature of candidates' ties with the FLN should be indicated, instructed Colonel Marzloff.[33]

---

[31] De Gaulle's order for the removal of officers from the CPSs said: "The moment has come . . . when the military must cease to be part of all organizations which bear a political character . . . I order that they withdraw without delay." *Le Monde*, October 14, 1958.

[32] *Ibid.*; *New York Times*, October 14, 1958, pp. 1:1, 10:1.

[33] *Le Monde*, October 12, 1958.

Just a few days before the election, Marzloff issued additional instructions to his men. According to the new order, the army was to remain wholly impartial. The army's task, however, was still a great one in that it had to promote the fusion of the two communities in Algeria, and "*to counsel and guide in particular the Moslem population.*"[34] In order to serve as "guides," the men of Marzloff's sector were told to "reinforce" their contacts with the Moslems, especially in veterans' organizations, youth groups, study groups, etc. Furthermore, the note continued, the army, "keeping itself wholly in an apolitical line . . . will remain in close liaison with the C.P.S."[35]

Contrary to its orders to maintain neutrality, the army again campaigned in favor of certain candidates, in some districts sponsoring "phantom opposition" lists to give the impression of the availability of free choice. Entering the campaign, the army stressed its favorites' viewpoints and its favorites were those who advocated *Algérie française*. One message from the Algiers military region declared: "It is necessary to undertake energetically a campaign of 'everyone must vote'. . . ." It was also necessary to support the men who wished to keep Algeria French, the message categorically added.[36]

Several candidates in Algeria complained of and denounced army partiality in the November elections (first round, November 23; second round, November 30). Charges of army maneuvers and pressures were frequent, and favored individuals were accused of benefiting from the active support of army officers.[37] In the final analysis, De Gaulle's hopes for a free election foundered on the actions of the army and on the lists presented by the Committees of Public Safety and the ultras. The choice open to the Algerians, either Europeans or Moslems, was a limited one, leading one observer to comment that of seventy-one seats filled in the National Assembly by Algeria, sixty were puppets of the *Algérie française* organizations, one of which was the army.[38]

Clearly, the army had not followed De Gaulle's injunctions of political neutrality. The October announcements of the army returning

[34] The note was dated October 28, 1958, *Le Monde*, November 12, 1958; (italics mine).

[35] *Ibid.*

[36] *Le Monde*, December 6, 1958.

[37] *Le Monde*, December 3, 1958; see also *Le Monde*, November 26, 1958; Kraft, *The Struggle for Algeria*, p. 226; Macridis and Brown, *The De Gaulle Republic*, pp. 252–53.

[38] Kraft, *The Struggle for Algeria*, p. 226.

to obedience were premature. Several days after sending his October 9 message to Salan, De Gaulle had held a press conference and proclaimed to the assembled reporters that he had directed the army to keep its distance from the November elections. "It has done so, on my order," stated De Gaulle.[39] He, too, was in error.

During the same press conference, held on October 23, De Gaulle made his "peace-of-the-brave" proposal. In order to end hostilities, announced the Premier, the FLN representatives had only to contact the French embassy in Tunis or Rabat and arrange for a security-guaranteed mission to France. Then conversations could be undertaken which would lead to a cease-fire. Exclaimed De Gaulle, "I have spoken of the peace-of-the-brave. What is it? Simply this: that those who have opened fire cease-fire and they return, without humiliation, to their families and to their work."[40] The rebels rejected De Gaulle's offer on October 25; their mission was independence, they avowed, and conversations limited to a cease-fire were unacceptable.[41] The army's mission of pacification was assured.

While the army was pleased with the political influence it had demonstrated in the referendum and the parliamentary elections, it also had seen signs that De Gaulle looked askance on its political activity. The military had been ordered to leave the Committees of Public Safety, and been told not to interfere in the November elections. Paris was apparently interested in the army's returning to a more traditional role. Yet Salan continued to hold both civil and military power; the army and its civilian allies, therefore, still felt secure.

However, at the end of November the story circulated that Salan was to be replaced by a civilian official.[42] It was soon bruited that Salan's civilian functions would be assumed by Paul Delouvrier and that General Maurice Challe would take military command in Algeria. Delouvrier was a former Resistance fighter, who, with Chaban-Delmas, had operated within occupied France, helping prepare the way for De Gaulle's return to Paris. Salan would be given the new post of Inspector General of National Defense. Left open was the question of the primacy of control in Algeria, whether it would be civilian or military.[43]

[39] De Gaulle's press conference of October 23, *Le Monde*, October 25, 1958.
[40] *Le Monde*, October 25, 1958.
[41] *Le Monde*, October 26–27, 1958.
[42] *Le Monde*, November 30–December 1, 1958.
[43] *Le Monde*, December 3, 1958.

De Gaulle made a four-day trip to Algeria beginning on December 3, a journey interpreted as having the administrative reorganization of Algeria as one of its main concerns. On December 12, Delouvrier was announced as the new Delegate General, to be assisted in matters of defense, territorial security, and the maintenance of order by General Challe. As rumor had promised, General Salan was to become the first Inspector General of National Defense.[44]

And the key question was answered; Delouvrier, the civilian, was to be assisted by Challe, the soldier. The separation between civil and military power in Algeria was established once again and manifested by the imposition of divided functions, with the army to resume its subordinate position in the administration of Algeria. The civil power was to be paramount. In a letter written to Salan in the early days of December, De Gaulle made clear that civilian supremacy was to return to Algiers. De Gaulle stressed the importance of the economic and administrative effort in Algeria and "in this perspective," read Salan in the letter from his Chief, "I judge it preferable to entrust this task to a specialized civilian personality, the military command resuming its former character."[45]

In the elections held on November 23 and 30, France again had said "yes" to De Gaulle. The Gaullist Union for the New Republic (UNR) was a nationwide victor in the second-round elections, winning all the seats in five departments, thirty-three out of fifty-five in Seine, eight out of ten in Gironde, and twelve out of twenty-three in Nord. A vote for the UNR was considered by many Frenchmen as a vote for the Premier, and as for other parties, "most . . . vied with each other in supporting General de Gaulle. . . ."[46] The people's faith in De Gaulle was demonstrated at the ballot box once more and his position as France's legitimate leader was reinforced. Yet the army's role as national guide had been vindicated by French voters, or so the army could believe, since the nation approved at the ballot box the regime installed by the army in May, 1958.

But those who believed that the November elections were a victory for civilian control, were reinforced in their belief when Salan left Algeria on December 18 to assume his functions in the Paris post which

[44] *Le Monde*, December 14–15, 1958.

[45] *Le Monde*, December 16, 1958.

[46] Macridis and Brown, *The De Gaulle Republic*, p. 266. For the election results see *L'Année politique 1958*, pp. 594–652.

had been specially created for him, a transfer generally interpreted as a "kick upstairs."[47] Three days after Salan left Algeria, De Gaulle received another vote of confidence from France, which to his mind, "cannot be France without greatness,"[48] as he was elected President of France, receiving 78.5 percent of the electoral college vote.[49] The man who had been haunted by the difficulties of legitimacy during World War II, who had maneuvered to maintain the legal procedures of investiture in May, 1958, now had a definite claim to the legitimate leadership of the France he loved.

At the beginning of 1959, De Gaulle was still all things to all men. Some looked to him for a liberal solution to the Algerian problem, others, like some officers, saw in him the resolution to keep Algeria French. After taking power in June, 1958, De Gaulle had allowed the words "*Algérie française*" to pass his lips in public only once; the word "integration" never. Yet the army and many others were convinced that De Gaulle would endeavor to keep Algeria French.

The partisans of French Algeria were reassured when Premier Michel Debré spoke in Constantine on February 23, 1959. Debré gave assurance in his speech that Algeria would remain French. "One cannot envisage," said the new Premier, "any separation between France and Algeria."[50] It was reported that Debré later told the mayor of Constantine that fears of France's leaving Algeria were baseless. According to Debré, the future would bring good days once more, "made possible by the indissoluble union of France and Algeria."[51]

President de Gaulle held another press conference on February 25, during which he too referred to Algeria. The President spoke of much work remaining to be done there, work which was "unimaginable without the presence and aid of France."[52] The President added that he did not prejudge, but that he was sure that the Algerians "*will desire that the destiny of Algeria be tied to that of France.*"[53] Was De Gaulle intimating that the Algerians would be given a chance to decide for themselves what future they wanted? And what kind of ties was the

[47] *Le Monde*, December 20, 1958.

[48] Charles de Gaulle, *The Call to Honour* (New York: The Viking Press, 1955), p. 3.

[49] Results of the election in *L'Année politique 1958*, pp. 653–54.

[50] *Le Monde*, February 24, 1959.

[51] *Le Monde*, February 25, 1959. Debré also commented in Constantine: "First, France is resolved to remain." *Ibid.*

[52] *Le Monde*, February 26, 1959.

[53] *Le Monde*, February 27, 1959; (italics mine).

President referring to? Such questions crossed the minds of De Gaulle's listeners, raising hopes in some, fears in others. De Gaulle had spoken also of a "new" Algeria, an ominous word for those dedicated to an "old" Algeria.

In August, 1959, De Gaulle again visited Algeria, accompanied by Minister of Armed Forces Pierre Guillaumat. Before De Gaulle left, the talk in Paris was that the President was going to Algeria to determine the military's state of mind. After his arrival, such speculation was verified since at every stage of his journey around Algeria, De Gaulle made it a point to visit with military men and eat at officers' messes.[54]

While sharing meals with the military men, De Gaulle asked and answered questions, putting many army men at ease by frequently referring to the necessity for pacification in Algeria. But he also spoke vaguely from time to time of some sort of self-determination, making it possible for the Algerians to choose their own future, since no solution would be successful without the support of the Moslem masses. For example, the officers at Zemmora learned from De Gaulle that they had to pursue their pacification task, but it was "necessary that the Algerians choose for themselves after pacification will have been achieved."[55]

When De Gaulle returned to Paris after his sixth trip across the Mediterranean since assuming power, he left the army with the idea that the Algerians were going to have some voice in selecting their future. He had disturbed many of his listeners, but simultaneously reassured them in repeating the necessity of pacification. Since Algeria would make its choice only after peace was restored, the task of continuing the mission of crushing the rebellion gave the military the prospect of the long-desired victory. Furthermore, many officers may have comforted themselves with the thought that the efficiency of the army's electoral campaign methods would ensure that the Moslems would decide correctly when the time for self-determination did arrive.

There were no new prospects for peace in De Gaulle's messages to the army, nor for political negotiations with the rebels. The army was pleased. Yet while satisfied as concerned the continuance of pacification, the army finally learned that De Gaulle was not necessarily committed to integration. The army, which had decided that the referendum of 1958 had settled the future of Algeria as part of France, now heard that

[54] See *Le Monde*, August 28, 1959; *Le Monde*, August 29, 1959.

[55] *Le Monde*, August 30–31, 1959; see also *Le Monde*, September 1, 1959; *Le Monde*, September 8, 1959.

this was not necessarily the case. Integration, the symbol of the insurrection of May, 1958, was being laid aside.[56] De Gaulle listened to his officers' opinions, but he also told them what his policy was going to be, and he told them he expected to be obeyed:

> You are the army of France. You exist only in the army, because of the army, for the army. You are at its service and it is your *raison d'être.*[57]

Even as the army was being told it must obey, it was receiving another confirmation of its political power. The President had come to the officers to listen to them and to inform them. Yet the nation would not receive the President's policy until almost three weeks later. Consultations were carried on in Algeria rather than in Paris, and De Gaulle "implicitly admitted that in the crucial Algerian question the mood in the officers' mess is more important to him than that prevailing in the lobbies of the Palais Bourbon."[58]

De Gaulle finally presented his Algerian policy to France on September 16, 1959. Three steps were involved, pacification, referendum, and solution. Pacification was the condition to be achieved before the Algerian people could choose their own future. Four years after peace was restored, the choice would be made, peace to be a condition when there were less than two hundred casualties caused by the rebellion in a year. At that time, voting in a self-determination referendum, Algerians could select secession, integration, or some form of federal autonomy. The last choice would mean Algeria's retaining close ties with France while enjoying a "government of Algeria by Algerians."[59]

The first choice, secession (complete independence), De Gaulle predicted would bring "appalling poverty," and "abysmal political chaos," which would be followed by "all-out slaughter," ultimately ending in a Communist dictatorship. (A form of partition of Algeria into French and Algerian zones was also referred to if independence should be selected.) Integration would bring complete equality before the law for all Algerians, and the same political and social level for all citizens. If the referendum ended in the third choice, a form of federal autonomy,

---

[56] *Le Monde*, September 8, 1959; *New York Times*, August 30, 1959, p. 9:1; *New York Times*, August 31, 1959, p. 5:1.

[57] *Le Monde*, September 1, 1959.

[58] "The French Army—I," *The Economist*, CXCIV (January 30, 1960), 433.

[59] *Le Monde*, September 18, 1959. See *L'Année politique 1959* (Paris: Presses Universitaires de France, 1959), pp. 631–33.

Algeria would be supported by France, and maintain close economic, defense, and foreign policy ties with her.

It was now official. Pacification, the army's coveted task, would continue and a referendum would take place only after Algeria had been peaceful for four years. Since the referendum was placed in a distant future, and only after pacification, the idea of the referendum was made palatable. Furthermore, many officers understood the President's self-determination proposals as being designed more for world consumption than for implementation. They easily assimilated this viewpoint, since the United Nations was due to take up the Algerian question in a short time. By his offer, De Gaulle was interpreted as bidding for world favor in France's treatment of the Algerian rebels. The same views had been entertained the previous October when De Gaulle had made his "peace-of-the-brave" proposal. Then, as in 1959, De Gaulle's overtures were turned down by the FLN, swinging international opinion against them.[60]

The army was not surprised at De Gaulle's speech since it had learned its essentials in August. Secession, as far as the army was concerned, meant another case of abandonment. The choice of internal autonomy was met with reservations by the army since an Algerian Algeria was still a retreat. Clearly, the option remaining was a French Algeria, with the Algerians free to choose their destiny when the time came, providing they chose France. For the army, the choice was the same as having the right to choose between good and evil.[61]

De Gaulle was operating from a position of strength. His prestige in France and in the world was high and the army had been performing

---

[60] The Provisional Government of the Algerian Republic replied to De Gaulle's September 16 address saying they were ready to engage in talks, but there was no question of a referendum while the French remained in Algeria. *Le Monde*, September 30, 1959. De Gaulle at a press conference on November 10 renewed his cease-fire offer and added that delegates of the GPRA's exterior delegation (representatives of the Provisionary Government in Tunis) could come to France for talks. *Le Monde*, November 12, 1959. The French Minister of Foreign Affairs had said in October that discussions for a cease-fire would be undertaken only with those who fought, saying thus that the external delegation of the provisional government would not be received. *Le Monde*, October 13, 1959. On November 21 the GPRA answered De Gaulle's press conference offer saying they confided to Ben Bella and his four co-prisoners the task of undertaking talks with the French government on self-determination. *Le Monde*, November 21, 1959. De Gaulle's reply to this was: "I speak of those fighting, not of those out of the fight." *Le Monde*, November 22–23, 1959. On the international aspects of De Gaulle's proposals concerning Algeria see Kraft, *The Struggle for Algeria*, pp. 218–52.

[61] *Le Monde*, September 22, 1959.

in obedience throughout 1959. Even in the municipal elections in Algeria in April, there were few protests that the army had behaved imprudently.[62] The White House had been pleased with the self-determination offer and even Nikita Khrushchev had given it his approval.[63]

De Gaulle had moved carefully, making pacification a prerequisite to self-determination in an effort not to offend the army. Yet many in the army considered that De Gaulle had gone too far in making the offer of self-determination, and troubled minds saw an Algeria being given the opportunity to steal another victory from the army. With his self-determination speech, De Gaulle challenged the army, although he had thrown down the gauntlet as gently as possible and had warned the army beforehand. But elements of the army dedicated to *Algérie française* felt the blow with resounding force. September 16, 1959, marks the divorce between De Gaulle and the army, as he reawakened the uncertainties and the fears of many French officers. Although they had heard De Gaulle's proposals earlier in general terms, the speech of September 16 made the proposals definite and official.

The army wasted no time in making its choice among the President's alternatives, and preparing for the still distant referendum. The same day De Gaulle gave his self-determination address, a colonel wrote his subordinates that they would continue to press the idea that France would be in Algeria indefinitely. The theme was to be developed in all the relocation centers, at all meetings with the civilian population, and in all individual contacts. The slogan to be used was: The army is here forever.[64] The population had to be further convinced that the army was fighting for it, not against it.

During the night of September 16–17, tricolor posters appeared in Algiers bearing the motto: *Algérie française* forever. The Algiers army staff denied giving the order for posting the signs, but French soldiers had been seen putting them up.[65] General Challe's order of the day on September 22 expressed the army's answer to De Gaulle. "We will remain," the order unequivocally proclaimed.[66] The same day Challe told his staff, according to Colonel Jean Gardes, "Of course we are all quite agreed; the army marches on the path of the second solution, that is to say, of integration. I give you the order to tell your subordinates.

---

[62] See *Le Monde*, March 12, 1959; *Le Monde*, March 24, 1959.
[63] Kraft, *The Struggle for Algeria*, p. 230.
[64] *Le Monde*, March 31, 1960.
[65] *Le Monde*, September 19, 1959.
[66] *Le Monde*, September 23, 1959.

Do not write it down. These orders are verbal only. And you will give your instructions verbally." [67]

Operation Resurrection was instrumental in bringing De Gaulle to power; Operation Veronica began in October, 1959, and had as its goal the return of De Gaulle to Colombey-les-deux-Eglises.[68] The leader of Operation Veronica was none other than the army's Chief of Staff, General André Zeller, who had been recalled from retirement to take his post as head of the army. Zeller's own strong views on the necessity of maintaining a French Algeria, plus his official position, made him a natural leader of De Gaulle's opponents. An order from Chief of Staff Zeller became an official directive; hence his importance at the head of any insurrectionary movement. As De Gaulle became increasingly liberal in regard to Algeria, and less in favor of integration, the discontented became more and more warm to Zeller. Zeller's contacts included officers and ultras in Algiers and these learned that a military directory was being planned to replace De Gaulle if the President did not alter his self-determination policy. The directory would consist of Generals Salan, Jouhaud, and Zeller.

The Chief of Staff learned in the first half of September that he was going to be returned to retirement on October 1. Therefore, the plotters, most of them civilian ultras, deemed it necessary to make their move by October 15. They thought that by then Zeller would have lost his contacts and the Zeller network would be rendered powerless. In general outline, the plan called for fifty deputies in the National Assembly to resign and leave the Chambers crying that De Gaulle's policy toward Algeria was treason, and declaring their own adherence to integration.

Concurrently, incidents would occur in Paris and Algiers, including assassinations. Finding its majority threatened, the Debré government would resign, recognizing that the self-determination policy was doomed. De Gaulle would then appoint Georges Bidault (a former teacher and resistance fighter) as Premier, or some other partisan of French Algeria. If Debré would not resign, if De Gaulle proved to be obstinate, then forceful action was to be taken. "Commandos" would

[67] Testimony of Colonel Gardes, Alain de Sérigny, ed., *Un Procès* (Paris: La Table Ronde, 1961), pp. 60–61.

[68] For the account of Operation Veronica presented here I am indebted to Merry Bromberger, *et al.*, *Barricades et colonels* (Paris: Arthème Fayard, 1960), pp. 37–66. For a brief mention of the outlines of the plot see Kraft, *The Struggle for Algeria*, p. 233, and Louis Terrenoire, *De Gaulle et l'Algérie* (Paris: Arthème Fayard, 1964), pp. 137–40.

invade the Palais Bourbon, the Hotel Matignon, and the Elysée Palace (respectively, the meeting place of the National Assembly, the Premier's residence, and the President's residence). De Gaulle would be escorted back to his country estate and France would have a directory imposed in his place.

Joseph Kraft asserts that De Gaulle was alerted to the plot by General Ely, Chief of the General Staff. De Gaulle did receive a plea from Ely, asking him to give the army four assurances: that all political negotiation with the FLN was excluded; that the army would assure the control of the eventual referendum; that terrorists would never be considered as combatants; and that the government would campaign for the French solution. Ely informed De Gaulle that if these assurances were not forthcoming he feared for the unity of the army. A worried Ely told De Gaulle that if another crisis occurred like the one in May, 1958, he feared that rather than risk division, the entire army would pass into dissidence.[69]

Immediately precautions were taken in Paris for the protection of the Elysée Palace, the Hotel Matignon, and the Palais Bourbon. Certain personalities who had been designated as eventual ultra victims were given protection and the police contacted former Gaullist fighters in case of the need to form a militia. Then De Gaulle moved his queen into checkmate position, or rather his general. The civilians who were busying themselves laying these plans were counting on the army's support. De Gaulle called General Challe to Paris.

De Gaulle first informed Challe that the speech of September 16 had contained the assurances the army desired. Then he added that political negotiations were not necessary for a cease-fire; as for the referendum, the army would of course oversee it, who else would do so? As to the French solution, "Who," asked De Gaulle, "can pretend that he is not for a French solution?"[70] Association was the solution to be sought, giving satisfaction to the Algerian dream of autonomy while maintaining close Algerian ties with France.

Challe returned to Algeria and relayed De Gaulle's words to his generals and colonels. A few officers, such as Colonels Antoine Argoud, Joseph Broizat, and Jean Gardes (all activist officers and advocates of revolutionary war), continued to condemn the self-determination proposals, but others felt that De Gaulle had satisfied the army's demands.[71]

---

[69] Kraft, *The Struggle for Algeria*, p. 233; Bromberger, *Barricades et colonels*, pp. 57–58.

[70] Bromberger, *Barricades et colonels*, p. 59.

[71] *Ibid.*, p. 60.

The civilian ultras of Algiers who had planned on the army's backing, especially Joseph Ortiz and Pierre Lagaillarde, soon learned that the army was not disposed to lend its support. For example, it was learned that General Jean Gracieux, commander of the 10th DP, had assured De Gaulle of his and his men's loyalty. And on October 10, Massu signed a communiqué saying, "I will maintain order!"[72] Massu had understood the army would remain in Algeria and he was satisfied.

Just in case of trouble, Plan Arsenal was put into effect by Paris. Eleven CRS companies and mobile gendarmes were sent from France to Algeria, paratroops were put on alert, and the protection of public buildings was assured. But deprived of the army's support by Massu's "I will maintain order!" the ultras of Algiers dared nothing. Ortiz and Lagaillarde would have to wait for another day.

In Paris, however, the activists initiated their plot, not having been warned that the army was no longer with them. On October 14, they tried to raise emotions and create a disturbing atmosphere by threatening deputies and disseminating lists of men marked for assassination. The names of men who would constitute the next government circulated,[73] while Guy Ribeaud accosted his former friends in the UNR darkly warning, "All those who betray the oath of the Forum will be eliminated!"[74]

The plot's end came suddenly during the night of October 14–15, 1959, when Alain de Sérigny, Jean-Baptiste Biaggi, Colonel Robert Thomazo, Pascal Arrighi, René de Cathala, and Guy Ribeaud attended a midnight meeting in Delbecque's office. Arrighi calculated that if the UNR deputies present at the meeting were to resign, fifty other UNR deputies would follow. They would be joined by the independents and others true to *Algérie française*. An opposition majority would result, and the government would fall. With this happy thought, the plotters issued a communiqué announcing their resignation, and added that others would join them.

At 3:00 A.M. the word came from Algiers. Arrighi gasped: "We have been betrayed by the army!"[75] Operation Veronica collapsed. Only on the fifteenth did the story of the plot break publicly in Paris; then stories spread of killers coming across the border from Spain and of a coup

[72] *Ibid.*

[73] Bromberger, *Barricades et colonels*, p. 61. The government was to be headed by Bidault, with Zeller as Minister of Defense. Also included were André Morice, Roger Duchet, François Valentin, Pascal Arrighi, Alain de Lacoste-Lareymondie, and Guy Ribeaud.

[74] *Ibid.*, p. 60.

[75] *Ibid.*, p. 63.

about to take place. At 10:00 A.M. Debré was told that an insurrection was about to break out. Debré, privy to the situation's true nature, answered that nothing would happen. The army would forbid all demonstrations in Algeria.[76]

When Albin Chalandon, secretary general of the UNR, publicly referred to the "October conspiracy," De Gaulle angrily reprimanded him: "How could you think of talking about a plot? One does not plot against France. And what could they do? I have all the army behind me!"[77] If De Gaulle could speak of having the army behind him, it was only in the sense that he had calmed and reassured the military activists just in time to prevent them from lending their support to the civilian activists. Without the army, the latter were powerless.

In the National Assembly on October 15, the government won the deputies' approval to follow the policy charted on September 16.[78]

[76] One assassination attempt did occur, or at least allegedly so, on the night of October 15–16. At 2:00 A.M. François Mitterand's car was machine-gunned, after he had time to jump out, climb a garden fence, and hide behind some trees. The attack brought a reaction from the government as it now had proof of a terrorist operation afoot. A hundred arrests of extreme rightists were made in Paris and the countryside. Kraft sees the Mitterand affair as a calculated attack designed to cultivate the fiction of a plot, once the real threat of the plot was removed. The government then had an excuse to move against enemies of the government's Algerian policy. Kraft, *The Struggle for Algeria*, pp. 233–34. The mystery surrounding the affair is seen in the statement that "the darkness hiding the scene has remained impenetrable to this day." James H. Meisel, *The Fall of the Republic* (Ann Arbor: The University of Michigan Press, 1962), p. 62.

[77] Bromberger, *Barricades et colonels*, p. 65.

[78] The vote was 441 to 23, *Le Monde*, October 17, 1959. In June, 1958, 42 percent of those queried in a French public opinion poll indicated that in their opinion Algeria would still be French in ten years; 18 percent replied they thought it would not, while 40 percent gave no answer. A poll taken in September, 1959, asked Parisians which of De Gaulle's three options had the best chance to succeed; 38 percent thought association had the best chance, 24 percent selected integration, and 17 percent secession. Twenty-one percent gave no answer. In a wider poll in October, 35 percent of those questioned selected association, 23 percent integration, 12 percent secession, and 30 percent gave no answer. In February, 1960, the poll showed 48 percent preferred association, 27 percent integration, 6 percent secession, and 19 percent with no answer. Cited· by William G. Andrews, *French Politics and Algeria* (New York: Appleton-Century-Crofts, 1962), pp. 18–19. French public opinion thus followed De Gaulle's preference for association, with a minority expressing the army's favorite, integration. As Andrews points out, "either there was a radical shift of opinion between June, 1958, and September, 1959, or De Gaulle convinced many of the 42 percent in the June, 1958, poll that 'association' is a French solution." *Ibid.*, p. 19.

Again the nation had given its approval, this time through its representatives, to De Gaulle and his policy. Those army elements that failed to accept the self-determination policy, seeing in it a denial of integration and a step on the path to abandonment, found their echo only in the minority opinion of civilians in France.

In the early days of November, the army received further assurances from the government. Minister of Armed Forces Guillaumat addressed a letter to Challe designed to mitigate the worries of certain army elements. Guillaumat praised the army for the military and humane actions being carried out in Algeria, and confirmed that the army would be in Algeria until the rebels ceased fighting, either by choice or force. He then stated that the army would be present at the referendum and control it, as the army had controlled the referendum and the elections in 1958. The army would "assure the liberty of the vote."[79] Many officers breathed more easily.

However, their breath was cut short on November 10, when De Gaulle held another press conference. In answer to a question concerning the evolution of the Algerian problem and the prospects for a cease-fire, De Gaulle stressed the Algerians' right to choose their own future. Their choice would be entirely free and all Algerians would take part in the campaigning and voting. Whatever their program, "whatever they may be, from wherever they may come . . ." all would participate without constraint.[80] De Gaulle then reiterated the offer to negotiate a cease-fire.

Thus the ultras, civilian and military, heard what they feared most: the possibility of a negotiated end to the fighting and the unequivocal right of the Algerians to choose their own future. A new plot developed the next day. As one unidentified officer exclaimed, "Each time De Gaulle opens his mouth, he provokes another uprising!"[81] For the ultras, cease-fire negotiations could have only disastrous results for their French Algeria. If the negotiations came to pass, they believed that Ben Bella would be freed, and the rebel leaders would be at liberty to roam Algeria in triumphant visits. They feared that the results of a referendum could only be in favor of the people's heroes, the rebel chieftains. The single remaining hope for the Europeans and *Algérie française* was, then, to have another revolution before negotiations

[79] *Le Monde*, November 8–9, 1959.

[80] *L'Année politique 1959*, pp. 635–36; *Le Monde*, November 11, 1959.

[81] Bromberger, *Barricades et colonels*, p. 67. The November plot is discussed in *ibid.*, pp. 67–85.

could take place. However, apparently waiting until political talks would accompany the military conversations, the FLN did not accept the new offer to negotiate. The ultras were thereby given time to prepare a new attack on the De Gaulle Republic.

In April, 1960, De Gaulle was scheduled to visit the United States. De Gaulle's opponents set the uprising for that month, when De Gaulle would be absent from the country. According to the plan, demonstrations would break out in Algiers in April, and civilian activists would occupy public buildings and entrench themselves. Fearing it might shed French blood, the army would refuse to attempt to dislodge them. Crowds would assemble the next day to acclaim the barricaded defenders of French Algeria, whose leaders would include Joseph Ortiz and Robert Martel, leader of MP 13 (Popular Movement of May 13).

Meanwhile, in mainland France, political and military personalities would announce in favor of the insurrection. Political friends of Bidault and François Valentin (president of the National Defense Committee of the National Assembly) would lend their support to the movement out of friendship and political sympathy. As agitation increased, the army would fear for its unity. If De Gaulle would remain in America, his government would collapse. Should he return, his prestige would be so lowered, thought the plotters, that he would have to renounce his course of self-determination and go back to the "promises" of May 13. If he refused, demonstrations, assaults on public buildings by activists, tanks from Rambouillet and Saint-Germain, troops from Pontoise, would carry the insurrection into the capital. De Gaulle would have to resign and go back to Colombey, being replaced by a provisional government whose members would be partisans of French Algeria. The composition of the government was apparently never definitely set; it was to be, however, a firm and tough government that would rule over the Sixth Republic.

Salan was approached by plotters, including Lagaillarde and Auguste Arnould, an Algiers veterans' leader, but he did not take the affair seriously, and is said to have broken into laughter at the propositions made to him.[82] General Zeller, shaken by the business of the previous month, felt little warmth for the movement and kept to himself, although General Jouhaud, born in Algeria and dedicated to *Algérie française*, was an eager advocate of the insurrection (Jouhaud was then air force Chief of Staff).

[82] *Ibid.*, p. 71.

Many persons and organizations became involved in the machinations. For example, Dr. Jacques Martin, promoter of a corporative system for France, Pierre Poujade and Jean-Marie Le Pen, both rightist deputies, and the Sidos brothers, founders of the extreme right-wing group, Young Nation. The Veterans of Indochina and the French Union, led by their secretary, Yves Gignac, were in the midst of preparations, ready as always to furnish "shock" troops when necessary. Philippe de Massey contacted military personalities, asking if they were ready to defend *Algérie française*. Secret agents operated in Toulouse, Avignon, Marseille, Saint Etienne, in the Vendée, Creuse, and Corrèze.

It is impossible to say how deeply the army was implicated in the plot. As in October, civilian activists both in Algiers and Paris seem to have taken the lead, depending upon the army to assure the success of their designs. That many officers were prepared to lend their support to the activists seems without doubt. Activist officers had been reassured by De Gaulle's words to Challe in October, and their withdrawal of support from the plotters brought about the collapse of Operation Veronica. The President's remarks on November 10 revived their opposition to De Gaulle. But the November plot, scheduled to burst in April, prematurely exploded in January when Ortiz and Lagaillarde took to the barricades.

When De Gaulle assumed power in 1958, it was necessary for him to restore discipline in the army. Transfer was one means, moving faithful Gaullists to key posts, removing the suspect, and putting others where they could be closely watched. No disciplinary action was taken against any officers because of their May 13 activities. Instead, promotions and honors were bestowed. In July, 1958, Massu was awarded another star and Salan was given another medal.[83] In December, 1958, the latter had left Algiers to become the Inspector General of National Defense, but in January he became instead the Military Governor of Paris, an honorific post and little else.[84] The recently instituted office of Inspector General of National Defense disappeared in February, and when Salan protested to De Gaulle, he was told that the General Staff had prepared the decrees.[85]

General Ely was recalled from retirement shortly after De Gaulle became Premier, and in January, 1959, was designated Chief of the

---

[83] *Le Monde*, July 13–14, 1958.
[84] *Le Monde*, January 30, 1959.
[85] Bromberger, *Barricades et colonels*, p. 41.

General Staff of Defense, a position which put him directly under the President. General de Beaufort, who was to have commanded Operation Resurrection in Paris, was made chief military adviser, thus also placed directly under De Gaulle. Colonel Gribius, who was to have brought his tanks into Paris for Operation Resurrection, was made a general and transferred to Algeria as commander of the West Algerian Zone. The metropolitan leader of the operation, General Miquel, was honored and then retired, one year in advance of his retirement age. General Allard, who commanded the Algiers army corps in May, 1958, was transferred to Germany while the officer who had acted as a liaison between Paris and Algiers, General Petit, became chief of the Premier's special staff, and thus under the government's eye. General Jouhaud, who had been commander of aviation in Algeria, was sent to Paris as air force Chief of Staff.

By the anniversary of May 13, 1958, only two officers remained in Algiers who had played an influential role the year before, General Massu and Colonel Godard. During that year, some fifteen hundred officers of the grade of major or above had been removed.[86] One tactic at the government's disposal—transfer—had thus been used extensively in its efforts to regain control of the army. Honors and promotions also were used by De Gaulle instead of disciplinary action to bring the army back into obedience. Such a maneuver could have had two effects, one salutary, one not. In the first case, the army was not called upon to punish its own men, a task which could have brought bitterness and destroyed respect for the new government. The army could rally to a regime which honored the army's officers. On the other hand, the transfer of activists to other posts gave them a chance to disseminate their ideas. Furthermore, and more important, the army had learned that it could oppose a government and not be chastised for it.

[86] See Williams and Harrison, *De Gaulle's Republic*, pp. 98–99. *Le Monde*, on May 9, 1959, published a list of the men most involved in the events of May 13, 1958, and their position a year later. See *Le Monde*, May 9, 1959.

CHAPTER IX

The National Arbiter

L'armée n'est pas une caste dans la nation, c'est la nation entière.
—RAYMOND POINCARÉ.

THE NOVEMBER PLOT, planned for April, 1960, was prematurely ignited by De Gaulle's recall of General Massu from Algiers in January. One of the last and certainly the most famous of the army partisans of *Algérie française* who had participated in the rebellion of May, 1958, Massu was to be taken away from the ultras.[1]

As early as September, 1959, Massu learned that his transfer was imminent. During an inspection trip that month, Minister of Armed Forces Guillaumat told the famous paratroop General that things were going to happen in Algeria which Massu would not like and offered him a command at Dakar. The General answered, however, that he preferred to remain in Algeria (Massu at this time was the Algiers army corps commander). Also in September, Zeller made his farewell visit as Chief of Staff to Algeria, and he too informed Massu of his forthcoming transfer. Zeller, who was being retired on October 1, told the hero of Algiers that he had delayed the decision, but now that he was leaving office Massu's removal would probably follow shortly thereafter.[2]

Massu was one of the last officers of May 13 left in Algiers, and the prospect of his assignment elsewhere alarmed the partisans of *Algérie française*. Massu, frequently referred to as the "Father of New Algeria," represented integration and continued French army presence. His absence would be interpreted as the army's future absence.

[1] On the ultras' mental state after De Gaulle's September 16 address, see Alain de Sérigny, ed., *Un Procès* (Paris: La Table Ronde, 1961), pp. 121–72.
[2] Merry Bromberger, *et al.*, *Barricades et colonels* (Paris: Arthème Fayard, 1960), p. 24.

The immediate cause of Massu's recall in January, 1960, was a sensational interview given by him to a German journalist. Hans Ulrich Kempski arrived in Algiers after promising the French Ambassador in Bonn that he would refrain from using any statements given to him by French officers which contained political significance.[3] Kempski was granted an interview with Massu which was published in the West German newspaper *Süddeutscher Zeitung* on January 18. The next day Massu was called to Paris.

During the interview, Massu stated that he wished the government would "finally help us to see clearly into the future, to see that we are going to succeed in keeping Algeria French." Kempski then remarked that De Gaulle must have some ideas on the subject of Algeria's future, to which Massu replied that if he did they were not the army's. Furthermore, added Massu, De Gaulle did not understand the Moslems, and if the President continued in his course, it would be interpreted by the Moslems as weakness.

Kempski then asked the General if the army in Algeria had the power to impose its conceptions of how to conduct the war in Algeria. Massu's reply was:

> The army has the power. It has not used it so far because the need has not presented itself, but it will have to use its force and intervene if the situation demands it. We no longer understand the policy of President de Gaulle. The army could not foresee that he would have such a policy. . . . Our greatest deception has been to see de Gaulle become a man of the Left.[4]

With these words, De Gaulle learned from an old comrade-in-arms that the army was prepared to intervene in the face of a policy with which it disagreed. Speaking of May 13, Massu remarked, "De Gaulle was the only man at our disposition. The army perhaps made a mistake." Then Massu uttered a thinly veiled threat. In answer to the question whether a successor to De Gaulle could be distinguished, Massu replied: "The first question to ask is when the successor to de Gaulle will come."

What Massu told Kempski he had already said many times in private to fellow officers who shared his sentiments. Arranged through General Challe, the interview with Kempski has been interpreted in two ways. One is that Massu, a blunt and undiplomatic officer, was offered to the

[3] Jean-André Faucher, *Les Barricades d'Alger* (Paris: Editions Atlantic, 1960), p. 58.

[4] For the interview see *Le Monde*, January 20, 1960.

journalist by Algiers to make De Gaulle aware of army sentiment. De Gaulle, apprised of the army's firm attitude in behalf of a French Algeria, would not then go beyond what the army was prepared to allow. After the interview, it was said that officers smiled and said, "Now . . . *le Grand Charles* will no longer be able to say he is unaware of what we are thinking." [5]

Another interpretation postulates that the interview was arranged to get Massu out of Algiers. Knowing that Massu would speak out and attack De Gaulle's self-determination policy, Paris is said to have arranged the interview in order to provide the government the pretext to remove the military's symbol of *Algérie française*. Massu was considered an obstacle to government policy, so the problem became one of getting rid of the obstacle. [6] In the agitation which could be counted on to follow Massu's removal, the government would be able to extend its powers and promote its policy.

Each viewpoint is interesting and engaging. However, the supposition that Massu was used to inform the President of the army's mental state appears faulty when one considers that De Gaulle, after his several trips to Algeria, must have been well aware of its position. Furthermore, in October, De Gaulle had the opportunity to learn the army's sentiments from Generals Ely and Challe. If Massu's interview was Algiers-inspired, there must have been more behind it than merely expressing army sentiment, for the gains to be made by Massu's public declarations would have to be quite large to justify placing him, Algiers' favorite, in a situation which provided justification for his transfer, already known to be under consideration. Moreover, an uprising was set for April. Why then take the chance of premature rebellion in January, instigated by the recall of Massu from volatile Algiers? Perhaps Algiers thought De Gaulle would not dare take action against Massu, for fear of what the ultras might attempt if Massu were sent to serve elsewhere. In this context, Massu's interview was more than a sounding of army opinion; it was another political challenge and Massu was the instrument used to deliver it. Given their previous successes, the activists could well have expected another and believed that De Gaulle would not discipline Massu for his indiscretion. Then the President would have his warning, Algiers would still have Massu, and the army would have defied De Gaulle and won a test of strength with Paris.

[5] Faucher, *Les Barricades*, pp. 64–75. See also "Army Speaks," *Economist*, CXCIV (January 23, 1960), 290.

[6] Bromberger, *Barricades et colonels*, p. 117.

The second hypothesis—that Massu was recalled to facilitate government action—is favored by the Brombergers, who maintain that it was De Gaulle's entourage that conceived the interview.[7] Whether De Gaulle was directly involved is not clear. In any case, the reaction of the President was as anticipated—the outspoken General was called to Paris and Algiers was deprived of Massu.

The Kempski trip had been preceded by a recommendation from the French Ambassador in Bonn and approved by the *Quai d'Orsay*. It was then cleared through General Challe, who directed Kempski to Massu, who has asserted that he (Massu) was ordered to give the interview. Before meeting Kempski, Massu had been informed by Captain Hotchot, one of Challe's aides, that the meeting would be a talk, not an interview. The subject of the conversation would concern an article which Kempski was going to publish toward the end of January. The General's name was not to appear in the article, and proofs were to be submitted to Challe before publication. Kempski, according to the captain, had agreed to these conditions. Since he was ordered to give an interview which was exploited, Massu became convinced he had been the victim of a plot to remove him from Algiers.

Massu later maintained that he had had no intention of taking a public position against De Gaulle. His next remark inclines one to believe him: "In any case, if ever I had the intention, I certainly would not have chosen a Teuton journalist in order to do it."[8] *L'affaire Massu* probably will join the ranks of other events of recent French history characterized by obscure origins and shadowy circumstances, such as the affair of the generals, the bazooka affair, and the Mitterand affair. It would appear that Massu was used as a pawn in a Paris-Algiers confrontation, and that he was the victim of political machinations. But whose victim remains unknown.

He arrived in Paris the night of January 19. Early Wednesday morning, January 20, he met with Guillaumat, who wrote a press communiqué for Massu, offering an official denial of the interview. The communiqué stated that De Gaulle enjoyed the Moslems' confidence, and that Massu supported De Gaulle without reservation.[9]

The day before, three visiting Algerian deputies who had come to plead the cause of integration heard De Gaulle say that the Moslems

[7] *Ibid.*

[8] De Sérigny, *Un Procès*, p. 100; see also pp. 96–103, and Claude Paillat, *Deuxième dossier secret de l'Algérie* (Paris: Le Livre Contemporain, 1962), pp. 339–40.

[9] Faucher, *Les Barricades*, pp. 73–74.

trusted him. The President told M. Portolano and his two companions, M. Laradj and M. Lauriol: "You can send the paratroops to the Elysée. Do you believe that will change anything of the fact that the Moslems have confidence only in Me?" Portolano then made the mistake of referring to the army, to a De Gaulle who had just finished reading Massu's remarks and who was still overwrought. "No, *monsieur le President*," said the deputy, "the Moslems who play the French card game have confidence only in the army. The others. . . ." De Gaulle cut him short: "The army? Ah! Tell me of the army. The army does nothing but stupid things. It was against Dreyfus. It was for Pétain, and now for integration." [10]

Massu's recantation was taken seriously by few observers. Until the night of January 21, Massu's followers in Algiers were hopeful that Massu would be returned to them and that his public disavowal of his interview would satisfy the President. De Gaulle would have his warning of the army's state of mind, and, being a military man, he could be expected to see that it would be tactically foolish to go beyond what the army would allow. But De Gaulle understood Massu's challenge to be a challenge from the army; the situation was not De Gaulle *versus* Massu, but De Gaulle *versus* the army. The question turned not on what the army would allow, but what the nation, as represented by Charles de Gaulle, would allow. If De Gaulle accepted the challenge, then the result would depend upon whether De Gaulle would be left in the political lurch by France as Pflimlin had been in 1958, or whether the nation would rally to support the state this time.

On the evening of the twenty-first, notice was sent to Madame Massu in Algiers that she could rejoin her husband in Paris. Massu was not to return to Algiers! Meanwhile, General Challe informed Massu that he was not invited to the conference to be held at the Elysée Palace set for Friday, January 22. Challe was in Paris for this meeting which would bring together high civilian and military leaders to discuss the Algerian situation. Then it was announced that Georges Bidault was banned from Algiers until February 1; Bidault had been planning to return on the twenty-third to continue his anti-self-determination campaign.

Emotions rose in Algiers when the word concerning Massu and Bidault was received, and unrest in Algiers reached its greatest pitch since the days of May, 1958. Communiqués were issued by ultra groups belaboring De Gaulle and the government, many containing ill-hidden

10 *Ibid.*, p. 69. On this same conversation see Paul Ribeaud, *Barricades pour un drapeau* (Paris: La Table Ronde, 1960), pp. 23–25.

threats of violence. The recall of Massu and the Bidault proscription attracted great attention in Algiers, as did the forthcoming meeting at the Elysée. The rumor was circulated that new decisions concerning Algeria and peace talks with the FLN were to be expected.

When the conference convened at the President's residence on Friday, January 22, De Gaulle confirmed that self-determination was the government's policy. In answer to Challe's insistence, he again granted that pacification had to continue, and acknowledged that political negotiation with the FLN was excluded. But De Gaulle told the army leaders that the army must respect the rules of discipline, that the policy of self-determination was determined and had to be respected by all. The orders of the government were to be obeyed without discussion.[11]

When the Massu question was brought up, De Gaulle brushed it aside as amounting to nothing: "No one will budge. The army is behind me...."[12] Not to be so easily denied, Challe warned that he would resign if Massu did not return to Algiers. Without Massu, said Challe, it would be impossible to assure order in Algiers. De Gaulle reminded Challe that he was the military commander in Algeria, and informed him that he had the support of the President of the Republic. "To maintain the authority of the state," stated De Gaulle, "Massu cannot return to Algiers. To maintain the authority of the state, you must return there."[13] Challe then warned that the unity of the army might break if riots erupted. "Let it come then," responded De Gaulle, "the army is true to me, with the exception of some malcontents. If it is necessary to use force, you will use it. You are the master of your means."[14]

Challe later in the meeting once more broached the Massu question, but De Gaulle refused to consider it again. The matter was officially closed. De Gaulle would meet Massu the next day and decide on his new command. The communiqué which was issued at the end of the meeting announced Massu's dismissal and the assumption of his command by General Jean Crépin. It further declared that measures to augment the war effort would be adopted, but emphasized that pacification was designed to lead to self-determination. Ultimately, Algeria would be given the right to determine its future, the only outcome worthy of

---

[11] Faucher, *Les Barricades*, pp. 91–93.

[12] *Ibid.*, p. 91.

[13] Bromberger, *Barricades et colonels*, p. 153.

[14] *Ibid.*, p. 154.

France. A warning to activists was sounded as the communiqué announced that the policy of self-determination would "not be changed."[15]

Extremists were shocked, new fears and resolutions arose, and activists meetings multiplied as a result of the President's firmness. Joseph Ortiz's group, the French National Front (FNF), had been growing rapidly since September 16, 1959, and now its leader let it be known that he had numerous army contacts who would support him when the time came. Major Navarro of Massu's staff kept in daily contact with Ortiz and although his function was probably to keep an eye on the extremists' activity, his presence led many to believe that he signified army support. The many contacts of psychological action officers with extremist groups strengthened the feeling of army backing.

Robert Martel told his followers that it was time for a new May 13. The actions of Paris would compel the army to forsake the government, said Martel, and then the men of MP 13 would be able to play the role of "army political auxiliaries."[16] Ortiz also warned that Paris would take decisions which would lead the army "to the solutions of despair."[17]

On January 13, Fernand Feral, president of the Assistance and Protection Movement, speaking to an audience of a thousand, promised that "our relations and our contacts with the army, with its officers . . . permits us to assure you that it will never tolerate the abandonment of French Algeria, even if a government of treason gives the order."[18] Feral urged his audience to organize and arm themselves. At his cafe, Ortiz stressed the point to eager listeners that "his [Ortiz's] friends in the army will never allow Paris the possibility of accomplishing the irreparable."[19] The European extremists were positive, because of their contacts with the army's extremists, that the entire army would react if faced with another abandonment.

The removal of Massu from Algiers impelled the civilian ultras to action. Paris had gone too far. Auguste Arnould, a moderate who belonged to none of the Algiers political movements, explained the

---

[15] Text of communiqué, *New York Times*, January 23, 1960, p. 2:5–6.

[16] Faucher, *Les Barricades*, p. 47.

[17] *Ibid.*

[18] *Ibid.*, p. 56.

[19] *Ibid.*, p. 45.

meaning of Massu's recall during the Barricades Trials: "He was a symbol; the last of the generals of May 13, when everything had been accomplished without firing a shot."[20] Civilian activists decided something had to be done. On the twenty-second, Ortiz waited for General Jacques Faure (in Massu's position until General Crépin arrived to take over as the Algiers army corps commander), to give the army's assent to action. Faure refused and counseled against demonstrations. But all was ready, according to Ortiz. Faure, however, was not convinced that the army would support an attack on the government. He maintained that the situation was unfavorable for an uprising, but Ortiz nonetheless resolved to proceed.[21]

The activists set January 30 as the day of insurrection, the day after a scheduled address by De Gaulle which was expected to reiterate the policy of self-determination. On the twenty-second the news swiftly spread in Algiers that Massu would not return; the activists were spurred to immediate action. Two days earlier Plan Balancelle had been put into effect by Delouvrier and Challe, the plan designed for serious trouble in Algiers. One of the three units which prepared to assure the maintenance of order was the Tenth Paratroop Division under General Jean Gracieux. The 10th DP was Massu's old division, a fact not missed by the population of Algiers.

Not only had the 10th DP won fame under Massu as the winner of the Battle of Algiers, but the unit had been stationed for a long while in the city. Numerous ties existed between the unit and the civilian population and several companies had men of Algiers in their ranks. The prospects of the unit firing on its neighbors, of its attacking the barricades and firmly opposing the insurgents, were remote. Familiarity between troops and an insurgent population is dangerous for an army's resolution to resist revolutionary activities, since the revolutionaries may be on good terms with the army.[22]

During the afternoon of the twenty-second, a meeting was held which Ortiz and other members of the FNF and several unnamed officers

[20] *Le Monde*, November 6, 1960.

[21] Bromberger, *Barricades et colonels*, pp. 157–58. Faucher maintains that the meeting of Ortiz and Faure has not been definitely determined. *Les Barricades*, pp. 97–98.

[22] On the fraternization of armed forces with insurgent groups and its effects see Katherine Chorley, *Armies and the Art of Revolution* (London: Faber and Faber, 1943), pp. 153–59. On the 10th DP see *Le Monde*, February 3, 1960.

attended. The civilians desired to know if the army would follow them:

> Ortiz looked at the officers. —"Alors?"
> The officers observed each other. The answer was clear, brutal:
> "—You can go to it. Algeria is ready. The army is at your side!"[23]

That evening a meeting of the FNF was held at which Jean-Jacques Susini spoke: "If they do not wish to return Massu to us, we will go to Paris to look for him."[24] Susini was a young man of the Algiers' Right (he was born in 1933) and was president of the General Students Association, a position he acceded to with the help of his predecessor, Pierre Lagaillarde. The time to act had arrived, announced Susini. According to witnesses, Lagaillarde was turned away from the meeting, under the pretext that he was not an FNF member.[25] Although he tried to become involved in the insurrection's preparations, Lagaillarde remained an outsider. He asked Ortiz at 10:00 P.M. on the twenty-second what was planned for the next day, but Ortiz told the ex-paratrooper that he knew nothing; it was necessary to wait.

Even as Susini was speaking to the FNF, tracts appeared in Algiers urging citizens to come with arms into the streets on Sunday morning. Others passed the word that a coup was planned for the next day, the twenty-third. "Be ready," the people were told, "the army will follow, it is certain. Ortiz has seen the generals. They have agreed."[26]

The word spread and it, plus their contacts with the activist officers, made the civilians feel certain that the army would support them as it had in May, 1958. However, the majority of officers had been again reassured by Friday morning's communiqué, issued following the meeting at the Elysée Palace, which had announced that pacification was to continue and no political negotiations were envisaged. De Gaulle in Paris believed that the army would remain obedient and suppress an insurrection if one broke out in Algiers. Ortiz and his men in Algiers

---

[23] André Euloge and Antoine Moulinier, *L'Envers des barricades* (Paris: Plon, 1960), p. 87.

[24] Faucher, *Les Barricades*, p. 98.

[25] Lagaillarde later maintained that he was not turned away from the meeting. He said he did not have time to attend, since he had an appointment for seven-thirty. (The meeting, according to Faucher, was held at six o'clock.) See Pierre Lagaillarde, *On a triché avec l'honneur* (Paris: La Table Ronde, 1960), pp. 81–82.

[26] Faucher, *Les Barricades*, p. 100.

relied on the army to join in opposition to Paris. In fact, the army neither fired on the insurgents, nor did it join the insurrection.

While the civilians were preparing their action against De Gaulle, Massu on this busy January twenty-second telephoned the Chief of Staff in Algiers, Colonel Antoine Argoud, from Paris. Massu told Argoud that although the conditions of his departure were heartbreaking, "it is not necessary to take any action. It is necessary to be calm. It is especially necessary to avoid a clash." [27] The next day at 11:00 A.M., a meeting was held in Algiers which included Ortiz, Colonel Gardes, Colonel Argoud, and General Faure. Faure repeated his arguments that the time was not ripe for an insurrection, and that the upper echelons of the army were undecided as to what course they would take. Ortiz maintained that the time could never be better, and added that the transfer of Massu, the living symbol of *Algérie française*, was the last blow. If the army in Algeria would follow, then the army in France would join the insurrection in a few days, Ortiz argued. Gardes interjected that it was too late to stop the insurrection anyway, and that it represented the last chance to save a French Algeria.

Argoud, whom Massu had left with the injunction to preach calm, asserted that the army would break in two. The army's opinion, according to Argoud, was far from unanimous because many officers had been convinced by De Gaulle's assurances. Argoud further warned that Challe was against an insurrection and was worried lest an insurrection would split the army. Finally, said Massu's Chief of Staff, the times were not like those of May 13. In January, 1960, the country was loyal to De Gaulle, as was the majority of the army. "The army corps will not march with you," Argoud concluded. But Ortiz announced that De Gaulle had led the country to the loss of Algeria. "We do not wish to die. We will demonstrate." [28]

At 3:00 P.M. Argoud received another call from Massu, who had just seen De Gaulle. Argoud was told that De Gaulle understood nothing. "I will keep you," Massu angrily reported De Gaulle as saying, "as if doing me a favor in not kicking me out of the army." De Gaulle then had said he would give Massu a good post, "as if, in this business, it was my future that was at stake and not that of Algeria." Then Massu said:

> Argoud, I am compelled to annul all my comments of yesterday. What I said to you no longer counts. On the spot is the place to

[27] De Sérigny, *Un Procès*, p. 116.
[28] Bromberger, *Barricades et colonels*, p. 173.

judge the action to take. Yesterday I said to you that it was necessary not to stir. Today, I no longer give any opinion![29]

Argoud understood Massu to mean the demonstration could take place and the army was not to interfere. He did not mention the phone call to the activists until the next day, but rumors of the call spread quickly.

The civilians were sure that the army would support them in an action against Paris. As Lagaillarde said at his trial, "We were aware of having the agreement of the military."[30] It seems certain that the civilian activists did have the support of some army elements, and that these few men relied upon the fear of breaking the army's unity to bring their comrades into an anti-Paris, anti-self-determination movement. How the majority of the army in Algeria would react to the demonstration provided the key to the action. With the army's support, another May 13 was foreseen; without the army, the civilians faced defeat.

Shortly after midnight on January 24, Delouvrier and Challe held a meeting attended by the leading military figures of the Algiers region. Challe had gone to Paris promising to bring Massu back to Algiers with him, but he had failed and now he explained his failure. Challe also repeated De Gaulle's enjoinder that order had to be maintained at any price. Someone asked Challe if this meant going so far as to give an order to open fire. Challe replied in the affirmative, resulting in several of those present voicing their disagreement.

It was obvious that an order to attack Algerian sympathizers of *Algérie française* would mean trouble. Colonel Argoud, who was present at the meeting, said to Delouvrier: "Sir, you do not honestly believe that we could open fire on these people ... who will shout for France and French Algeria? As for me, that is completely out of the question. I would never execute the order; furthermore, I shall never give formal orders to my men to obey it."[31]

In the morning, leaflets appeared in Algiers announcing a demonstration to take place at 10:00 A.M. The Territorial Units (UTs) were called out, but it is not known who gave the order for these home defense

[29] *Ibid.*, p. 176. At the Barricades Trials, Massu recalled saying to Argoud, "I take no responsibility. . . . I render void my telephone call of yesterday evening and I leave you free." De Sérigny, *Un Procès*, p. 116.

[30] *Le Monde*, November 17, 1960.

[31] From the testimony of Colonel Argoud at the Barricades Trials. Colonel Antoine Argoud, *Sans commentaire* (Paris: Editions de Minuit, 1961), p. 49.

organizations to assemble.[32] Victor Sapin-Lingières, commander of the Algiers UT (which numbered twenty-five thousand men), asked Ortiz who had summoned the unit, but Ortiz insisted he did not know. General Crépin, who had replaced Massu, questioned the UT commander, but Sapin-Lingières could only deny having any responsibility for the order which was assembling the men.[33]

Two command posts appeared, one under Ortiz and another under Lagaillarde, who had determined to enter the actions despite his exclusion from the preparations. Leaflets were widely distributed and orders were given, apparently by everyone but Delouvrier. Enthusiasm was absent from the demonstration which finally took place. There was some applause and singing, but then the crowd began to disperse for lunch. Just after the noon hour, Ortiz received a request to visit General Challe. When Ortiz left for the General's office, he told the demonstrators that if he did not come back, they knew what remained to be done.

In his meeting with Challe, Ortiz was asked what he wished to accomplish. The insurgent leader replied that he was not the crowd's master, and that he had not called out the Territorials. Challe then gave Ortiz permission to demonstrate, and informed him that the army would not oppose him. However, if the crowd approached the Forum, the army would receive the order to charge. Ortiz gave his word that no public buildings would be occupied.

Ortiz considered the summons from the General a show of weakness. He became convinced that he could now force the army to rally to the insurgents' side, as it had done in May, 1958. When Susini heard the results of the meeting from Ortiz, he was appalled. An insurrection that failed to take over public buildings, a coup d'état which left the officials in place, made little sense to him.

[32] The UTs were created in 1955 by General Paul Cherrière to make up for the shortage of army personnel. They were used in a guard capacity, freeing regular troops for operational duties. Reservists in Algeria served three days a month in the UTs, assuming their army grade, and serving under officers who were also in the reserves. An armored UT was also formed, consisting of tank corps veterans who served six days a month on active duty and who participated in regular military operations. See Jean-Raymond Tournoux, *Secrets d'état* (Paris: Plon, 1960), pp. 189–90; Paul Gerin, *L'Algérie du 13 mai* (Paris: Gallimard, 1958), p. 22.

[33] One explanation which has been offered is that the UTs' appearance was spontaneous: "... it seems the territorials 'jumped the gun' and formed a 'soviet' of their own, which issued the mobilization order." James H. Meisel, *The Fall of the Republic* (Ann Arbor: The University of Michigan Press, 1962), p. 67; see also Faucher, *Les Barricades*, p. 130.

Back at his command post, Ortiz appeared with Colonel Gardes (Gardes had recently been reassigned from his position as head of the Algiers Fifth Bureau to a new post at Saïda; he had not yet left Algiers to assume his new functions). The presence of the officer with Ortiz convinced many observers that the army was indeed with the demonstrators. Ortiz had promised that his demonstration would stay within certain limits, and when several young men began taking up paving stones to erect a barricade, Ortiz forbade their actions. However, the missing emotional spark for the demonstration was provided later in the day and the situation left Ortiz's control.

At four-thirty in the afternoon, an order to erect barricades was issued, but not by Ortiz, the order probably coming from Lagaillarde's camp. Immediately barricades construction started, while at the Memorial to the Dead, police and crowds clashed. Rumors spread, one saying that in Paris, De Gaulle had been wounded. At six o'clock, a mobile gendarme unit received orders to advance and disperse the crowds. Colonel Joseph Broizat (commander of the First Colonial Paratroop Regiment, the 1st RCP), and Colonel Henri Dufour (commander of the First Foreign Legion Paratroop Regiment, the 1st REP), were to lead their units from separate directions and aid the gendarmes in clearing the streets. The gendarmes advanced first, at twelve minutes after six. As they moved down the street, firing broke out, and both gendarmes and civilians fell. Dufour's men belatedly arrived in jeeps, which they moved between the crowd and the gendarmes. But the fusillade had already claimed nineteen lives and wounded 141 others. Conflicting stories exist as to who fired the first shot, and the Barricades Trials failed to reveal the originators of the firing. Whether the first shot came from the gendarmes or the crowd remains unknown.[34]

Disorder reigned among the demonstration's chiefs and in the staffs of the forces of order. The army waited for orders that did not come, watching the Territorials and civilians go behind the barricades which were to become the symbol of the insurrection. The idea of the barricades, proposed by Lagaillarde and accepted by Ortiz, was for the rebels to enclose themselves in entrenched camps, issuing calls asking others to join them. When their number reached one hundred thousand, the Forum, the GG, and finally De Gaulle would fall according to Ortiz's and Lagaillarde's reasoning, without demonstrators having to

[34] See Faucher, *Les Barricades*, pp. 146–51; Bromberger, *Barricades et colonels*, pp. 224–46; see also De Sérigny, *Un Procès*, pp. 187–255.

move from behind their barricades. Ortiz's promise to Challe would be kept, but the government would collapse.

Delouvrier, remembering May 13, feared an attack on the GG, and had it surrounded with gendarmes and Republican Security Company troops. In his concern over the Forum and the GG, he left the rest of the city to the insurgent leaders. Meanwhile, the failure of the army or police to attack the barricades reinforced the belief that Challe and the army were with the insurgents, and the men of the barricades proceeded to demonstrate that for them the best attack was to remain in their camps. They believed that the army would not fire on fellow Frenchmen who shared their sentiments for a French Algeria, and also were convinced that the army would rush upon the men behind the barricades not to attack them, but to join them. To rally the rest of Algiers and the army to the cause of *Algérie française*, was the ultras' objective. The barricades as weapon and symbol appeared in a message from the entrenched men: "The barricade does not separate us; it unites us. It is a sign of the union between military, Territorials, and civilians."[35]

By the night of the twenty-fourth, fifteen hundred men had taken refuge with Ortiz or Lagaillarde, while Challe called Paris and talked to General Ely and Guillaumat. He told them he could give the order to clear the barricades by force. One of two results would follow: either the army would obey or it would not. "If they do not obey me, it is anarchy. I cannot risk such an eventuality."[36] In Challe's opinion, the only way to solve the problem was by persuasion, for men of the army could not be relied upon to fire upon Frenchmen.

The activist officers depended upon the unity of the army to insure their success. Although they were prepared to challenge Paris, the activists realized they could not stand against the government alone. Their success or failure depended upon the remainder of the army, which would have to decide whom it was going to follow—the government or the dissident officers. But unlike May, 1958, a government was now in control in Paris, led by a man resolved to see that his regime endured. What would the mass of the army do this time? Would the sacred concept of unity carry it into dissidence, or would the army obey the legal authorities? The week of January, 1960, was a week of doubt.

The activist officers recognized the fact that the army was in a peculiarly strong position. If they chose to leave the barricades, the

[35] Euloge and Moulinier, *L'Envers des barricades*, p. 114; (broadcast on radio Algiers, January 26, 1960).
[36] Bromberger, *Barricades et colonels*, p. 252.

insurgents could not take the rest of Algiers if the army decided to oppose them. On the other hand, the barricades could not be suppressed without army help. The army was therefore the key factor in the situation, giving it the opportunity to play the role of arbiter between Paris and the barricades, and to do so in the army's interest. The activists felt they were in a position to force De Gaulle to modify his position on self-determination. Unless he did so, decided these officers, the barricades, the symbol of revolt, could stand unmolested by the army. To gain political concessions, it was necessary that Ortiz, Lagaillarde, and their men remained undisturbed. The proper course for the army was to do nothing, thought the activists, at least for the present. If the army had joined the insurgents, it would then have entered into open opposition to the government. As it was, the army became a middleman, the role the activists prescribed.

On the twenty-fifth Algiers was paralyzed by a general strike. The barricades had been strengthened during the night, and paratroops calmly chatted and exchanged cigarettes with the men behind the heaped-up paving stones. Men entered and left the entrenched camps without interference. As the hours passed, it became clear that the army would not fire on the barricades. Guillaumat, knowing how repugnant a fire order would be to the army, telephoned Challe in the afternoon and asked him what he would do if he received the order to fire. Challe answered that he would probably hesitate to transmit the order, and that if he did give the command to fire, he probably would not be obeyed.[37]

In Paris the big question was whether the army would fire if ordered to do so. Members of the municipal council in Algiers wondered the same thing, and sent a delegation to see Challe and Delouvrier. Their leader reported back that Challe and Delouvrier agreed that force should not be used against the citizens of Algiers. The council was not satisfied and sent another delegation to the two men. Their leader, M. Bouharaoua, later affirmed that Challe and Delouvrier "were fully and definitely in agreement and gave the assurance that the army would not fire."[38]

A Cabinet meeting was held in Paris and the following communiqué was issued: "The President of the Republic and the Government are determined to maintain the Algerian policy they have adopted and to assure the quickest possible return to public order."[39] Premier Debré

[37] Faucher, *Les Barricades*, p. 183.
[38] *Le Monde*, January 27, 1960.
[39] *New York Times*, January 26, 1960, p. 1:8.

and Guillaumat, Minister of Armed Forces, flew to Algiers at De Gaulle's behest to bolster the government's position. The President saw them off telling them, "I desire that all be over this night.... Tomorrow, there must no longer be a single insurgent in the entrenched camp." [40]

Challe immediately informed Debré of the army's position when he arrived in Algiers. The army did not want to join the insurgents, nor did it want to fire on them. Delouvrier agreed that force could not be used in Algiers because of the prevailing state of tension. Colonels Dufour and Brechignac (the last named commander of the Ninth Colonial Paratroop Regiment [9th RCP]), told the Premier that the government would have to take care not to issue orders the army could not execute. A crisis of conscience, said the colonels, must be avoided. Debré replied that this would mean giving the insurrection *carte blanche*, but Brechignac and Dufour assured Debré such would not be the case. The rebels would not leave their camps; order would be maintained. All that was desired was that the army should not have to fire on men who shared the army's feelings. The Premier assured the two colonels that there would be a French solution to the Algerian problem and that it would be confirmed when he returned to Paris. The army's strategy appeared to be working. [41]

In his meetings with other officers, Debré heard the same general comments: fears of great losses if the army should fire; civil war if the order to fire came; probably mutiny if the troops were ordered to fire. General Gracieux bluntly told Debré he would not give a fire order, and the Premier could arrest him if he so wished. Debré also met with ten regimental commanders, all colonels, to learn their views. They concurred that the use of force was out of the question, adding that an order to fire on fellow Frenchmen would be considered a criminal act. Furthermore, the army agreed with the men of the barricades that the government must renounce the policy of self-determination. The high passions of the situation broke out in one colonel's exclamation: "Instructions of the President of the Republic or not, they will not fire!" [42] The consensus was that the army would not obey an order to fire—an order which could mean civil war.

Debré asked Colonel Argoud what, in his opinion, should be done. He answered that De Gaulle must retreat on the issue of self-determina-

[40] Faucher, *Les Barricades*, p. 183.
[41] See *ibid.*, pp. 194–97.
[42] Bromberger, *Barricades et colonels*, p. 284. On Debré's visit see *ibid.*, pp. 283–87.

tion. If he refused, then Challe should take over and preserve the unity of the army. Should Challe refuse, then, said Argoud—a future chief of the Secret Army Organization—"I see no other solution than a junta of colonels whatever may be their names."[43] To avoid such an eventuality, certain actions had to be initiated. The army would have to be given all necessary means to achieve pacification, including peremptory justice; as for self-determination, the President would have to indicate his preference for integration; and the campaign of demoralization carried on by the metropolitan press would have to cease. Debré listened and did nothing; he was convinced a military putsch was in the offing if he acted against these outspoken colonels.[44]

While his Premier heard the firm views of the officers, De Gaulle spoke to the nation. In his broadcast of January 25, the President proclaimed the situation in Algiers a blow against France both in Algeria and in the world. He asked the demonstrators, "led astray as they may be by lies and slander, to return to order." He expressed his confidence in Challe and Delouvrier and ended his speech with, "as for me, I will do my duty."[45] The battle was engaged. The combatants were the President and the army; the battlefield was again Algiers; the stake was control of the government's policy.

De Gaulle well understood his position. If he drew back, he would be considered a puppet, dangling on strings that would cross the Mediterranean. He was convinced of his policy's correctness, a policy which recognized that Algeria sooner or later would determine her own destiny. To fail to acknowledge it would be to struggle uselessly in the face of reality. De Gaulle felt that if he were to cede one point, another riot would soon occur, and a new ultimatum would be presented by the army.[46] When De Gaulle talked with Colonels Georges de Boissieu, the chief of Challe's staff, and Dufour, sent to Paris on the President's request, De Boissieu asked the President to at least say, "*Algérie française.*" "I have already said it," declared De Gaulle. "It is up to the Algerians to say it."[47]

Badly shaken by his conversations with the officers of Algiers, Debré heard Guillaumat say on the flight back from Algiers that he was no

[43] *Ibid.*, p. 287.

[44] See *ibid.*; and Bernard E. Brown, "The Army and Politics in France," *The Journal of Politics*, XXIII (May, 1961), 270–72.

[45] *New York Times*, January 25, 1960, p. 1:5.

[46] Explained by De Gaulle to Marshal Alphonse Juin on January 26, 1960. Bromberger, *Barricades et colonels*, p. 295.

[47] *Ibid.*, p. 300.

longer useful as Minister of Armed Forces—the army would not obey him. At the Elysée Palace, Guillaumat was heard to say again, "I have become useless. The army no longer obeys me."[48] In such an atmosphere, Debré showed the President the text of a speech he had drawn up, giving the officers in Algeria the assurances he had promised would be forthcoming from Paris. De Gaulle adamantly refused to give the speech, despite Debré's impassioned argument that he had talked with the army leaders and the government had to announce for integration if the army was to be placated. In despair, Debré offered his resignation to De Gaulle, but the President merely said they would discuss it later. For the present, Debré must obey. A new draft was then written, excluding the words which had been promised the colonels.[49]

Meanwhile, the position of the government appeared to weaken. The afternoon of the twenty-sixth, it was learned that if the order to fire were given, Marshal Alphonse Juin, France's highest ranking living officer, and Generals Zeller, Salan, and Miquel, would publicly pronounce against the government action. At six o'clock in the evening, radio Algiers broadcast that the barricades were not a separation, but a symbol of unity. In Paris some understood this to mean that the two sides of the barricades had joined, since the station over which the commentary was heard was army controlled.

Debré spoke to the nation at half-past six, using his voice, but De Gaulle's words. Order had to be established in Algiers. If it was not, nothing would be possible in Algiers and all might be lost. The colonels listening closely in Algiers learned that their pressure on Debré the previous evening had been in vain. Although Debré had been influenced by their arguments and emotion while in Algiers, in Paris there was Charles De Gaulle.

The conflict between De Gaulle and the army sharpened as the barricades in Algiers grew stronger, and fraternization continued between the forces of order and the rebels. No order to fire on the men of the barricades had been given; technically, the army remained obedient. Yet the army's pressure was felt everywhere, and in France there was a sensation that the government was losing and with it, the Fifth Republic. Readers of the *New York Times* were informed by Henry Giniger, in an article datelined Paris, January 26, that "French democracy hung in the balance tonight."[50]

[48] *Ibid.*, p. 299.
[49] Faucher, *Les Barricades*, pp. 208–9.
[50] *New York Times*, January 27, 1960, p. 1:8.

During the Cabinet meeting held the day after Debré's speech, De Gaulle rendered homage to the army, and denied the existence of any plot, reminiscent of May, 1958, when Pflimlin expressed his confidence in the army. De Gaulle added that the government had no intention of entering political negotiations with the rebels. The army could be expected to take heart at these words, but the ones which followed attested to De Gaulle's undeviating position—the policy of September 16 would not be changed.[51] Meanwhile, in Algiers, the crowds assembled in front of and behind the barricades shouted, "The army is with us!" With friendly gestures the paratroops responded, and free access and exit from the barricades continued as the government's opposition to the barricades remained verbal only.

"The army," wrote Benjamin Welles from Algiers, "holds the key to the French crisis."[52] The same army which had brought De Gaulle to power to implement an integration policy now challenged the President by inaction, while from the barricades, Ortiz, Lagaillarde, and their men watched the army and the government silently wrestle. On January 27, General Challe spoke to the people of Algiers. Painful days had passed, he said, and in order not to cause bloodshed the army had been patient. However, the situation could not continue in its present state because the interests of Algeria dictated that order must be restored. "I repeat once more," Challe reminded Algeria, "the French army is fighting to see that Algeria remains French indefinitely."[53]

The next day the army in Algiers found itself squarely faced with its responsibilities. At 5:00 P.M. Delouvrier made an impassioned speech, calling on Moslems, Europeans, and the army to rally to De Gaulle. The Delegate General first addressed himself to metropolitan France, saying there were no insurgents in Algiers; there were only resolute men ready to die to save France. The French army, and it was not an unruly army, and these resolute men had been brought face to face by a "tragic misunderstanding." The men on one side of the barricades feared they would no longer be French; the army, also French, was on the other side of the barricades because it had to obey, and neither side dared fire. "Every bullet weighs on the conscience of the man who fires and thus kills a brother who is fighting for the same cause."

The drama of the crisis of conscience had affected everyone in Algiers, said Delouvrier. De Gaulle or bloodshed was the choice which had to

51 Faucher, *Les Barricades*, p. 235.
52 *New York Times*, January 28, 1960, p. 3:1.
53 *Ibid.*, p. 3:3.

be made. Delouvrier reported that he had "brutally" asked several officers what their choice would be. "I saw on the faces of these soldiers, faithful to the Republic, indecision. I saw in their eyes tears of the crisis of conscience. That is the truth, Frenchmen of France."

The army, stated Delouvrier, was experiencing a crisis in its unity. Would Algiers be obeyed or Paris? The army's constitutional head was in Paris, therefore to disobey him would mean opposition to the national leader of France. Delouvrier cautioned his army audience to listen carefully. May 13 could not be repeated: "There is no de Gaulle in reserve." If De Gaulle were forced to return to Colombey, would the nation forgive the army, asked Delouvrier. "That is your dilemma, men of the army. There is one way of escaping from it, and one alone: you must obey General Challe, who obeys the President of the Republic. Army of Algeria, it is a supplication, but it is also an order: close ranks behind General de Gaulle."

Next, the Moslems were asked by the Delegate General to turn out in processions crying: "Long live De Gaulle!" and he urged them to send telegrams to Paris declaring their support of the government. Delouvrier then addressed himself to Ortiz, Lagaillarde, Sapin-Lignières, and the Europeans of Algiers exclaiming: "I cry to the metropolitan area that I salute your courage, children of the motherland." Delouvrier then proposed that he, Ortiz, and Lagaillarde should walk hand in hand to the Memorial to the Dead when the difficulties were settled.[54]

What Delouvrier was trying to do was obvious. He was attempting to prevent a split within the army, and between Algiers and Paris. The appeal, unsanctioned by Paris, left De Gaulle infuriated. A communiqué was issued publicly disavowing the words of the government representative in Algiers, adding that Delouvrier's offer in no way reflected the government's intentions.[55] Many officers who had been moved and who had wavered in their support of the barricaded men, were again thrown into confusion by the government's disavowal of the speech.

Following his broadcast, Delouvrier dealt another surprise to Paris and Algiers as he and Challe left for a secret command post in the countryside.[56] Algiers was left stunned by the departure of both the

[54] Text of the speech, Bromberger, *Barricades et colonels*, pp. 361–69.

[55] *New York Times*, January 29, 1960, p. 3:1.

[56] Henry Giniger reported from Paris that Delouvrier and Challe had been ordered out of Algiers on command from the government to "prevent their submergence by

civilian and military commander. It was widely thought that legal authority had left the city to the insurgents. But the move, according to the Brombergers, was a masterstroke in that it took away the army's ability to play middleman in the Paris-Algiers struggle and the army now had to make its choice: the government or the insurgents.[57]

While the flight of Delouvrier and Challe later did prove to be a masterstroke, at the time it appeared to be a sign of government weakness. It seemed that the city was left to the insurgents and they now had a definite chance of success. Several officers gained the impression that Delouvrier had fled because the 10th DP commander, General Gracieux, had shown signs of sliding to the insurgents. Earlier on the twenty-eighth, an attempt had been made to get the Moslems in the Casbah to demonstrate and recreate the atmosphere of May 13, 1958, an effort Gracieux had favored. He, like many officers, wanted to shed no blood, yet did not want to join the insurgent Europeans either.

These officers shared the sentiments of the men of the barricades in that they too desired to see De Gaulle retreat from his September 16 position. Therefore, the idea of Moslems demonstrating on behalf of their desire to remain French grew and earned army support. However, Lagaillarde opposed the move because he envisaged his barricade as a military affair, not to be vitiated by Moslem mob action. Ortiz was also against the demonstration since he wanted a purely European movement, and feared that the Moslems would appear shouting "*Vive De Gaulle.*"

Several officers, led by Colonel Argoud, nonetheless decided to try the Moslem demonstration. Arnould was enlisted to lead the rallying of the Casbah. If he was successful, the colonels reasoned that Paris would be shown that the people of Algiers were still, as first shown in May, 1958, united in a fraternal desire to remain French, and De Gaulle would have to make concessions. The night of January 26–27, a meeting was held in Challe's office where the matter of the demonstration was considered. Present were Argoud, Colonels Cousteau and Rouquette (both staff officers), General Gilles, inspector of airborne troops, and

---

the settlers' insurrection against Paris." *New York Times*, January 29, 1960, p. 1:8. However, both Bromberger and Faucher indicate that Delouvrier's move came as a surprise to De Gaulle. Bromberger, *Barricades et colonels*, p. 373; Faucher, *Les Barricades*, p. 268. Giniger may have been reporting what was assumed to be the situation.

[57] Bromberger, *Barricades et colonels*, p. 372; see also Thomas Brady's analysis of the "flight" of Delouvrier and Challe as forcing the army to choose between loyalty and the insurgents, *New York Times*, January 29, 1960, p. 1:4.

seven or eight other superior officers. Also present was Jean Mamert of Debré's special staff, sent as a special emissary to Algiers. Delouvrier also made an appearance and appeared provoked by the conference.

Someone said that there was only one way to persuade De Gaulle to change his mind, and that was to prove Algeria was completely united against self-determination. Mamert agreed that would change Paris' viewpoint. At four in the morning Mamert announced he had to telephone Debré, but Delouvrier interrupted and announced that it would be he who would call Paris. The Delegate General did so, and asked Debré what Mamert would probably have asked. What did he think of a Moslem demonstration? "Very good idea," answered Debré, "on the condition they cry 'Long live de Gaulle'." [58]

The colonels were taken aback, but continued with their plans. The result was a dismal failure. The Moslems failed to follow their European prompters, and only a few of them, lacking enthusiasm, arrived at the scheduled meeting place, the Plateau des Glières. It was later charged by Paul Ribeaud that Colonel Santani, whose Zouaves patrolled the Casbah, had prevented the Moslems from leaving the area. While Jean-André Faucher feels that it may be going a bit too far to credit the Zouaves with checking the demonstration, he acknowledges that Santani, a loyal officer, would not have been upset to see the movement fail.[59] But the Moslems' own lack of interest was probably the most important factor in the demonstration's stillbirth, with the result that the army could not pretend to have the backing of the non-Europeans of Algiers.

Many in the army saw in Delouvrier's flight a fear that Gracieux was sliding toward the insurrection, as mentioned earlier. In fact, the Delegate General was well aware that several officers were involved in promoting the Moslem demonstration, and had seen even General Challe at the meeting discussing the project. But beneath the appearances of Delouvrier's flight, remained the real reasons, four in number

[58] Bromberger, *Barricades et colonels*, p. 320. At the Barricades Trials, Colonel Argoud testified the meeting had consisted of himself, Generals Challe, Ely, and Gilles, plus Mamert. During the meeting, according to Argoud, Challe had exclaimed, "It's settled then. The thing to do now is to confront General de Gaulle with a *fait accompli*. I am going to call on the Moslems to come out and demonstrate for French Algeria. Hurray for the army, Brothers All! Then, when de Gaulle sees that the people are all of one mind, well, that's the moment to make him reverse his policy. . . ." See Argoud, *Sans commentaire*, pp. 70–71.

[59] Ribeaud, *Barricades pour un drapeau*, p. 150; Faucher, *Les Barricades*, pp. 256–61, 276; Bromberger, *Barricades et colonels*, pp. 352–53.

according to Delouvrier's own explanation: to free himself from appearing in Paris' eye to be the prisoner of the insurgents; to free himself of the same suspicion in the eyes of the Algerians; to show the illegality of the insurgents' action in Algiers; finally, to throw the insurgents and their supporters into confusion by demonstrating that one could govern from outside Algiers (a situation many in Algiers thought impossible since Algiers was the political center of Algeria), and thus force the army to face its responsibilities. The army was left in Algiers with power, but without civilian leadership. Only if the army rallied to Paris could the chain of command be kept intact. The alternative was to be cast adrift, without legitimate foundation or connection.

The departure of Delouvrier and Challe accomplished exactly what the Delegate General had anticipated: the activist officers were confronted with a dilemma. Colonel Argoud had prepared a manifesto, signed by a number of superior officers, stating their solidarity with the insurgents. In the "Manifesto of the Colonels," General Challe, whose signature block was included, and his men were allegedly presenting the army's unanimous position that General de Gaulle must "resolve the question," and do so by altering his policy of self-determination. But when Argoud attempted to present the manifesto to Challe, he was unable to see the General.[60]

Delouvrier, however, was found by Argoud and a group of activist officers. "*Messieurs*," remarked the Delegate General, "you desire responsibilities. I am going to give them to you."[61] His speech followed in the evening, and the "Argouds" found themselves with power but without legitimacy. The fear of the military man was realized; there no longer was a hierarchy. In Constantine and Oran demonstrations and incidents had broken out, and Generals Jean Olié, the commander in Constantine, and Fernand Gambiez, the commander in Oran, called Algiers and told the army there to make its decision. They admitted that their regiments were divided in their anti-De Gaulle and pro-De Gaulle sentiments, but the unity of the army was endangered if Algiers continued to "temporize with the insurrection."[62]

In the countryside around Algiers, the troops of the Algiers army corps expressed their wish to remain loyal by joining the Oran army corps under Gambiez. Even within Algiers, opinion was divided in the army and in the paratroop units. Colonel Broizat, commander of the 1st

[60] For the text of the manifesto see Bromberger, *Barricades et colonels*, pp. 354–58.
[61] *Ibid.*, p. 358.
[62] *Ibid.*, p. 350.

RCP, asked his officers for their opinions. Some wanted to join the men behind the barricades, others demanded to proclaim their loyalty to De Gaulle. When the men of the Twenty-fifth Paratroop Division under Colonel Ducourneau appeared in Algiers, they accused the 10th DP of being plotters against the Republic.[63]

The activist officers, who constituted a minority, but an important minority because they were willing to take the initiative, had to decide what to do. They could have proclaimed a Committee of Public Safety or a junta, but they realized that the metropolitan area was against them, and even some army units in Algeria. Without supplies, without credits from France, Algeria could not hold out for long. Then too, General Lauris Norstad, the Supreme Allied Commander, had hinted, or so they thought, that North Atlantic Treaty Organization forces might be used if the French army in Algeria became a rebellious force.[64] Finally, there was the threat of civil war.

In the meantime, General Ely had been active in Paris and on the twenty-eighth obtained the words of appeasement he desired. First, De Gaulle, in his speech scheduled for the next day, would say he was for the most French solution; second, the affair of the barricades would be settled by negotiation. Ely left for Algiers at 3:00 A.M. on January 29 to deliver the news personally. Behind him in Paris, rightists were being arrested and their homes searched.

In Algiers, the army and the Europeans still faced each other across the barricades, the "symbols of unity," but the time had come for them to disappear. On the evening of the twenty-eighth, Gracieux had sent Colonel Broizat to see Ortiz and Lagaillarde to discuss the possibility of peacefully leaving the barricades and joining in a demonstration on the Forum, but nothing came of the negotiation attempt. However, the next day events carried the barricades closer to their disappearance.

On January 29, Ely arrived at Reghaïä (twenty miles east of Algiers), and met with Delouvrier and Generals Challe, Crépin, Olié, Gambiez, and other high-ranking officers. Ely brought them the President's speech, which Ely hoped would satisfy the dissatisfied army. At 8:00 P.M. De Gaulle spoke, wearing his general's uniform to stress his role as general as well as president. He announced that there would be no political negotiations with the rebels; that he desired that the Moslems

[63] *Ibid.*, p. 351.

[64] Norstad said: "It is in the interest of all NATO member countries that a solution be found for the Algerian crisis. The situation in Algeria constitutes a grave incident for a NATO member which interests the entire alliance." *Ibid.*, p. 349.

should choose the most French solution and that he himself would promote that solution; that the army would continue pacification in both its destructive and constructive aspects; and that the army would guarantee the liberty of the referendum when it came. Once more the army listened to words dear to its heart.

But De Gaulle again stressed that there was to be no retreat from the policy of self-determination, the only one worthy of France. The army, which sometimes seemed to consider that the Algerian war was its war and not that of France, was put on notice that its mission did not include equivocation and interpretation. The loyalty of the army, said the Commander in Chief, was not subject to conditions. As the man responsible for France and its destiny, De Gaulle insisted that he be obeyed by all French soldiers.

He acknowledged that Delouvrier and Challe may not have wanted to unleash a battle in Algiers by storming the barricades, but no soldier was henceforth to associate with the insurrectionists. Although the means to achieve it could vary (leaving the means to Delouvrier and Challe, again pleasing the Algiers army), order would have to be restored: "I have given, I give the order for it." [65]

De Gaulle's firmness won him the army's respect; his assurances encouraged it. A paratrooper who had been sitting and watching the barricades for almost a week voiced the feelings of many of his comrades when he said after hearing the President speak: "That's a chief." [66] A captain, shored up by the President's remarks, answered, when asked what would now happen to the Europeans behind the barricades, "Either they come back into peaceful order or we go in and get them." [67]

De Gaulle's resoluteness found its way into the army. Ely left Reghaïa promising to replace the questionable Gracieux, and Delouvrier and Challe decided to move the 10th DP out of Algiers and replace it with other units. Shortly after De Gaulle's address, the Territorials were ordered mobilized by their commander, Sapin-Lignières, on orders from General Gracieux, the orders' effect being to draw away from the barricades a great source of strength, since these home guardsmen had constituted a large proportion of the men of the barricades. Also, the Territorials were ordered to interfere neither with essential public services nor with the resumption of limited bus service

[65] *New York Times*, January 30, 1960, p. 2:2–5.
[66] Quoted by Henry Giniger, *New York Times*, January 30, 1960, p. 1:8.
[67] Quoted by Thomas Brady, *New York Times*, January 30, 1960, p. 3:1.

in Algiers. The Territorials, who had been enforcing the general strike, were now told not to interfere with the relaxation of the strike.

The Twenty-fifth Paratroop Division appeared in Algiers on the thirtieth, arriving from service on the Tunisian frontier. The Twenty-fifth, which had no ties with Algiers, closed off the barricades area. A little after noon, the total blockade order was issued, with only one street remaining open so that men could evacuate the barricades. The Territorials were ordered to report to their headquarters by 4:00 P.M. or be considered deserters. In eastern and western Algeria, insurgent activity completely died away.

Debré sent orders to Algiers that the Broizat proposals were annulled, and General Gracieux was instructed to send another officer to negotiate on a much more restricted basis. Colonel Yves Godard replaced Broizat and met with the barricades leaders, offering immunity to men who left the barricades and joined special units to fight the FLN. The insurrection chiefs, however, would be at the government's disposal. Ortiz accepted on the condition he be allowed to fight the FLN under certain generals, for example, General Faure. Lagaillarde flatly refused.

On the thirty-first, more troops entered Algiers as the 10th DP marched out. General Toulouse replaced Gracieux as commander of the 10th DP and from midmorning to sunset soldiers held back crowds which tried to reach the barricades, some thirty persons being injured as the army's lines held fast. General Crépin was given full powers by Delouvrier to re-establish order, and the insurgents knew that Crépin could be relied upon to be energetic in the suppression of the barricades.

At 10:15 P.M. on January 31, Colonel Dufour, commander of the 1st REP, met with Ortiz, Lagaillarde, and Martel and the terms of surrender were agreed upon. The leaders would be put at the government's disposition, with their men to be given the opportunity to enter a special commando unit to be joined to the 1st REP. Lagaillarde returned to his men and told them he did not think the terms could be rejected.[68]

Before dawn on February 1, Ortiz made an unimpeded exit from his camp and disappeared in a black car. Most of Ortiz's men left their barricade soon after his departure. The next morning, Lagaillarde and his remaining 420 men marched in military formation from their position. Lagaillarde's redoubt throughout the week had been a miniature army under his strict command, in contrast to the loose organization of

[68] See Lagaillarde, *On a triché*, pp. 132–33.

Ortiz. As the insurgents left their camp, Dufour's legionnaires rendered honors to them, whether to the flag they carried or to the insurgents themselves one is left to guess.

Twelve hundred men had been in the barricades the morning of the thirty-first, but far less than half that number chose to join the 1st REP, the remainder electing to go home during the night. Of those who opted for the commando unit and who left in paratroop trucks for Zeralda, the 1st REP headquarters, many were on their way back to Algiers a few hours later, one hundred and fifty automobiles appearing at Zeralda to take home the men who had already changed their minds. Lagaillarde was flown to Paris where he was taken to Santé prison, and Ortiz and Martel went into hiding. A month after the fall of the barricades, the commando unit made up of Lagaillarde's and Ortiz's followers was dissolved after having served in one operation against the FLN.

Changes in the French army in Algeria came swiftly. General Jacques Faure, commander of the Twenty-seventh Infantry Division, was relieved of his command and recalled to Paris. Faure was generally assumed to have had no role in the insurrection, but was known for his opposition to De Gaulle's policies. Generals André Gribius and Henri Mirambeau, commanders of the West Saharan Zone and the Thirteenth Infantry Division respectively, were likewise recalled to Paris and relieved of their Algerian commands. Also summoned to France were Colonels Gardes, Argoud, Bigeard, and Broizat. Colonel Marcel Bigeard, two hours before De Gaulle's speech, had written one of his own claiming the army was with the insurgents. For some unknown reason the speech was never circulated, although copies did make their way to Ortiz's fortress where they "remained stacked up between sandwiches and bottles of beer." [69]

When the Council of Ministers met on February 10, the Territorial Units were dissolved and the psychological service sections decentralized. Pierre Messmer replaced Guillaumat as Minister of Armed Forces, and key military posts went to generals who were known for their devotion to the idea of soldiers not becoming involved in politics. General Crépin, who had an outspoken dislike of political soldiers, replaced Challe as Commander in Chief in Algeria, with Challe promoted up and out to the position of Commander in Chief of the Central-European Zone of NATO. Adolphe Vezinet was given Massu's old post as commander of the Algiers army corps, now vacated by Crépin.

[69] Ribeaud, *Barricades pour un drapeau*, pp. 156–57.

Suspected because of his behavior during the Week of the Barricades, General Gracieux was transferred from Algiers to become inspector of airborne troops. His replacement was a faithful Gaullist, General Bernard Saint-Hillier. General Jouhaud, who had played no part in the January uprising but was known for his integrationist sympathies, became Inspector General of the air force, leaving his more elevated post as air force Chief of Staff to General Paul Stehlin.

Hundreds of officers were transferred out of Algeria during 1960, but of the nineteen persons who were brought to court in the Barricades Trials—one of the longest trials of French judicial history, the case lasting over four months—Colonel Gardes was the only active-duty officer indicted.[70] Of the nineteen accused, only twelve were present before the judges and all of these were acquitted, plus one individual, Jacques Laquière, who was acquitted *in absentia*. Although Pierre Lagaillarde, Jean-Jacques Susini, and Marcel Ronda had fled after the trial opened, they were tried as if present. Lagaillarde was sentenced to ten years, Susini to two years suspended sentence, and Ronda to three years and the loss of his reserve officer grade. Ortiz was sentenced to death *in absentia*; Robert Martel to five years *in absentia*; and Jean Meningaud to seven years *in absentia*.[71]

During the Week of the Barricades, the army activists had attempted to use the men behind the redoubts and the unity of the army for their own ends. They had placed themselves between the insurgents and Paris and from there tried to play the role of national arbiters. For a time their position appeared strong since officers had expressed doubts that their men would fire if so ordered, and indeed many officers had warned that they were unwilling to give such an order. But the order never came.

[70] *Le Monde*, January 25, 1961, carried a listing of the then current positions of the main figures of the Week of the Barricades. Among those listed were Colonel Godard, director of security of Algiers in 1960, commander of a subdivision of Nevers in 1961; Colonel Gardes, former head of psychological action in Algiers, on provisional liberty as one of the accused of the Barricades Trials in 1961; Colonel Argoud, Chief of Staff of the Algiers army corps in 1960, Chief of Staff of the Sixth Military Region at Metz in 1961; Colonel Bigeard, commander of the Saïda sector in 1960, commander of the Sixth Overseas Regiment at Banqui, French-Equatorial Africa, in 1961; Colonel Dufour, commander of the 1st REP in 1960, confined to quarters since December, 1960; General Faure, commander of the Twenty-seventh Infantry Division in 1960, without command in 1961; General Mirambeau, commander of the Thirteenth Infantry Division in 1960, without command in 1961; General Gribius, commander of the West Saharan Zone in 1960, commander of the Fifth Armored Brigade in Germany in 1961.

[71] *Le Monde*, March 4, 1961.

Perhaps it never came because it was feared the army was untrustworthy and would divide, resulting in an internecine conflict. Perhaps there was a reluctance to give the command which would have meant, if obeyed, French soldiers would fire on the Europeans of Algiers. Perhaps, rather than risk disobedience, rather than call upon French soldiers to fire upon men devoted to France, Paris preferred the stalemate that the Week of the Barricades became.

Ortiz and Lagaillarde had hoped to entice the army behind the barricades with them. The movement would spread, like a *tache d'huile* (spot of oil), and De Gaulle would have to reverse his Algerian policy or resign. The activist officers reinforced the civilians' belief that the army would join them; the fraternization of the 10th DP with the men of the barricades convinced them. However, the paratroops of Massu's old unit were not the entire French army, and when it became obvious that the army was going to obey De Gaulle, the end of the barricades was in sight. The European ultras had planned on the army coming to their aid as in 1958, but in January, 1960, the majority failed to follow their active, though few in number, fellow officers. And even those who had encouraged Ortiz and Lagaillarde had done so only to use these men as pawns in their own game to checkmate the king in Paris.[72]

How successful was the "national arbiter" in January, 1960? Several authors have written that De Gaulle gave in and granted concessions to win over the army. The promises of continued pacification, of desiring the "most French solution," of assuring the army it would control the referendum when it did come, were seen as the cost of obedience.[73] However, De Gaulle's firmness far outweighed his concessions and he remained adamant in his policy of self-determination, the policy the movement was initiated to reverse. Furthermore, these same "concessions" had been granted the previous October by the President. De Gaulle gave away nothing, and asked for everything from his army—he demanded obedience. The officers who saw in the "concessions" of the January 29 speech a retreat by De Gaulle, seem rather to have been retreating themselves. These officers, caught in a now untenable position, grasped De Gaulle's "concessions" because they afforded the

[72] See Edward Behr, *The Algerian Problem* (New York: W. W. Norton, 1962), pp. 173–75.

[73] See for example Henry Tanner, *New York Times*, February 14, 1960, IV, p. 4:5–6; Joseph Kraft, *The Struggle for Algeria* (Garden City: Doubleday and Co., 1961), p. 236; and the view of one writer that "in order to incite the Army to act, he [De Gaulle] virtually guaranteed the Army a free hand in Algeria." Brown, "The Army and Politics in France," p. 273.

excuse to return to obedience. They said the President had retreated. Actually, they had.

The insurgents' situation was well exemplified by the remark of a paratrooper following De Gaulle's call to order. Mused the soldier, "You know, he is right." And then he said to a comrade, indicating the men behind the barricades, "They are getting to be a bore." [74] The nation and most of the army had grown tired of the situation in Algiers.

In the beginning of the week, the unity of the army had been used as the clarion call to prevent the army from attacking the barricades, but within a few days the barricades had demonstrated that the unity of the army was a fiction.[75] In Algeria and in France, while some officers had engaged in antigovernment activity, others had taken clear stands for the Republic and its policy, making it known that they would refuse to rally to the insurgents, and if necessary were ready to fire on the barricades. They took a clear position in favor of legitimate authority in Paris, and warned their dissident fellow officers that the unity of the army could no longer be relied upon to take them down paths they dared not or desired not to tread. One of the lessons of the Week of the Barricades was that the unity of the army could no longer be used as a battering ram for movements attempting to bring down the regime.[76] However, to be forewarned was not to be forearmed; in April, 1961, military activists would again depend upon the unity of the army to present a solid front against the Republic.

Another result of barricades week was the division that henceforth would separate the army and the Europeans of Algeria. Officers had disliked the *colons* for some years because of their attitudes and practices toward the Moslems, but their dislike had been overshadowed by the common goal of keeping Algeria French. They had united their forces and with a single voice, chanting *Algérie française*, had exerted tremendous pressure on Paris, particularly in May, 1958, and on many other less spectacular occasions. However, the feeling that engulfed the *colons* after barricades week, of having been abandoned and betrayed by the army, drove a wedge between the civilian ultras of Algeria and the army.[77]

[74] Quoted by Thomas Brady, *New York Times*, January 30, 1960, p. 3:1.

[75] Paul-Marie de la Gorce, *The French Army* (New York: George Braziller, 1963), p. 506. De la Gorce also takes the position that the "concessions" of January 29 were a reiteration of those of October, 1959, with roughly the same consequences.

[76] See the article by Jean Planchais, *Le Monde*, March 11, 1960.

[77] See Jules Roy, *Le Monde*, June 9, 1960; also Philippe Herreman, *Le Monde*, June 2, 1960.

In their attempt to bring down the Fourth Republic, the *colons* and their army allies were successful because France had abdicated power to Algiers. "We are in May 1958," wrote Maurice Duverger. "Then the nation had let the established regime die because it was incapable of ending the Algerian war, because General de Gaulle had seemed to the nation to bring the hope of peace...."[78] The nation, therefore, had followed the army's lead and accepted De Gaulle. But in 1960, there was no De Gaulle to turn to, and the army had either to back the President or legalize their insubordination by creating a new "legal" government.

No such attempt was made, and the Week of the Barricades demonstrated that De Gaulle was at the head of a strong and generally accepted government. When the barricades went up there apparently was some doubt on these points, but by the end of the week, De Gaulle had proved the strength of his Republic. The contest for control was won by the scepter, not by the sword, and the army, which had found its opening to power in an absence of Parisian power in 1958, could not repeat the performance when power reappeared in Paris. In January, 1960, the army came to realize that De Gaulle had the nation behind him and the army followed the will of the nation. As Professors Macridis and Brown have observed, "metropolitan public opinion was overwhelmingly critical of the uprising."[79]

Professor Meisel has written that the crisis of the army in 1958 was not recognized for what it really was, "the crisis of the state itself."[80] In similar fashion, the Week of the Barricades was a crisis of the state, a test of the Fifth Republic's strength, a struggle between the army feudal lords of Algeria, determined to hold their fief, and the distant sovereign whom they themselves had crowned.[81] De Gaulle could have avoided the clash by accepting Massu's denial of the Kempski interview and returning the famous General to the Court at Algiers. But the Chief of State chose to accept the challenge as another step in the direction of reducing the army's political power.

Yet in spite of the victory of civilian Paris over military Algiers, certain army elements continued to think of reversing the government's

[78] Maurice Duverger, *Le Monde*, June 30, 1960.

[79] Roy C. Macridis and Bernard E. Brown, *Supplement to the De Gaulle Republic* (Homewood, Illinois: The Dorsey Press, 1963), p. 19.

[80] Meisel, *The Fall of the Republic*, p. 156.

[81] See "The King and the Barons," *Economist*, CXCIV (February 6, 1960), 500–502.

self-determination policy. A note was passed in Algiers on March 21, 1960, purportedly written by a group of officers, which read:

> Our army has given proof of its discipline, of its unity, and of its political maturity. It has kept its reason in spite of calls to its heart. In refusing to fire on the Algerian people it has shown that it will never be for the state against the country.
>
> One knows equally well that the army of draftees is not in opposition to the professional army. That the army of the *bled* [countryside] is not in opposition to the army of Algiers. That the paratroops are not in opposition to the infantrymen. Keep in mind that there is only one army, and this one army fights to keep Algeria French.[82]

The Fifth Republic and civil authority won a victory in January, 1960, but not the contest. Once again elements of the army would rebel, next time without the civilians. But De Gaulle would be ready for new challenges. On the evening of the barricades' surrender, the German Ambassador arrived at the Elysée Palace. De Gaulle greeted him with: "*Eh bien, monsieur le Ministre . . .* we have just gone through a bit of a jostled week. Let us look at the problems of Europe."[83]

[82] *Le Monde*, March 23, 1960.
[83] Bromberger, *Barricades et colonels*, p. 444.

CHAPTER X

Charles and the Dragon

l'Idéal de l'Etat sain, celui où la force de la loi prime la loi de la force.
—PIERRE-HENRI SIMON.

THE FIFTH REPUBLIC emerged from the Week of the Barricades still committed to self-determination for Algeria, enjoying increased prestige and support after Ortiz and Lagaillarde had failed in their effort to rally the army to their side and change De Gaulle's policy.[1] Jules Roy exclaimed: "Never has a chief of state had more authority and inspired more respect and confidence than General de Gaulle. . . . The army will blindly obey the President of the Republic and would obey him even if he imposed on it the solution of the Algerian problem most contrary to its wishes. . . ."[2] But in the following months, and particularly in April, 1961, army activists demonstrated they were not prepared to accept that most contrary to their wishes—an independent Algeria.

Shortly after the barricades were torn down in Algiers, Paris acted to reduce further formal military political power in Algeria. A decree issued on February 20, 1960, enunciated the primacy of civilian authorities

---

[1] Of the three choices to be given to Algeria, De Gaulle preferred association over frenchification or secession. A survey taken in October, 1959, showed that 35 percent of Frenchmen also preferred association. In February, 1960, the figure had risen to 48 percent. The figures for frenchification were 23 percent and 27 percent; for secession 12 percent and 6 percent; no answer, 30 percent and 19 percent. Cited in William G. Andrews, *French Politics and Algeria* (New York: Appleton-Century-Crofts, 1962), p. 21.

[2] Jules Roy, *Le Monde*, June 8, 1960. Roy, an ex-colonel of the French air force and a third-generation French-Algerian, wrote a book in which he expressed his feeling that social injustice had caused the rebellion and kept it going. He asked for peace, with the Algerians "having a nation in their turn," thus bringing an end to torture and murder. See his *The War in Algeria* (New York: Grove Press, 1960), p. 120.

over the military in Algeria: "Under the authority of the government's Delegate General, the regional inspectors, the general prefects, the prefects and sub-prefects exercise in their respective districts, the functions normally devolved to civil authority."[3] Charged with the maintenance of public order, the army in this field could give instructions to the civilians. In certain parts of Algeria, those most directly threatened by the FLN, the military continued to be able to use the civilian police in maintaining order. The army also continued to exercise in these areas control of persons, vehicles, and goods.

A De Gaulle directive a few days later reiterated the decree's stipulations. Wherever possible, the President emphasized, civilian control must be resumed. Certain functions not properly military (such as teaching, public health, and administrative affairs), that the army had performed because of the circumstances in Algeria, were progressively to return to civilians. As far as possible, the prefectural administrations were to recover the direction of civilian affairs. In conclusion, De Gaulle ordered that "the military command hold itself above political discussion and electoral operations . . . and concentrate on the operational actions which must render them possible."[4]

Speaking to a veterans' organization in Oran on the last day of February, General Gambiez, the Oran army corps commander, defined the army's new political posture: "A soldier must no more contest the political strategy of the Chief of State than he would discuss the military strategy of his chiefs."[5] During the early days of March, De Gaulle once again appeared in Algeria. His trip took him to several military command posts where he talked with officers, apparently another journey to confer with the army in Algeria and determine its state of mind. Although De Gaulle had strengthened his position, he still deemed it necessary to go to the "mess-halls" to talk, to listen, to probe the officers' attitudes toward a cease-fire, the European uprising, and the new administrative organization.[6] The President demonstrated by his trip that the army remained a political factor to be reckoned with.[7]

While in Algeria, De Gaulle assured the army a long tenure in Algeria, since the Algerian problem, he declared, would be resolved

[3] *Le Monde*, February 23, 1960.

[4] *Le Monde*, March 4, 1960.

[5] *Le Monde*, March 1, 1960.

[6] *Le Monde*, March 2, 1960.

[7] See Anthony Hartley, "Thunder on the Right," *The Spectator*, CCIV (June 10, 1960), 828.

only after the army had achieved a complete military victory, and the accomplishment of this would be a long-term affair. Allowing that he could not see into the future, he added that it was necessary for the French to remain in Algeria. At Menas he said, "Algeria must not be separated from France. It is of the nature of things that Algeria be bound to France. Under what form? I do not prejudge that. That will depend upon the situation of the world and the vote of the population."[8]

Elsewhere De Gaulle reassured his troubled officers by saying, "I repeat that I do not specify under what form France will remain in Algeria, but I am sure that she will remain there."[9] At a military conference at Assiz, De Gaulle expressed his preference for some form of association with Algeria, first explaining that the former arrangement between France and Algeria was impossible, as was also a completely independent Algeria. At the far-off referendum when Algeria would decide her future, De Gaulle believed Algerians would choose "an Algerian Algeria bound to France."[10]

Again the army had heard from the Chief that it would continue fighting until the long-sought military victory was won. Since it would take a long time to defeat the FLN, the army's prolonged presence was assured; and when the day for decision arrived, the President had implied that the army would still be there in an Algerian Algeria which would have close ties with France. Yet during the same trip De Gaulle told the army that it would not remain in Algeria indefinitely, for at Barika he had said: "You are the sword of France *here for the moment, and one day, eventually elsewhere*. It is always necessary to think of that. *You are not destined always to be the French Army in Algeria*."[11] During his trip, De Gaulle mentioned two important concepts: first, he had used the words, an Algerian Algeria; second, the army was told that it would not always be in Algeria. However, the present was given to the army and enough of the future to pacify some of its officers.

Following the President's return to France, a communiqué was issued which summarized his trip. Once order was restored, Algeria would determine her own future, which would probably be an Algerian Algeria (the words now used for the nation to hear) since a return to yesterday's domination was impossible, as was complete independence which would bring chaos. The most important part of the communiqué

---

[8] *Le Monde*, March 6–7, 1960.
[9] *Le Monde*, March 5, 1960.
[10] *Le Monde*, March 6–7, 1960.
[11] *Ibid.*; (italics mine).

followed: the people of France learned De Gaulle had reminded the army that Algeria, important a problem as it was, was only one of France's problems. "It is necessary, then, that the army, while accomplishing its current task in Algeria," read the communiqué, "equally have its mind fixed on the missions which may fall to it elsewhere. It is to its duty to the whole, and not only to a local and momentary phase, that the French army must adapt itself and prepare itself morally and materially." [12] Could the words "elsewhere," and "local momentary phase," be interpreted as meaning that the army's Algerian role was drawing to a close? Was it for this eventuality that the army had to prepare itself, "morally and materially"?

Local elections were scheduled in Algeria for May, and the army received word it was to keep itself impartial and support no candidates. [13] Pierre Messmer, the Minister of Armed Forces, made it clear in a May 4 press conference that the army was to take no part in the electoral campaigns, and declared that the army's "*raison d'être* is not to enter into the struggles, but to maintain a strict neutrality." [14] Three days before the elections, it was reported that the army was conforming to the directives, [15] and it was later said that the only army political activity during the election was the efforts of some military men to keep down abstentions. Remaining neutral as ordered, these men had counseled the Moslems to go to the polls to prove they were not under the orders of the FLN, which was telling them to stay home and not vote. [16]

On election day, no soldiers were seen at the polls and the army was forbidden to provide trucks to transport voters. However, in some districts menaced by the FLN, military vehicles were used to bring voters to the polling places. Philippe Herreman of *Le Monde* was assured by several mayors that the army would observe strict neutrality, [17] and they apparently were correct in their judgment. The army that in 1958 had played such a predominant campaign role, in May, 1960, was adjured to remain on the sidelines and obeyed. [18]

12 *Le Monde*, March 9, 1960.
13 *Le Monde*, April 28, 1960.
14 *Le Monde*, May 6, 1960.
15 *Le Monde*, May 27, 1960.
16 *Le Monde*, May 24, 1960.
17 *Le Monde*, May 28, 1960; *Le Monde*, May 29–30, 1960.

18 In these local elections, in which the army's political role was limited to trying to keep down abstentions, the voter turnout was 58 percent; the voter turnout for the legislative elections of November, 1958, was 67 percent; the September, 1958, election voter turnout was approximately 80 percent. *Le Monde*, May 5, 1960.

In May, Pierre Messmer told members of the foreign press that the army's collective attitude was above suspicion, and although he acknowledged that some individual officers questioned certain policies he pointed out that their opinions were being legitimately presented, normally and as to be expected in a democratic regime.[19] Indeed, during the spring and summer of 1960 the French army was a politically quiet body, at least on the surface, despite the fact that, in June, De Gaulle renewed the offer to talk with the FLN, and conversations, although inconclusive, did take place at Melun from June 25 to 29.

Attracting little attention and no fanfare, General Salan retired from the army in June and went to Hydra, in Algeria, where for the next three months little was heard from him. Then, on September 14, Salan issued a sensational communiqué which put him in open conflict with the government. There was no authority, according to the retired General, which could abandon a part of the national territory. Yet, queried Salan, had not the President of the Republic said to the Moslems that they could choose to be no longer French? He, Salan, would have nothing to do with a policy of self-determination. In effect, Salan accused the President of violating the constitution, perhaps even of being a deserter and a traitor.[20]

Within a week, Salan was summoned to Paris and was confronted by Messmer. Salan defended his statement on the grounds that he had spoken as President of the Association of Combatants of the French Union (a post to which he had been elected in June), not as an officer, and in his judgment he was guilty of no transgression. Messmer felt differently, and informed Salan that the communiqué was of a nature to encourage enemies of De Gaulle's Algerian policy. Salan was ordered not to return to Algeria. When the news of Salan's proscription reached Algeria the reaction was little more than Salan's wife issuing a statement declaring that Salan would be "our protector in Paris as in Algeria."[21]

Salan was not silenced, however. The next month *Le Monde* carried a column by the retired General which called the free world's attention to the dangers in store if the Communists gained an African foothold.

[19] *Le Monde*, May 15–16, 1960.

[20] *Le Monde*, September 16, 1960. Article 6 of the Fifth Republic Constitution provides that the President "shall be the guarantor of national independence, and of the integrity of the territory. . . ."

[21] *Le Monde*, September 25–26, 1960; see also *Le Monde*, September 20–22, 1960; September 24, 1960.

Algeria could not be abandoned, according to Salan, because it was the last bulwark across the Mediterranean which could bar the route to Soviet imperialism and the conquest of the world.[22] Toward the end of October, Salan went to Barcelona, at first telling reporters he would be returning to Paris. It soon developed he would be staying in Spain.

During October, another general firmly attached to *Algérie française* retired, air force General Edmond Jouhaud, a *pied noir* (a European born in Algeria) and former air force Chief of Staff. The retired Jouhaud returned to Algeria and became the honorary president of the National Association of the Repatriated French of North Africa. Although he infrequently appeared in public, he established numerous activist contacts, especially in Constantine, and also established relations with Salan who was now in Madrid.

A tract was clandestinely distributed in the army in October which demonstrated that the activists in military circles had by no means accepted the government's declared policy. "The army does not intend to be deaf and blind, to be a simple 'instrument of power,'" announced the pamphlet. "It pays with its blood and its sacrifices for the right to have its voice heard with the same right as other national bodies. . . . The army must play a determining role in the solution of the 'Algerian problem.'" On May 13, according to the authors, the army had supported integration, but the government had since favored France's enemies and discouraged her friends. In conclusion, the writers (unidentified) announced that they stood by the unity of the Republic and the integrity of its territory.[23]

A few days after the appearance of the tract, one of the officers who had received a copy wrote an open letter to *Le Monde* giving another viewpoint. The tract, said the anonymous officer, spoke for a minority of the army while pretending to speak in the army's name. But the majority of officers, said the correspondent, "would categorically refuse to follow . . . in the path of the pronunciamento and anarchy."[24]

It has been said that "the IVth Republic had its crises; the Vth had its plots."[25] De Gaulle, speaking on November 4, convinced some of his listeners that the time had come for the President to go, reminding one again of the officer who had reflected in 1959: "Each time de Gaulle

[22] *Le Monde*, October 13, 1960.

[23] *Le Monde*, October 12, 1960.

[24] *Ibid.*

[25] Jacques Fauvet and Jean Planchais, *La Fronde des généraux* (Paris: Arthaud, 1961), p. 7.

opens his mouth, he provokes another uprising!"[26] De Gaulle announced that the future Algeria would not be governed by France, but would be an Algerian Algeria. He then spelled out what he meant: the new Algeria would be an emancipated Algeria in which the Algerians themselves would decide their destiny; the responsibility for their country would be in their hands, "an Algeria which, if the Algerians wish it— and I think this is the case—will have its own government, its own institutions and its own laws."[27]

Algeria's tomorrow, promised De Gaulle, would be decided by the Algerians and France would not protest the result. The previous March, De Gaulle had said a completely independent Algeria was impossible, that some form of association was necessary. Now he opened wide the door to independence. At least such an eventuality could be interpreted from his words, and many did not fail to so interpret them. It is often difficult to interpret De Gaulle's speeches since many meanings can be found in almost any of his public pronouncements, particularly as regards Algeria. Perhaps De Gaulle was not thinking of complete independence, but still in terms of some sort of association. An Algerian Algeria, governed by its own institutions yet associated with France, was not precluded in his November 4 remarks. Furthermore, on October 28, De Gaulle had again expressed his opinion that complete independence was the road to chaos.[28]

A few days after the November 4 declaration, De Gaulle announced that a referendum would be held both in France and Algeria to determine popular approval of the government's self-determination policy. From San Sebastian, Spain, came Salan's reaction: "For me, the referendum on Algeria has already taken place. It took place in September, 1958, and its result is well known: Algeria must remain French, absolutely French."[29]

[26] Merry Bromberger, *et al.*, *Barricades et colonels* (Paris: Arthème Fayard, 1960), p. 67.

[27] *Le Monde*, November 6–7, 1960.

[28] At a luncheon held at the Chateau de Rambouillet and attended by senators and deputies opposed to De Gaulle's Algerian policy, the President had answered questions and appeared to be trying to appease these enemies. One parliamentarian opined that an Algerian Algeria would lead inevitably to independence. De Gaulle, we are told, answered that in no case would it lead to an independent Algeria. For one reason, the army would not allow it. He added that if Algeria did become independent, against his taste and contrary to what he currently envisaged, he would not stay on as Chief of State, but would return to Colombey. Reported by Pierre Viansson-Ponté, *Le Monde*, October 30–31, 1960.

[29] *Le Monde*, November 18, 1960.

On the surface, the army remained quiet. In mid-November, Messmer and General Ely went to Algeria on what appeared to be a trip to explain government policy to the army and to alleviate army worries. Long discussions were held with officers concerning Algerian policy, and the visitors from Paris spoke particularly about the international complications to be kept in mind when considering Algeria. The army was told that its role would be to help keep Algeria in close contact with France, and that it would have to assure the liberty of the vote at the forthcoming referendum. Messmer and Ely strongly underlined the fact that there was no question of delivering Algeria to the army's arch foe, the FLN, which did not, in their opinion, represent all Algerians.[30]

On November 22, Louis Joxe, a senior diplomat, was appointed Minister of State in charge of Algerian affairs, and assigned the task of carrying out the President's program of preparing Algeria for self-determination. Under Joxe, Algerian administration would progressively be turned over to Algerians, starting at the local level. In the second week of December, De Gaulle left for Algeria to speak to the Algerians, both European and Moslem, and to talk and listen to the army. Since it was felt that the army would play an important role in the forthcoming referendum, set for January 8, 1961, the army's attitude was of vital concern to the government.[31]

De Gaulle explained during the course of the trip that the army's proper role consisted of maintaining order and acting as a fraternal bond between the Moslems and France. At Blida, De Gaulle said that to pretend Algeria was a province such as Lorraine or Provence was in vain; there was only an Algerian Algeria which was growing more Algerian every day. Yet France was needed by this new Algeria as was the French minority in Algeria. France's support would be offered in brotherhood promised De Gaulle, "in that respect, the role that the army has played and is playing is essential because it has not belonged to any faction. The army does not have its own interests on this soil, unless that interest be the honor of France and military duty."[32] Having no interest or factions of its own, the army was the servant only of France. "The army has no policy," stated the President, "it is not the army's place to declare a policy. The honor of the army, the duty of the army, is simply to serve. And that must be done in unity. Let the army be exemplary."[33]

[30] *Le Monde*, November 17, 1960.
[31] Pierre Viansson-Ponté, *Le Monde*, November 18, 1960.
[32] *Le Monde*, December 11–12, 1960.
[33] *Le Monde*, December 14, 1960.

While De Gaulle was speaking, riots and strikes were taking place in various parts of Algeria. Before his arrival, rumors and pamphlets had been circulated by ultras calling for public disturbances and demonstrations. Naturally the army's position was questioned: would it maintain order or would it sanction disorder as it had for a time the previous January? The question was put to General Crépin, the Commander in Chief in Algeria, who replied: "One of the army's permanent missions is to have order respected and maintained. Everyone must be convinced that the army will fulfill its mission here as elsewhere." [34]

In Algiers, Oran, Orléansville, and elsewhere, General Crépin proved to be right. When De Gaulle arrived on December 9, the Europeans in Algeria called for protest strikes against his Algerian policy. In Algiers, steel-helmeted police fought European demonstrators all day on the ninth, until the army moved in with tanks and finally subdued the European demonstrators.[35] Violence continued across Algeria the next day as the Europeans persisted in their protests against self-determination. On the tenth, a new factor was added to the situation when the Moslems left the Casbah in Algiers to demonstrate against the Europeans and to yell for an "Algerian Algeria," and to cry "*Vive De Gaulle!*" In Orléansville, a city 105 miles southwest of Algiers, Moslems and Europeans clashed beneath the windows of the building where De Gaulle was staying, the Europeans shouting, "De Gaulle to the gallows!" and "*Algérie française*," while the Moslems punctuated their blows with "*Vive De Gaulle.*"[36]

The President was in Bône on the thirteenth when Europeans again demonstrated. Called upon to restore order, the army obeyed and fired on the demonstrators, killing two and wounding fifteen more. To the Europeans' dismay and shock, the troops that had obeyed the order to fire were Foreign Legion paratroops, the men most admired by the Europeans.[37] The effects of the bullets did not stop with the killed and wounded. January, 1960, had illustrated that the army was no longer trustworthy as an ally in the fight for *Algérie française*. The week of December tenth demonstrated that the army could not only no longer be trusted, but had turned into an enemy force which would fire on Europeans.

Other lessons emerged from this week. A wave of nationalist fervor had swept the Moslems, and they proudly marched carrying FLN flags,

[34] *Le Monde*, December 9, 1960.
[35] *New York Times*, December 10, 1960, p. 1:8.
[36] *New York Times*, December 11, 1960, pp. 1:7, 3:2.
[37] *New York Times*, December 14, 1960, p. 1:6.

and banners asking for independence. Once the marchers had passed, with their flags and banners, their voices jubilant, the myth of integration and fraternity could no longer be invoked by anyone: Algerian nationalism was a reality.[38] The army did not challenge the nationalist display, even though the Moslems carried the hated FLN flag. When mobs got out of hand, whether European or Moslem, the army restored order.

Algérie française was destroyed by the chanting Moslems. The referendum of January 8 was won a month before the balloting by the Moslems' demonstration that their Algerian Algeria would be an independent Algeria. The slogans of December 11 were transformed into ballots on January 8, 1961. On that day 70 percent of the votes in Algeria registered "oui" to a government bill concerning self-determination for Algeria and the organization of public powers before self-determination.[39]

The referendum also proved France had accepted an Algerian Algeria, which would mean negotiations with the FLN in spite of De Gaulle's earlier guarantees given to the army that negotiations would not take place until military victory had been secured. The Europeans of Algeria were adrift. France had abandoned them and the army could no longer be depended upon.

For many officers the situation was a bitter one; however, they recognized that no path remained open but discipline or a split with the nation which had again demonstrated its support of the government's policy.[40] Many officers were appalled, but most resigned themselves to the will of the nation. Maurice Duverger marked January 8 as a signal day for France and wrote that De Gaulle, the man who had shielded France for two and one-half years from an army dictatorship and the plots of the Right, realized the fruits of his toils at the referendum. Duverger felt that by the heavy "yes" response in France and Algeria, "the ultras [were] crushed and the army restored to its tradition of discipline."[41]

In the weeks following the referendum, the government further restricted army civil functions in Algeria and set in motion the machinery for negotiations with the rebel forces. An early March directive informed the army that henceforth any proceedings or arrange-

---

[38] See *ibid.*, p. 2:3.

[39] The results published by the Constitutional Council showed that 70 percent of those voting in Algeria voted "yes"; the figure for France was 75 percent. See *Le Monde*, January 15–16, 1961.

[40] See Jean Planchais, "La discipline de l'armée," *Le Monde*, December 21, 1960.

[41] *Le Monde*, January 13, 1961.

ments touching persons, and particularly measures restricting individual liberty, would be taken only by civilians. The military could advise such action but the civil authorities would be the implementing instruments. The number of districts in Algeria where the army held all police powers were reduced in number from thirty-nine to seventeen. Those remaining were on the frontiers and in operational zones in Kabylia and North Constantine.[42]

France and the Provisional Government of the Algerian Republic (GPRA) announced on March 30 that talks would begin at Evian on April 7. However, on the very day of the announcement Minister Joxe managed to bring events to a standstill by remarking at a conference in Oran that he would meet with representatives of the Algerian National Movement (the MNA, a rival nationalist group under Messali Hadj). Negotiation preparations were halted the next day by the GPRA which labeled the MNA "valets of colonialism."[43]

Paris on April 7 again announced its desire to open negotiations, and De Gaulle held a press conference on the eleventh during which he said: "France has no interest in maintaining under its law and under its dependency an Algeria which would choose another destiny." France would place no obstacles in the path of the creation of an Algerian state, declared De Gaulle. The President admitted it was impossible to pretend that the Moslem masses wished to be part of France.[44]

A few days later, while on a trip through southwest France, De Gaulle spoke of peace and association, meaning by the latter an "organic cooperation" between France and Algeria, which would include a preferential system of cultural and economic exchange, and the concession of bases and facilities useful "to our defense."[45] Cooperation, preferential system, concessions, all indicated an independent Algeria. Frenchmen learned on April 20 that the GPRA was prepared to negotiate. During the preparations for the talks, the army remained outwardly calm, apparently resigned to the forthcoming conversations which would end the war and create an independent Algeria. "The political problem," according to one officer, "is the business of the government. We think it will err in resolving it, but that is the government's concern."[46]

[42] *Le Monde*, March 3, 1961.

[43] *Le Monde*, March 31, 1961; *Le Monde*, April 1, 1961.

[44] *Le Monde*, April 12, 1961.

[45] *Le Monde*, April 18, 1961.

[46] *Le Monde*, April 6, 1961.

But other officers considered it more than the government's concern, and activist literature continued to be circulated. "Some, to tell the truth, are neither resigned nor in the process of becoming accustomed to the idea of negotiation. Here and there partisans of a political 'clash' remain. It is asserted that they are few in number," reported Marcel Thiebault from Algeria.[47] That all was not halcyon was made apparent in a communiqué, issued on March 16 by the Algiers army corps commander, General Vezinet: "The forces of order will oppose with the greatest firmness every attempt to disturb calm and security *from wherever it comes.*"[48] On April 21, the attempt came from the army itself.

Because of the failure of the Week of the Barricades and the transfers which followed, the activists attached to the idea of *Algérie française* became more careful and discreet in their operations. Little is known of the early stages of the plotting unleashed by De Gaulle's November 4 pronouncement, but that a movement was initiated shortly after the speech was confirmed by Colonel Brothier who testified in September, 1961, at the Algiers Putsch Trials. Colonel Brothier revealed that before the end of 1960, when he was commander of the First Foreign Legion Paratroop Regiment, he had received two messages from retired Generals Jouhaud, Salan, and Gardy.[49] Gardy was particularly concerned as to the fate of the Foreign Legion (in which he had spent his career), should Algeria be lost. In the messages, the colonel was asked what the Legion's reaction would be in case it was asked to join in a military uprising. Brothier replied that he thought any such movement would meet with failure unless it emanated from France, but that in any event the nation would never accept a military dictatorship.[50]

Early in 1961, the four leaders of the forthcoming putsch were widely separated. Salan was in Madrid; Jouhaud was in Algiers; Zeller had gone to Paris; and Challe, in Fontainebleau, had joined his companions in retirement at the end of January. Toward the end of March, the preparations for an uprising gained momentum, the much-discussed Evian talks impelling the plotters to greater activity. Between March 25 and April 1, Challe was contacted by several persons asking

[47] *Ibid.*

[48] *Le Monde,* March 17, 1961; (italics mine).

[49] General Paul Gardy retired in 1959, but maintained his associations with activist officers still on active duty. He is known to have visited Salan in Madrid in November, 1960. See *Le Monde,* April 24, 1961; *Le Monde,* April 24, 1962.

[50] Maurice Cottaz, ed., *Les Procès du putsch d'Alger et du complot de Paris* (Paris: Nouvelles Editions Latines, 1962), p. 193.

him to join in a strike against the regime. Challe's assent was deeply desired because of his prestige and fame as a leader, one who could rally men who otherwise would be cool to such an action.

"Come with us," Challe was enjoined, "many military men are ready. We will show we can pacify Algeria and not abandon it."[51] Challe held back, telling his callers that he was at heart with them but his conscience was troubled. He asked for time to think. Challe communicated with General Jouhaud, and told him he had been contacted by political and military figures asking him to head an insurrection in Algeria. Challe informed Jouhaud that Zeller felt that if he, Challe, did not take over as head of the action, anarchy would result since there would be no one capable of coordinating action.

General Challe asked Jouhaud his opinion. Jouhaud responded that if Challe thought the movement possible—even if difficult—he would be behind him. The three generals decided to wait for De Gaulle's April 11 speech, "with a last little hope in their hearts."[52] When, on that day, De Gaulle announced that no obstacles would be placed in the way of the creation of an Algerian state, "it was the end of French Algeria," Jouhaud sadly testified.[53] Challe, Zeller, and Jouhaud took the irretrievable step the next day: "On April 12, Generals Zeller, Jouhaud, and I," recounted Challe, "fixed the date for the 20th."[54]

General Salan played no part in the putsch's final preparations. At Salan's trial in 1962, his former aide-de-camp, Captain Ferrandi (who had followed Salan to Spain even though Ferrandi was still on active duty), testified that Salan learned of the army's uprising by radio. Upon hearing of the events in Algiers, Salan decided that it was his "duty" to go to Algeria and join the insurrection. During his trial, Salan admitted that he had played no part in organizing the rebellion.[55]

Although talk of an insurrection had been going on since the previous fall, the final preparations were obviously rapidly made, with the setting of the date of insurrection just eight days from the day of decision. Large-scale and detailed plans were apparently thought unnecessary since the generals, prompted by Colonels Broizat, Gardes, Godard, and Argoud, were sure of the adhesion of the mass of the army. Challe was

---

[51] *Le Procès des généraux Challe et Zeller* (Paris: Nouvelles Editions Latines, 1961), p. 39.

[52] *Ibid.*, p. 40.

[53] *Le Procès d'Edmond Jouhaud* (Paris: Editions Albin Michel, 1962), p. 32.

[54] *Procès Challe*, p. 40; see also *Procès Jouhaud*, p. 32.

[55] *Le Procès de Raoul Salan* (Paris: Editions Albin Michel, 1962), pp. 92, 84.

assured by the colonels that in all their contacts they were told, "If he [Challe] comes, everyone will march."[56] The consensus of the conspirator colonels was that the army was on the verge of revolt. There was no need for lengthy planning; when the uprising came, the army would follow Challe. Clinging to its oath never to abandon Algeria, the army would turn on the government of abandonment.

Colonel Charles Lacheroy, the revolutionary war theorist, sent Challe encouraging reports from a trip made to Algeria on April 16, "taking his desires for realities and vague promises for firm engagements," according to Jacques Fauvet and Jean Planchais.[57] In the words of Colonel Godard, "everything was O.K."[58] The insurgent leaders were convinced that the entire army would follow them over the parapet in their attack against Paris. Their putsch would have been successful, later mused Challe, "if as they had told us, the greatest part of the army had waited for us. . . ."[59]

By April, 1961, the prospect of abandonment and of an Algerian Republic was too much for some military men to bear. Not only was the enemy to be engaged in negotiations, but in March a secret order was distributed telling commanders to prepare for a unilateral cease-fire.[60] The FLN would not be defeated after all, and the French army would lay down its weapons first. Feeling betrayed, deceived, and robbed of victory, Challe and his followers struck the spark which would fail to grow into a flame. There was no other course of action, felt Jouhaud: "We were in a revolutionary situation, in rebellion against the fate to which Algeria did not wish to submit. One defends oneself as one can. It is life or death."[61]

As the activists planned their assault on Paris, they relied on the one asset they were positive was theirs. The officers involved in the planning and execution of the putsch depended upon the unity of the army to bring their comrades to their side. They believed that as long as the principle of unity was intact, the mass of the army was at the mercy

[56] Fauvet and Planchais, *La Fronde*, p. 90.

[57] *Ibid.*, p. 91.

[58] *Ibid.*

[59] *Procès Challe*, p. 39.

[60] See the testimony of Colonel Roca, Cottaz, *Les Procès du putsch d'Alger*, p. 122; also Walter Kerr, "The French Army in Trouble," *Foreign Affairs*, XL (October, 1961), 91.

[61] *Le Monde*, April 13, 1962. For Challe's remarks on his decision to revolt see *Procès Challe*, pp. 22–45. See Fauvet and Planchais, *La Fronde*, p. 120; Henri Azeau, *Révolte militaire* (Paris: Plon, 1961), pp. 112–13, 131–40.

of a minority acting in the army's name. The conviction that "the army will not fire on the army," was one of the principal weapons in the activists' armory.[62]

During the night of April 21–22, the military *coup de force* struck Algiers. General Gambiez, who had been named Commander in Chief in Algeria in February, received information on Friday afternoon (April 21) that there was something afoot for that night. Gambiez and Vezinet (the latter was the Algiers army corps commander) alerted the Algiers forces, and later, about 12:30 A.M. Saturday morning, Vezinet called Gambiez and told him gendarmes had reported truck movements in the area of Zeralda, the headquarters of the 1st REP. Gambiez called the paratroop base, which was eighteen miles from Algiers, and talked to Major Denoix de Saint-Marc, since the commander was on leave. De Saint-Marc assured his Commander in Chief that "all was absolutely tranquil at Zeralda and that the greatest calm existed."[63]

Still worried, Gambiez called the Zeralda transportation section and was informed that no trucks had left the motor pool. No sooner had Gambiez hung up, than he was called by Colonel Moulet at Algiers-Sahel who told him that troops were moving on Algiers. Gambiez then set out for Zeralda, but on the way met a column of army trucks heading for Algiers and tried to stop it. However, the column leader, Lieutenant Philippe Durand-Ruel of the 1st REP, refused to halt the vehicles. Gambiez shouted that the lieutenant was under arrest. Durand-Ruel blandly replied that he would take his arrest in his car, drove around the General, and continued on his way to Algiers.

Gambiez followed the trucks into Algiers and there unsuccessfully attempted to prevent the paratroops from entering public buildings. The General now found himself being told by Durand-Ruel that he was under arrest. Gambiez attempted to drive off, but as his car started to move, the lieutenant shot out one of its tires. Gambiez admonished the lieutenant: "When I was a lieutenant in the Legion, lieutenants did not arrest generals." Replied Durand-Ruel: "Then generals did not sell out the Empire,"[64] and put Gambiez under the guard of legionnaires for the next few days.

Another column, led by Major de Saint-Marc, made its way through

---

[62] See *Le Monde*, April 25, 1961; *New York Times*, April 22, 1961, p. 11:4; *New York Times*, April 25, p. 14:1.

[63] *Procès Challe*, p. 76. See Georges Blond, *La Légion étrangère* (Ottawa: Le Cercle du Livre de France, 1965), pp. 413–16.

[64] Cottaz, *Les Procès du putsch d'Alger*, p. 77.

a barrier outside Algiers which had been erected by General (then Colonel) Moulet, the commander of the Algiers-Sahel region. Moulet's barricade was manned by men of the CRS and gendarmes who refused to fire on the men of the 1st REP for two reasons, according to Moulet.. First, the paratroops were a superior fighting force; second, testified Moulet, "we were not prepared to fire on our brothers-in-arms." [65] Moulet was also arrested by the Legion, but his concern for unity was still evident at the trial of the man who had arrested him. Moulet told the court that he regretted being a witness against De Saint-Marc, adding, "I do not think there was a cheap or a shabby motive in him, certainly not." [66]

Many officers, like Moulet, when called upon to appear for the prosecution in the trial following the putsch, appeared to be on the defendants' side. When called to testify against Durand-Ruel, Gambiez first praised the Foreign Legion, then turned to the men on the accused bench, where sat the officer who had arrested him, and announced: "I keep my esteem for those among you who adhered to the movement in order not to be cut off from your comrades. I am ready to render it to the others as soon as they have thrown off the mask of bravado." [67]

The fear of shooting fellow Frenchmen spared the men of Major Forhan, commando-paratroops, from being fired upon by a gendarme detachment under Major Guyard. Forhan's men occupied the Palais d'Eté and captured Robert Buron, the Minister of Public Works who was visiting Algiers, and the Delegate General, Jean Morin. Guyard's gendarmes stood by as the building was occupied after Guyard had assured Forhan he would never fire on French troops.[68]

However, in South Oran and in the Kabylia region, the principle of unity brought only a few adherents to the putsch. Challe ordered Colonel Roca to take command of the Kabylia region, where Roca had been a sector commander, recently vacated by the retirement of General Simon. Stressing the unity of the army, Roca asked his "subordinate" sector commanders to join the revolt, but several of them refused. When General Simon, still in the vicinity, was urged to join the insurgents, he replied that although he understood their ideals, he could not join them. However, he said he was not opposed to them: "I have

[65] *Ibid.*, p. 13.
[66] *Ibid.*
[67] *Ibid.*, p. 86.
[68] *Ibid.*, p. 101.

already had to fire three times on Frenchmen, I will not do it a fourth." [69]

The scene was repeated in South Oran, where the commander, General Philippe Ginestet, told Major Julien Camelin, Argoud's emissary, that he submitted to Challe's insurrection only to spare his soldiers a fratricidal struggle. Later, during the trials, Ginestet would ask the court to be lenient with Camelin, who, Ginestet informed the court, was born in Algeria and wanted a French Algeria. A simple disciplinary measure would suffice, the General advised the court. [70] In the summer of 1962, shortly before Algerian independence, General Ginestet would be the victim of a Secret Army Organization assassin.

In May, 1958, the army's actions had been covered by a cloak of legality. In 1960, the Week of the Barricades found the army hesitating but not in open rebellion. But in April, 1961, army elements attacked the authority of the state in open defiance, in a military coup led by four retired generals—Challe, Zeller, Jouhaud, and Salan. Word of the revolt first reached Paris at 1:00 A.M. on April 22, when Morin was cut off in the middle of a telephone call to Paris while asking for CRS reinforcements. When he was called back, Morin was allowed to say only that he was no longer free. By 2:30 A.M., Algiers was in the hands of the Legion's paratroops. [71]

In the forenoon of the twenty-second, Joxe and General Jean Olié, the Chief of Staff of National Defense, left France for Algeria and landed at the naval base at Mers-el-Kébir, after stopping at Marseilles to wait for word that they could land in safety. Olié was immediately designated Commander in Chief in Algeria to fill the gap left by Gambiez's capture. [72] Elsewhere in Algeria, General Marie-Michel Gouraud, commander of the Constantine region, wavered, then placed his command under Challe. The commander of the Oran region, General Henri de Pouilly, refused to join the rebellion, but he was forced to move his command post to Tlemcen, some seventy miles from Oran, in the face of civilian demonstrations and the mutiny of the Legion paratroops in the city. Colonel Argoud went to Oran to take command until General Gardy could arrive to assume power. [73]

[69] *Ibid.*, pp. 122–23.
[70] *Ibid.*, pp. 109–10.
[71] *New York Times*, April 23, 1961, p. 2:5.
[72] *Ibid.*
[73] See *New York Times*, April 23, 1961, p. 1:8; *Le Monde*, April 24, 1961.

Challe issued a proclamation on Saturday announcing: "I am in Algiers with Generals Zeller, and Jouhaud, and in liaison with General Salan, in order to keep our oath, the army's oath, to keep Algeria, so that our dead may not have died for nothing."[74] Communiqués soon followed over the radio, one of which announced a state of siege in Algeria, and the passing of all civilian authority to the military, now commanded by Challe.[75] This announcement was soon followed by the declaration that "*Algérie française* is not dead. There is not, there will not be, there never will be, an independent Algeria."[76] A short while later, radio listeners heard that "the army has taken in hand the destiny of Algeria."[77]

On Sunday, April 23, Salan arrived in Algiers only to learn from his comrades that in spite of the first night's success, the movement was on the verge of collapse.[78] The mass of the army had not followed as had been expected, and France was rallying to the support of De Gaulle. In France, from political parties, labor unions, and other quarters, came announcements of resolve to stand with the President. However, on this Sunday of April, 1961, it still outwardly appeared that the revolt was strong, and it was declared that the insurrection had spread to the Constantine region. Paris feared an imminent airborne invasion, and the city was put on a state of alert. Extreme right-wingers in Paris were arrested, one of the seized being Jacques Faure.

De Gaulle spoke to the nation that evening and to the army. "An insurrectional power has established itself in Algeria by a military pronunciamento," De Gaulle began.[79] He then stigmatized the quartet of generals and their adherents who had risen against the government as a group of ambitious and fanatical men embarked on an odious and stupid adventure. In the name of the state and of France, which these

[74] Azeau, *Révolte militaire*, p. 265; see also *Le Monde*, April 23–24, 1961; Fauvet and Planchais, *La Fronde*, pp. 116–17.

[75] *L'Année politique 1961* (Paris: Presses Universitaires de France, 1962), pp. 650–51.

[76] *Le Monde*, April 23–24, 1961.

[77] *Ibid.*

[78] *Procès Salan*, p. 84. At his trial, Challe was asked by the court's president if he had been satisfied with the arrival of Salan. Had it been awaited or had it been a surprise? Challe was asked. The accused replied, "I prefer not to answer, Mr. President." *Procès Challe*, p. 64.

[79] Text of the speech in *L'Année politique 1961*, pp. 651–52; see also *New York Times*, April 24, 1961, p. 3:6.

men had flouted and defied, De Gaulle ordered that all means be used to subjugate the uprising:

I forbid all Frenchmen, and first and foremost, all soldiers, to execute any of their orders. The argument according to which it may be locally necessary to accept their command under the pretext of operational or administrative obligations will deceive no one. The only chiefs, civilian and military, who have the right to assume responsibilities are those who have been regularly named for that purpose.[80]

The special-powers provisions of Article 16 of the constitution were then invoked by De Gaulle.[81]

Charles de Gaulle, the man who in 1940 had called upon the French army to disobey, again in 1961 freed soldiers from the necessity of obeying their immediate superiors. He took away the army's discipline and gave the men of the army a choice: the rebel leaders of Algiers, or the legitimate government in Paris. The military hierarchy could not be used to hide behind—men had to choose. The myth of the unity of the army was destroyed by De Gaulle as he divided the army into two camps, the loyal and the disloyal. In 1940, De Gaulle had asked the army to be loyal to France and disobey her government. In 1961, he asked it to obey the government, for now obedience lay in the course of disobedience to the insurgent leaders in Algiers.

Shortly after De Gaulle spoke, Debré took over the microphone in a call to the nation. The putsch leaders, warned Debré, were planning an attack on France, particularly on Paris. Airplanes stood ready in Algeria, according to the Premier, to drop paratroops on the French capital. Orders had been given and precautions taken to repulse the attack, said Debré. He then made an astonishing request. The people were asked to go to the airdromes at the sound of the sirens, on foot or in cars, "to convince these misled soldiers of their grave errors."[82]

---

[80] *Ibid.*

[81] Article 16 of the Fifth Republic constitution provides in part: "When the institutions of the Republic, the independence of the nation, the integrity of its territory or the fulfillment of its international commitments are threatened in a grave and immediate manner and when the regular functioning of the constitutional governmental authorities is interrupted, the President of the Republic shall take the measures commanded by these circumstances." Article 16 remained in effect until September 30, 1961.

[82] See *L'Année politique 1961*, p. 652; *New York Times*, April 24, 1961, p. 1:8.

Were the entreaties of the Parisians supposed to halt the returning battle-scarred, embittered "paras" and legionnaires?

On the night of April 23–24, Paris was again in a state of alert. With the powers of Article 16, De Gaulle ended all sea and air traffic and mail and financial communications with Algeria. Reservists were called up in France, enough to constitute a division, and additional squadrons of gendarmes were assigned to each department. In Paris, about fifteen hundred civilian volunteers were ready to take arms at a moment's notice.

The night passed without incident. On Monday, April 24, aircraft began arriving in France from Algiers, but not loaded with paratroops. Challe was deprived of the means to transport his forces, because the pilots had decided to go home, to obey their President. The same day Challe learned that the army would not follow him. All over Algeria, the draftees had gone on strike, despite Challe's April 23 attempt to neutralize them by announcing that the conscripts' term of service would not be affected by the uprising and that they would go home on time. Nonetheless, the draftees chose Paris, not Algiers, and the army's situation deteriorated to the point that "in many units privates are denouncing noncommissioned officers, the noncommissioned officers are denouncing officers, and the officers are denouncing each other." [83] Officers who had revolted against the state found that their own men revolted against them, and enlisted men took over units and arrested their disloyal officers. The draftees had made their choice.

The insurgent generals had become generals without an army. As one conscript asked: "If the officers can disobey de Gaulle, why can't we disobey our officers when they turn against the nation?" [84] Several telegrams to De Gaulle revealed the sentiments of the mass of the army. One of the many received read: "We obey only one chief: General de Gaulle, President of the French Republic. . . ." [85] It was signed by men who were draftees. The conscripts' refusal to oppose Paris was diagnosed by the activists as Communist inspired. [86]

---

[83] *New York Times*, May 1, 1961, p. 14:1. On the conscripts' release see *Procès Challe*, p. 62.

[84] *New York Times*, May 1, 1961, p. 14:1.

[85] *Procès Challe*, p. 62.

[86] Challe and Zeller maintained in their trials that the conscripts were infiltrated by Communists who had influenced them to act as they did. *Ibid.*, pp. 41, 43; *Procès Jouhaud*, p. 34. On the role of the conscripts see Fauvet and Planchais, *La Fronde*, pp. 217–19, 234; John Terraine, "The Army in Modern France," *History Today*, XI (November, 1961), 742. According to Louis Terrenoire, "Challe and his telephone

The insurrection's end came swiftly. The combination of De Gaulle's firmness plus the nation's solidarity was too much for the outlaw generals and colonels. On Tuesday afternoon, Challe announced to his three comrades that the situation was lost and he intended to surrender. Zeller at first disagreed, but then he too agreed to give himself up. Salan and Jouhaud refused. Salan had hopes of spreading the insurrection by arming civilians and re-establishing the Territorial Units, arguing that if they had failed on the military front, they would continue on the civilian.[87] While Challe wished to surrender, Salan wanted to rally the civilian population and continue the struggle against Paris' policy of abandonment.

A torn document, bearing the date of April 25 and signed by Salan, revealed his intent. According to the order, certain units in France were to revolt, and in Algiers the reborn Territorial Units were to enter action.[88] That night a broadcast announced that the Territorials were reorganized (probably without Challe's concurrence) and it was further declared that the conscripts who had served over eighteen months would be sent home. The defense of Algeria would be assured by Algeria's Europeans. In addition to the reactivation of the Territorial Units, young Algerians would be called into service to replace the men from France who would be returning home. But it was too late for the announcement to have any effect. By the time the message was broadcast, the putsch was crumbling.

Declarations of loyalty came to Paris from all over Algeria on Tuesday, and Oran and Constantine returned to loyalist control. At 10:30 P.M., troops faithful to the government began moving into Algiers, and gendarmes reached the center of the city by eleven o'clock. A broadcaster on the rebel radio began shouting for all to rush to the Forum. Thousands answered the call, carrying rifles, pistols, shotguns, and other assorted weapons, and milled about the huge square waiting for word from the generals who were in the GG.

Just before 1:00 A.M., April 26, the quartet of defeated generals appeared on the balcony. Challe was the only one who appeared to have any spirit left. The others were grim and sullen, particularly Salan. Their attempts to make a farewell address were, like their insurrection, unsuccessful; the microphones were dead. Zeller, dressed in civilian

---

were beaten by De Gaulle and the radio." *De Gaulle et l'Algérie* (Paris: Arthème Fayard, 1964), p. 230.

[87] See Fauvet and Planchais, *La Fronde*, p. 238; *Procès Salan*, p. 93.

[88] *Procès Salan*, pp. 93–94.

clothes, slipped away. At one-thirty Challe, Salan, and Jouhaud boarded military trucks and left the Forum as the occupation of the city by loyal forces continued. Slowly, the crowd vanished, and within an hour the great square was empty. Around Algiers scattered shots continued through the night. "As it began, the insurrection was ending in angry frustration—pointless gunfire in the dark of the North African night." [89]

Challe was taken the next day and sent immediately to Paris. Arriving at the military field of Villacoublay, he left the aircraft carrying his own suitcase and wearing rumpled civilian clothes. As he descended from the aircraft he reportedly stumbled at the bottom of the ramp, and the vanquished General returned to France falling on his knees. He stepped into a waiting police van and Santé prison gained a general. [90] Ten days later Zeller was captured. Salan and Jouhaud remained at large, to embark upon their work in the Secret Army Organization.

The generals had counted on the unity of the army to bring them success, but even within the leaders' circle, unity was lacking. Salan was the leader of the political viewpoint and the advocate of continuing the struggle. His arrival in Algeria was apparently not welcome news to Challe, for Salan's views of integration were feared to be the same as those of the civilian ultras: a means to continue to hold the Moslems in subjection. [91] For Challe and the others, integration meant full Moslem equality with the Europeans.

Challe had joined the putsch with the conviction that military victory in Algeria was possible. Given freedom of action, Challe believed that in three months he could subdue the rebels and present De Gaulle with a pacified, peaceful Algeria. Challe denied having any political ambitions in executing the putsch. His aims were purely military, he told Colonel Pierre Goubard on Saturday, April 22. He "had not come to alter the government or to constitute a new one, but to lead a purely military action." [92] With a pacified Algeria, a French Algeria could no longer be questioned.

Generals Jouhaud and Zeller also maintained that their goals were not political, but military. At his preliminary investigation, Zeller declared the goals of the putsch did not include taking power in Paris; its aim was only to show the Europeans of Algeria that the army would

---

[89] *New York Times*, April 26, 1961, pp. 1:6, 14:4.

[90] *New York Times*, April 27, 1961, p. 8:3.

[91] Fauvet and Planchais, *La Fronde*, pp. 178–79.

[92] *Procès Challe*, p. 106; see also pp. 40, 107, 187, 188; *Le Monde*, April 26, 1961.

continue to protect them.[93] Tenth Paratroop Division Colonel Ceccaldi, whom the insurgents were trying to win over, was told by Zeller on April 22, "We have no personal ambition, neither Challe, nor Jouhaud, nor myself [Salan's name is conspicuous by its absence]. Our goal is not political."[94]

Jouhaud, like Challe and Zeller, disclaimed any political ambition or motivation. Jouhaud said at his trial: "Never have I thought to modify the institutions of the French Republic. I am a republican of old stock . . . by my parents and by my education. I was classed as a republican officer and never . . . have I thought to modify the institutions of the Republic."[95] General Jouhaud spoke, he said, for all those men who had joined the putsch out of dedication to French Algeria. At his trial (which opened on May 29, 1961, and ended June 1, 1961) Jouhaud stated: "What I have done, I have done for my poor country, I have done for the little people."[96] He went on to say that he had abandoned everything for Algeria, his native country. He had nothing more to attain in life, he told his judges, since he had received all the honors one could hope for and had taken a good job after his retirement from the service. "I have only one regret," he lamented, "I would have desired with all my soul to die on Algerian soil. Apart from that I regret nothing."[97]

But for all their protestations of leading a military action and not a political one, the fact remains that their insurrection was a challenge to the state. The end to be attained was a reversal of government policy, a policy which had been approved in a national referendum and adopted by the government. There is no escaping the fact that the ends of the putsch were political. Accordingly, the High Military Tribunal, which was instituted on April 28, 1961, was to try those involved in crimes against the security of the state.

The rebellious generals claimed that their interest was only in the military aspects of the Algerian problem, but the fact that political implications were present in their minds was seen in a meeting which took place on April 22 between putsch leaders Challe and Zeller and General Georges Héritier (chief of the interservice staff in Algiers), and Colonel Lennuyeux, a former Challe aide. After both the latter men

[93] *Le Monde*, May 12, 1961.
[94] Cottaz, *Les Procès du putsch d'Alger*, p. 70.
[95] *Procès Jouhaud*, p. 39.
[96] *Ibid.*, p. 46.
[97] *Ibid.*

refused to join the putsch, the colonel asked the rebel generals what they expected to gain in Algeria. He was told that a clear military victory was foreseen; then no one could any longer doubt that Algeria was French. Lennuyeux then asked Challe and Zeller what plans they had for France.

According to Héritier, the answer was unclear, and he gained the impression the insurgent generals had not specifically prepared for any action against the metropolitan area. Héritier did recall they had mentioned that De Gaulle would resign when confronted with military success in Algeria, and then perhaps a military government would be implanted in Paris. But this result would apparently be a side effect of the primary goal of seeing that Algeria remained French.[98]

Lennuyeux remembered saying to Challe that even if the army in Algeria followed him, France would not. Challe, according to Lennuyeux, answered: "It will follow against de Gaulle; we have not acted like children; I have seen trade unionists and even some employers and they agree."[99] Zeller entered the debate after Lennuyeux expressed doubts as to the solidarity of this support, averring, "In France, we will have a government that will be with us; at first it will be military. Later we will allow the creation of a government run by politicians."[100] It appears that the purely military motives of the insurrection may be questioned.

But as for the insurrection's execution, it was a purely military operation. In May, 1958, and January, 1960, civilians had played important roles, indeed, it had been civilians who had initiated the action in both previous insurrections. But April, 1961, was of another cast. Civilians were not wanted and were not accepted in the putsch, a military action not to be sullied by civilian contacts. The ultras' motives were suspect, for example, in their attitude toward integration. It was in the French national interest that the officers were revolting, not for the special interests of the *colons*. Only on the last day of the abortive attempt did Salan mention bringing in civilians to spread the infection of the insurrection, but he could not convince Challe and Zeller that civilian aid should be enlisted.

Jacques de Mari, who had served in Salan's civilian cabinet in 1958 and who had an unfailing faith in the General, went to him when he heard Salan had arrived in Algiers. The civilian placed himself at

[98] *Procès Challe*, p. 95.
[99] *Ibid.*, p. 101.
[100] *Ibid.*

Salan's disposal, who, without giving his admirer an exact job, told him to find an office and wait for orders. The orders never came.[101] When Morin, the Delegate General, was captured the first night of the putsch, he was put under the guard of paratroops. When civilians appeared in the morning and offered to relieve the soldiers, their commander refused and the military guard remained.

The civilians' consternation was overheard by Colonel Goubard on Saturday, April 22 (Goubard was then the aide to General André Arfouilloux who commanded the South Algerian Zone). While waiting to see Challe, Goubard listened to the conversation of a group nearby, who were bewailing that it was inconceivable they were not included in the coup. The ultras were ready to furnish men, arms, and information, yet they were not received. "They have the air of not wanting us," lamented one of the civilians, "the military has the air of wishing to treat the affair all alone. . . ."[102] And indeed they did.

On April 22, Colonel Goubard heard Challe remark that their movement would have numerous friends and sympathizers in France. The French public, Challe felt, would understand the rebels and their deep feelings, rally to their support, and force the government to modify its policy. Goubard asked Challe if a coup was foreseen in Paris. "The response was negative."[103] It will be recalled that Paris had expected an airdrop and that Debré had called for the citizens to go to the airdromes to counsel the wayward paratroops. However, the testimony of several witnesses indicates that action in France was never contemplated by the putsch leaders.

Many individuals recalled asking putsch participants if an action against Paris was planned and all received the same answer: nothing foreseen for France. Challe many times expressed himself as harboring no wish to see Frenchmen fighting among themselves, a conflict an airdrop would have precipitated.[104] Challe repeated his desire to avoid a conflict to Lieutenant Jacques Favreau of the 1st REP on April 25, in response to Favreau's asking if an airdrop on Paris was being prepared. Challe replied there never had been a question of such a thing since it would mean civil war.[105] Even Colonel Argoud agreed that no action should be taken in France, and he earnestly informed General Léon

---

101 Cottaz, *Les Procès du putsch d'Alger*, pp. 186–87.
102 *Procès Challe*, p. 109.
103 *Ibid.*, p. 108.
104 *Ibid.*, p. 134; see also *ibid.*, pp. 126, 146; *Le Monde*, May 6, 1961.
105 *Procès Challe*, p. 185.

Perrotat, who was commander of the Twenty-ninth Infantry Division and the Central Oran Zone, that France would not be attacked. "Besides, it would be useless," Argoud asserted, "the metropole will follow by itself."[106]

When the question of invading France was raised at Challe's trial, Colonel Goubard testified that an airdrop on Paris had been logistically impossible. According to Goubard, with the available aircraft, Challe could have sent only two thousand men to France. Perhaps that would have been enough in 1958, said Goubard, but not in 1961. Challe claimed he never even had made such a calculation since the operation had never been considered. Goubard added he did so only after the coup had collapsed.[107] When Challe was directly questioned as to whether a strike against France had been planned, he answered, "in no case, Mr. President; in no case. . . ."[108] He stated he did not have enough men for such an enterprise, nor had he wanted to start a civil war. In answer to the argument that Algeria could not survive without France for the three months Challe needed for a victory, Challe responded that his friends in NATO would not have let him down. The allies did not want communism in Algeria and North Africa either.[109]

Although the denials of action foreseen in France were numerous, the trials which followed the putsch disclosed the Paris plot. Twenty-two men, military and civilian, were tried from September 11 to 22 for actions taken in France. In the car of one of the plotters, Bernard Sabouret Garat de Neddes, a plan for taking Paris had been found. It was known as Plan Godard and indicated Paris was to have been invested by three military columns coming from Auxerre, Orléans, and

106 *Ibid.*, p. 130.

107 *Ibid.*, pp. 109–11.

108 *Ibid.*, p. 54.

109 Fauvet and Planchais, *La Fronde*, p. 213. The thesis that the allies would help to keep the Communists out of Algeria by keeping Algeria French was echoed in the rumor which circulated during the putsch that the generals were encouraged to revolt by the United States Central Intelligence Agency. Agents had been in contact with the generals' circles, but there is no evidence that they proffered aid. One observer has written that "the evidence indicates there were CIA operatives who let their own politics show and by doing so led the Challe rebels to believe that the United States looked with favor on their adventure." Andrew Tully, *CIA: The Inside Story* (London: Arthur Barker, 1962), p. 57; see pp. 50–57. See also Alexander Werth, "The CIA in Algeria," *The Nation*, CXCII (May 13, 1961), 433–35; and *Procès Challe*, p. 95.

Rambouillet.[110] The columns were to have been increased in strength by civilians who would join the movement along the path to Paris. During the night of April 21–22, the project was put into motion, apparently involving only the civilian elements of Plan Godard. However at 4:00 A.M. the men received the order to go back home. It is not known where the order came from, nor why it came.

The leader of the Paris plot was the old conspirator, General Jacques Faure. Challe had disclaimed any intentions of action in the metropole, yet Fauvet and Planchais state that Faure was acting under Challe's orders.[111] During the trial it was revealed that Sabouret had met Colonel Godard and was told that the Algerian movement could not fail to have consequences in France. Therefore, the operation in Algeria would have to be supported in France.[112] Evidence of other meetings, conversations, and letters was produced during the trial which exposed plans for action in the metropolitan area. The judges concluded that the plots of Algiers and Paris were parts of a whole.[113]

The actions taken against the army after the April putsch were not this time limited to transfers. Between June, 1961, and January, 1962, over one hundred French officers stood trial for their part in the April putsch attempt with results ranging from acquittal to fifteen years imprisonment. The two sections created out of the fifth bureaus after the January, 1960, uprising were abolished, and just two days after the collapse of the insurrection, it was announced that three paratroop regiments and a special group attached to the air force known as the air commandos would be dissolved. Two of the paratroop units disbanded were Regular army formations, the other was the 1st REP, the insurrection's spearhead.

The 1st REP had been formed after World War II and had won a glorious history for itself in Indochina and Algeria. Twice the regiment had been decimated in Indochina, and after being reconstituted in Algeria in 1955, it had put out of combat almost eight thousand FLN

110 See Fauvet and Planchais, *La Fronde*, pp. 149–65.

111 *Ibid.*, p. 151.

112 Cottaz, *Les Procès du putsch d'Alger*, p. 212.

113 For a summary of the Paris plot trials, see *ibid.*, pp. 207–35. Seven of the accused received prison sentences ranging from one to ten years. General Faure was one of those receiving the ten-year penalty. The other fifteen accused were acquitted. See Appendix.

members, while losing three hundred of its own men and suffering some five thousand wounded. More than three thousand decorations for bravery were won by men serving in the 1st REP. When the regiment's officers were loaded on buses to be taken to Algiers for punishment, they departed from Zeralda singing a song made famous by Edith Piaf, "*Je ne regrette rien*" ("I Regret Nothing").[114]

On June 8, by virtue of the powers given him by Article 16, De Gaulle decreed that until October 15 military men of all grades could be put on special leave or removed from active duty. The same measure provided that officers who had not yet achieved the requisite time in grade for promotion to lieutenant general could have the seniority requirement waived. Messmer first denied the decree was due to the putsch, but later admitted that exceptional situations had to be met with exceptional measures. No figures are available on the number of officers who "had their departure facilitated," but it was estimated that the figure would reach into the hundreds. The waiving of the seniority rule made possible the advancement of younger officers to replace senior officers who were involved in the insurrection.[115]

Actually, those who participated in the planning and execution of the putsch were but a fraction of France's officers and enlisted men. The rest of the army remained loyal, although some wavered and some took a sitting-on-the-fence position, waiting to see whether Algiers or Paris would prevail. When it became clear that De Gaulle had millions of Frenchmen behind him, Robert C. Doty reported, "The waverers fell off, the loyalists took heart, and the generals were left with nothing in the end but about one company of Legionnaires. . . ."[116]

Before it even began, the putsch of the generals was doomed to failure. The plotters depended on the unity-of-the-army myth to rally their brothers-in-arms to the cause of keeping Algeria French, yet the myth of army unity had been shown to be a fiction in January, 1960. That the army did not follow Challe and his cohorts into rebellion should have come as a surprise only to the insurgent leaders who refused to recognize that the unity of the army could no longer be used as a weapon against the state. January, 1960, held another lesson which the perpetrators of the putsch failed to comprehend. The Fifth Republic

[114] See *Le Monde*, April 29, 1961; *New York Times*, April 28, 1961, p. 7:1; *New York Times*, April 29, 1961, p. 1:8.
[115] See *Le Monde*, June 9, 1961; June 11–12, 1961; June 15, 1961; June 22, 1961.
[116] Robert C. Doty, *New York Times*, April 27, 1961, p. 8:3.

had not bent to the will of the Week of the Barricades' arbiter, the army, because France had rallied to its government and accepted its Algerian policy. A further indication of the nation's solidarity and its acceptance of the government's course was provided by the referendum of January 8, 1961.

The principal reason for the failure of the April, 1961, insurrection (and January, 1960) was that most men of the French army refused to follow a course contrary to that of the government and the people of France. The government was not a weak, unpopular one, but enjoyed strong national support. It has been said that many officers wavered and hesitated in the first hours of the revolt. Their hesitancy ended when they discerned that the civilians of France were unsympathetic to the Algiers uprising.

A frequently noted aspect of the putsch was the attitude of the draftees (the *contingent*), and the fact that they failed to rally or even to obey their dissident officers has been frequently commented on. Henri Azeau observes that the true lesson of April, 1961, was the emergence of the *contingent* as a political force, and attributes to it the principal reason for the failure of the putsch.[117] However, the *contingent*'s behavior was a reflection of opinion back home. The *contingent*, drawn from all sectors of French life, is revealed not as a political force, but as a body of men who shared the ideas of the mainland. These men, in uniform for a relatively brief time, did not have the same loyalties as those who had made a career of the army; nor had they taken the oaths, nor had they fought in the jungles of Indochina, nor had they been absent from France for the long periods their professional comrades-in-arms had. Their ties were with France, not with Algiers. Their reaction to the putsch was the natural one.

In December, 1960, two articles appeared in *Le Monde* which referred to the draftees in Algeria. One article described the *contingent*'s stabilizing role, and its knowledge that France would no longer accept a French Algeria; the other quoted a tract which had been distributed to draftee units, which told its readers that the *contingent* had a clear duty: to listen to the nation, and be the image of its will.[118] Walter Kerr plays down the actual role of the *contingent* in the putsch's failure, but feels that "its current belief that it did much must stand as a constant warning to the officer corps that another time *drafted men may*

[117] Azeau, *Révolte militaire*, pp. 180, 213.
[118] The tract was reprinted in *Le Monde*, December 2, 1960.

act as the civilian population at home would want them to act."[119] But most officers, not only reservists in the *contingent* units but the professionals as well, behaved as the civilian population desired. In commenting upon the April, 1961, putsch two scholars summarize the significant factors in its collapse as follows:

> Among the important reasons for this failure were lack of cohesion on the part of the insurgent generals, opposition within the armed forces and particularly on the part of the conscriptees, and above all the determination of General de Gaulle, supported by public opinion, to resist.[120]

General Olié declared that the revolt collapsed because of the army's loyalty, sense of honor, and spirit of discipline. These were manifested, he maintained, in the ranks of the superior officers, among the professional troops and the draftees. They did their duty, Olié averred, in doing what the nation expected of them.[121] The last phrase is the significant one: they did what the nation expected of them.

Maurice Duverger observed during the Putsch Trials that the accused repeatedly referred to honor, faith, and oaths taken. However, these were used in relation to collectivities other than the nation, especially to Algeria, to the Moslems, and to the army. Absent from the trials, wrote Duverger, was France. It was true that Algeria and the Moslems were important problems, wrote Duverger, but secondary after all to France itself.[122] The activists had lost sight and contact with France, and had attempted to interpret her interests themselves. The will of the people, as expressed on January 8, had no meaning for them. When the national interest as interpreted by the army became paramount to the national interest as interpreted by the government and accepted by the people, praetorianism was not far behind.

A significant effect of the putsch was to unite France behind De Gaulle. Men, both civilian and military, had to decide whether they would follow and accept the principles which motivated the rebellious generals or the General who presided at the Elysée Palace. It was an

---

[119] Kerr, "The French Army in Trouble," p. 94; (italics mine).

[120] Roy C. Macridis and Bernard E. Brown, *Supplement to the De Gaulle Republic* (Homewood, Illinois: The Dorsey Press, 1963), p. 21.

[121] *Le Monde*, April 28, 1961.

[122] See Maurice Duverger, "L'Armée et les procès," *Le Monde*, June 11–12, 1961.

hour of decision, for Frenchmen and therefore for France. The decision was made, and the Fifth Republic proved able to defend itself, unlike its predecessor when it had faced military revolt in Algeria. With a consolidated regime, the end of the Algerian war came that much closer.

From 1958 on, De Gaulle had striven to prove that he ruled France, that he made policy and not the army. He had denied the army's right to be an arbiter in 1960, and in April, 1961, came "the showdown between the president and president-makers." [123] De Gaulle won, and consequently the April putsch may be said to have been the consummation of the De Gaulle Republic's legitimacy, "the baptism, as it were, that washed away the original sin of its birth," as a writer for the *Economist* explained.[124] Although De Gaulle had been returned to power by the army, he refused to be the army's political servant; the army's role was to obey orders, not to give them, and this was finally made clear in the spring of 1961. The men of the army who were adamantly opposed to the government's self-determination policy, discovered the army no longer served as an effective political instrument, and they disappeared into the clandestine activities of the Secret Army Organization. By so doing, they acknowledged that the army was no longer a political power in France.

[123] "Fall of the Dinosaurs," *Economist*, CXCIX (April 29, 1961), 420.
[124] *Ibid.*, p. 419.

CHAPTER XI

Return to Silence?

Varus, redde legiones.—EMPEROR AUGUSTUS.

WITHIN THREE WEEKS of the April putsch's failure, French and Algerian provisional government representatives were engaged in talks at Evian-les-Bains. The conversations began on May 20, the same day France ordered a month's unilateral cease-fire to French forces in Algeria, and announced that six thousand Algerian prisoners would be released.[1] The Evian talks ended on June 13, with the representatives departing in disagreement concerning guarantees to be provided Europeans in a new Algeria, and, in particular, respecting the question of sovereignty over the Sahara. Despite the inconclusive results, two days after the conclusion of the Evian negotiations, France announced she would continue her suspension of offensive operations and her liberation of prisoners.

Speaking at Verdun on June 28, De Gaulle spoke of an "independent state" if that was what Algeria wanted, and he added, "We know the Algerians want independence."[2] Two days later, speaking at Epinal, he again referred to an independent Algeria: "All our effort, all our will, is directed toward substituting for the old relation between France and Algeria, some relation between two sovereign and independent countries, yet cooperating in all areas where cooperation is possible."[3]

De Gaulle announced on July 12 that the transfer of French military units back to the homeland would begin shortly, and he further let it be known that the conscripts' service commitment would be shortened

[1] *Le Monde*, May 21–22, 1961.
[2] *Le Monde*, June 30, 1961.
[3] *Le Monde*, July 1, 1961.

by several weeks (the length of service was then twenty-seven months and twenty-four days).[4] He then again referred to Algeria's new status and announced: "France accepts without reservation the fact that the Algerian populations could constitute a completely independent state."[5] France was ready, declared the President, to work toward that end with Algeria's political elements, particularly with the FLN, in the framework of self-determination.

France and the GPRA on July 17 jointly declared that meetings would again take place, to begin three days later at Lugrin, France. The talks lasted but eight days, the Saharan issue again bringing negotiations to a close. However, this obstacle soon came tumbling down as De Gaulle, in a press conference on September 5, commented, "The Sahara must be a part of Algeria." Sovereignty over the vast desert region would be exercised by the new nation, De Gaulle conceded. In return, Paris asked that France be given rights to oil and gas resources, resources France had been in the process of developing for some time.[6]

Over two thousand members of the military services, including eighty generals and admirals, heard De Gaulle speak at Strasbourg on November 11, 1961. Certain army elements had formed a limited conception of their own wishes, said De Gaulle, and limited conceptions of the country in which they fought. De Gaulle now repeated for the benefit of his military listeners that Algerians would have a sovereign state of their own if they so desired. Self-determination "was, it is, the solution decided by the Chief of State, adopted by the government, approved by parliament, ratified by the French people."[7]

Some in the army would like to have things as they desired, continued the President, instead of as they actually were, "but since the state and the nation have chosen their path, the path of the military is clearly outlined."[8] The army, the instrument of the state, had described

[4] *Le Monde*, July 14, 1961.

[5] *Ibid.*

[6] *Le Monde*, September 6, 1961. Two days later, the OAS made an attempt on De Gaulle's life; see *Le Monde*, September 10–11, 1961. One of the arrested following the assassination attempt was Raoul Girardet, author and professor at the Paris Institute of Political Studies. Girardet, the son of a French army officer, was considered an intellectual of the Far Right. He was arrested the night of September 8–9, and released October 1. See *Le Monde*, September 9, 1961; October 3, 1961; January 6, 1962.

[7] *Le Monde*, November 24, 1961.

[8] *Ibid.*

for it by its civilian chief the traditional concept that the army's obligation was to obey.

In the last days of December, it became known that French and Algerian representatives were engaged in secret negotiations. Meeting somewhere near the French-Swiss border, representatives of the two governments were attempting to settle their differences and agree to a cease-fire. Their efforts were successfully concluded on February 20, 1962, when France and Algeria, after almost eight years of fighting, agreed upon general peace terms.[9] The next step called for open conversations to fill in the details, and preparations were made for a conference which would finally bring an end to the Algerian war. Representatives of France and the GPRA met at Evian-les-Bains for this purpose from March 8 to March 18.

The day prior to the opening of the conference, Pierre Messmer arrived in Algiers for an unobtrusive and little-noticed trip. His mission was similar to that of Joxe who had visited Algeria a week earlier. Both had the task of explaining the latest developments concerning Algeria and the preparations for a cease-fire to the army, both apparently to inform the army and judge its reactions. Acting in the former capacity, Joxe had met with over one hundred officers at Reghaïä and revealed to them the main lines of the forthcoming military agreements with the FLN.[10] On previous occasions, De Gaulle had taken it upon himself to cross the Mediterranean to explain and listen to the army when important developments were in store for Algeria. It is perhaps indicative of a lessened concern with the army's political voice that this time the job was performed by seconds. It may be indicative too of a greater trust in the army.

With the close of the Evian conference, one hundred and thirty-two years of French control of Algeria came to an end.[11] A cease-fire was signed on March 18, which provided that French military strength in Algeria would progressively be reduced to eighty thousand men (from over five hundred thousand) within a twelve-month period following

[9] *New York Times*, December 30, 1961, p. 1:8; February 20, 1962, p. 1:8.

[10] *Le Monde*, March 3, 1962.

[11] Representing the French side at the conference were Louis Joxe and two of his aides, Robert Buron and Jean de Broglie, plus General de Camas and Colonel de Seguin-Pazzis, both military counselors of Joxe's Cabinet. For the GPRA, there were Belkacem Krem, the vice-president of the GPRA; Ben Tobbal, the GPRA Minister of State; Saad Dahlb, the GPRA Minister of Foreign Affairs; and Mohammed Yozid, the GPRA Minister of Information. *Le Monde*, March 8–9, 1962.

self-determination, with those remaining to be removed within another twenty-four months. A few concessions were granted by the GPRA: for example, the naval base at Mers-el-Kébir was leased to France for a period of fifteen years with provisions for renewal, and France was granted the use of a number of airbases and installations for five years.[12]

On the nonmilitary side, the agreement signed at Evian called for a self-determination referendum to be held in both France and Algeria. Furthermore, guarantees were provided for the Europeans of Algeria, an interim political regime was provided for, and joint exploration of the Sahara was agreed upon. Finally, broad amnesties were to be declared by both sides.[13] The day after the signatures were added to the text, the cease-fire went into effect. In the referendum held on April 8, 1962, the French voters gave their overwhelming support to the Evian accords as 90 percent voted "yes" to Algerian independence. The Algerians exercised their right of self-determination on July 1, 1962: of those voting a resounding 99.72 percent voted "yes" for independence.[14] Algeria and France had clearly chosen.

At a special meeting of the Council of Ministers on July 3, De Gaulle formally granted Algeria its independence:

By the self-determination poll of July 1, 1962, the Algerian people decided in favor of the independence of Algeria in cooperation with France. In consequence, the relations between France and Algeria being henceforth based on the conditions defined by the governmental declarations of March 19, 1962, the President of the French Republic declares that France solemnly recognizes the independence of Algeria.

Done in Paris, July 3, 1962
Charles de Gaulle[15]

[12] Among the installations retained by France were the nuclear testing sites at Reggane, Colomb-Bechar, and In-Ekker, *Le Monde*, March 3, 1962.

[13] The text of the agreement is in *Le Monde*, March 21, 1962; and Roy C. Macridis and Bernard E. Brown, *Supplement to the De Gaulle Republic* (Homewood, Illinois: The Dorsey Press, 1963), pp. 107–11.

[14] In Algiers, abstentions amounted to 8.12 percent of the eligible electorate. The percentage of "yes" votes in relation to the registered voters was 91.23 percent. *Le Monde*, July 4, 1962.

[15] *Le Monde*, July 4, 1962. See also "Text of the Declaration of General de Gaulle President of the French Republic Proclaiming Algerian Independence," *French Affairs*, No. 140, July 3, 1962, Ambassade de France, Service de presse et d'information.

The French army, which had so long considered Algeria one of its havens, where it had played such a responsible and important role, was now not even responsible for the maintenance of order. Following the referendum, units of the French army were found at only four hundred locations in Algeria; previously they had occupied over four thousand. After the proclamation of independence, the army had neither territorial responsibility nor responsibility for keeping order, although the army could be called upon by Algerian prefects to help maintain order if they first contacted the French representatives to the new government. In an emergency, the French army could be directly summoned by Algerian authorities. But most of the time, the army, in its remaining camps and forts, dedicated itself to drill and instruction.

The negotiations on the way to peace which have been briefly summarized here, were accompanied by a campaign of terror—plastic bombs of the OAS and assassinations executed by OAS agents. Discovering that the army could no longer be used to change government policy, the activists deserted and took to the underground. Propelled by their faithfulness to Algeria instead of to France, by commitment to their own doctrines instead of to those of the nation, these men descended to secret, terrorist warfare, and earned for themselves the title of "*les soldats perdus*," the lost soldiers.[16]

But it is with the Regular army, not a secret army, that we are concerned. Hence, let us return to those men who chose discipline. Many did so in anger, despair, or sadness. Yet they chose discipline. Confronted with the government's self-determination policy, some officers concluded they could not remain in uniform and live at peace with themselves. They resigned from the army, taking the honorable course of the military man who finds he no longer can obey. Between January, 1960, and November, 1961, over thirteen hundred French officers left the army voluntarily.[17]

Among those who retired were several general officers who requested release before reaching the age limit of their grade. General Olié, for example, who had replaced Ely as Chief of the General Staff of National Defense in February, 1961, asked for two months' leave for health reasons in September. It was widely known that disagreement with De

[16] De Gaulle gave them this title at his November 23, 1961, speech at Strasbourg: "Outside of its rules there can be, there are, only the lost soldiers." *Le Monde*, November 24, 1961.

[17] Revealed at *Le Procès d'Edmond Jouhaud* (Paris: Editions Albin Michel, 1962), p. 323.

Gaulle over military policy, not health, prompted his resignation which came the following month.[18]

The same month that Olié asked for his two months' leave, General André Beaufre, French representative to the NATO permanent military group in Washington, D.C., submitted his retirement papers. Generals such as Olié and Beaufre had come to the conclusion they no longer could serve a government with which they so greatly disagreed. Not only Algerian policy, but policy concerning NATO and the plans for a nuclear strike force led these men to leave the service. In addition, the atmosphere which reigned in the army following the April putsch, and then the Putsch Trials, created an environment many found unbearable.[19]

At least one officer found the burden of abandonment too great to bear. On February 2, 1963, General Joseph Loiret disappeared. He had been loyal to the government, and, in fact, had received threats on his life from the OAS. His body was found April 12 in the Garonne River, but there was no trace of wounds on his body, and no indication that he had been murdered. *Le Monde* did not say whether Loiret's life had been taken forcibly or whether he had committed suicide, but he had been known to be depressed. The General had a special interest in the *harkis* (Moslems who had served with French forces in Algeria) and they had been the victims of reprisals after independence. Readers were left with the impression that Loiret had taken his own life out of despair for his deserted *harkis*.[20]

The unsuccessful April putsch initiated a purge in the French army which removed its most politically conscious elements, a purge which was both government implemented and self-imposed. Those most intoxicated by psychological warfare doctrines and by the desire to play a political role, went into jail, into hiding, or into retirement.

In 1961 and 1962, calls for discipline and obedience to civil authority were made by officers who remained on active duty. General Charles Ailleret, who assumed military command of Algeria on June 7, 1961, and who held the post until April 18, 1962, declared in a June, 1961, order of the day that he would serve in the most absolute discipline. Then addressing himself to both the draftees and the professionals under his orders, Ailleret reminded them they were in the same army.

[18] See *Le Monde*, September 9, 1961; October 27, 1961.

[19] *Le Monde*, September 9, 1961. General de Pouilly, who had been made prisoner by the rebels in April, 1961, resigned in August, 1961, *Le Monde*, August 26, 1961.

[20] *Le Monde*, April 13, 1963.

"Your duty is identical," he said, "devotion to the nation in strict obedience of the laws, outside of which there is only incoherence, division, and adventure."[21]

The fact that the unity of the army could not be used in an insurrection to bring the army to follow a minority of their number was recognized by the dissidents after April, 1961. In September of that year a remarkable secret letter was received by officers in Algeria which granted that not all of them would join in another "popular explosion." For those who would choose not to join, the letter asked that they concern themselves with fighting the FLN and keep free of the dispute between Paris and Algiers. "To assure the security of the country and of the two communities, *without involving yourselves in political life*, such will be the line of conduct which will be asked of you," announced the letter. The officers were asked either to join in a new movement when it came, or to neutralize themselves. The appeal was now to the traditional attitude of apoliticism rather than unity. At the same time, as Jean Planchais pointed out, it asked them to stand aside and give a free hand to those who would attempt an insurrection.[22]

In 1958 the words of the psychological action advocates had dominated military writing and speaking in France. In 1961 and 1962, the familiar words became obedience, law, and loyalty, replacing the politically loaded implications of the "Lacheroys." Ailleret's 1961 Christmas Day message to his troops described them as being the true image of France, in the exclusive service of the nation. Referring to his command, he stated: "They will, I am sure of it, conclude their work in the spirit of strict discipline *vis a vis* the state."[23] It was clear that the army was to be at the service of the state, and not above it as a frequently unsolicited counsel and/or veto power.

The traditional soldier spoke through General Coste at the Barricades Trials in January, 1961. While giving testimony, General Coste remarked, "Certain statements here demonstrated an extraordinary deviation from the traditional conception of the army. They have furnished proof that an order is no longer an order, but a basis for discussion."[24] That such a situation should no longer exist was made clear to an audience of young air force officers who listened to General

21 *Le Monde*, June 22, 1961.
22 *Le Monde*, September 16, 1961; (italics mine).
23 *Le Monde*, December 27, 1961.
24 *Le Monde*, January 18, 1961.

Leroy, director of air force teaching, point out at the air base at Creil in December, 1961: "Your profession subordinates you directly to the state, whose form has been chosen by the men of this community."[25] No room here for equivocation; room only for obedience.

On the day he issued the cease-fire order for Algeria, Ailleret told his men: "Today as yesterday, in peace as in combat, the French army remains true to the tradition of duty."[26] After over twenty years of firing, French guns were silent. What was in store for tomorrow's French army? De Gaulle had given the answer in 1959. Speaking at the Ecole militaire on November 3 of that year, De Gaulle had told his student listeners what the future army would be like. France would have its own nuclear strike force (*force de frappe*),[27] and the new French army would be a modern army. In his 1962 New Year's message, De Gaulle foretold that the coming year would witness the modernization of the greater part of the army,[28] and added on February 5 that "before the end of next year we will possess the first operational element of a French atomic force."[29]

In 1962, the French armed forces began their transformation into three types of defense units: a strategic nuclear defense force of bombers and missiles; intervention forces (staffed by men from the navy, air force, and army), armed with conventional and nuclear weapons and designed for emergency assignments outside France; and interior defense forces stationed in France and capable of being rapidly expanded by national mobilization, whose duty was the protection of France itself. The strategic bombers and later missiles, the intervention forces, able to move swiftly and massively to the support of the new African Republics which might ask for help, and the interior defense forces, with the mission of defending the homeland against subversive war or direct enemy attack, were to prepare France for any type of conflict at any point, using both conventional and nuclear weapons.[30]

25 *Le Monde*, December 22, 1961.
26 *Le Monde*, March 20, 1962.
27 *Le Monde*, November 6, 1959.
28 *Le Monde*, December 31, 1961–January 1, 1962.
29 *Le Monde*, February 7, 1962.
30 See *Le Monde*, January 21–22, 1962; Pierre Messmer, "The French Military Establishment of Tomorrow," *Orbis*, VI (Summer, 1962), 205–16; "Aperçu général sur les armées," Service d'Information, d'Etudes et de Cinématographie des Armées, Cabinet du ministre, Ministère des armées, October, 1962; *France and its Armed Forces*, Ambassade de France, Service de presse et d'information, December, 1964.

Look ahead and not the past, the army was told. In the past lie the memories of World War II, Indochina, Morocco, Tunisia, and Algeria. General L. J. de Puloch relates:

> It has been necessary to lift the sights of our young officers beyond the field of battle of a psychological war toward other disciplines, such as social and technical sciences. The results have been more than we hoped. These warriors of the jungles who dreamed of nothing but swamps and forests . . . threw themselves with the same ardor and the same intelligence into this new field of activity.[31]

A once-more strong France is the promise of the future, where there will be a France capable of defending herself with her own new and modern weapons. By devoting itself to that day, to military renovation and reorganization, the army may be less prone to nonmilitary activities. Demonstrating the connection between a nation and the army which it serves, that an army is the emanation of the nation, De la Gorce writes:

> By embarking on the path of modernization and seeking to bring about a revolution in military concepts, the young officers would be modeling themselves on a society filled with enthusiasm for techniques and productivity, turned away from values and abstract ideas, and contemptuous of the past, but looking forward to the future as an era of wealth, security, statistics and well-being. These officers would be at one with their age.[32]

The French army is being given a new job to do, and its perspectives are oriented toward a proud future instead of a humiliating past. With its new commitments, the army, as De la Gorce perceives, may well be drawn closer to the temper and values of the France from which it had become separated.

Frenchmen are much concerned with bringing the army into the nation, of making it a truly French army once more, for they have experienced the consequences of an alienated army. They desire to end the army's alienation and integrate their "lost soldiers." A program of information and education is called for to bring to France and her army an air of reciprocal understanding. The job is one for the schools, the

[31] General L. J. de Puloch, "Future of the French Army," *Military Review*, XLIV (November, 1964), 47.

[32] Paul-Marie de la Gorce, *The French Army* (New York: George Braziller, 1963), p. 552.

universities, and particularly the military academies, traditionally islands in the midst of a surrounding civilian sea, instilling their own values, creating their own men for their own world. A wall of mistrust and misunderstanding has separated the civilian and military branches of the French family, a wall which will have to be removed.[33]

A taste of political life in May, 1958, gave the army a predilection for it. But even though De Gaulle assumed power through the army, he had no intention of being forever grateful to it and carrying out its wishes. If army and Gaullist policy differed, the army would have to give way. To convince the army of this arrangement was no overnight process, and the curtailing of the army's political power, which it so relished in 1958 and 1959, was a delicate operation which necessitated feints and parries.

The army had guillotined the Fourth Republic, but it hesitated to remove what was in large part its own creation—the De Gaulle regime, even when it learned the regime was not going to be true to the ideals of May 13. But when elements of the army discovered they had no other recourse, they again faced Paris in open rebellion in the spring of 1961. The defeat of their attempt, the April putsch, was the defeat of the French political army. Until then, De Gaulle had been constricted by the limits imposed by army sentiment concerning Algerian policy. It took four years to bring peace to Algeria, years during which De Gaulle consolidated his power and broke the army's, years during which he demonstrated that Paris, not Algiers, governed France.

May, 1958, signalled the baptism of the political army (it had been born earlier); April, 1961, sent it into retirement, although perhaps not yet its grave.[34] In the meantime, De Gaulle had to consider that behind him was always the threat of an army veto on his policies. De Gaulle was not a free agent, as Professor Meisel puts it, and to those who ask why it took him so long to bring peace to Algeria, Meisel answers:

> They forgot the army mortgage on his property, when he recovered it in 1958. The creditor could not be paid off all at once; he would take small installments only. . . . The creditor was very nervous, he

---

[33] See Jean Planchais, *Le Monde*, March 2, 1962; and *Le Monde*, July 28, 1962; also a letter from an unidentified French officer to *Le Monde*, May 5, 1961; see the comments of General Jean Valluy on the necessity of broader education and contacts for military officers, *Le Monde*, January 31, 1962; and *Le Monde*, February 23, 1962; see Messmer, "The French Military Establishment," p. 216.

[34] See Edgar S. Furniss, Jr., *De Gaulle and the French Army* (New York: The Twentieth Century Fund, 1964), esp. Part II.

was loath to part with his control—twice he refused; one time by proxy, openly the second time.[35]

The revolutions of May, 1958, January, 1960, and April, 1961, denote the evolution of France from the chaotic government situation of May, 1958, and decisive military intervention, to stable government in 1961 and the ineffectiveness of army machinations. The army's political actions between the revolts demonstrate the declining political strength of the army as that of civilian authorities increased. Army political activity was at its height in the summer of 1958 when De Gaulle had just taken power, but as his authority increased, the army's began to diminish. According to Professor Finer:

> *Treize Mai* demonstrated that the army could intimidate a government into resigning—provided the army had powerful civilian support. But it received such support only by adopting as its candidate one who was a masterful public figure in his own right, and a politician to boot. April 22 demonstrated, *per contra*, that by defying this figure it brought against itself the full weight of civilian resistance, and that in the face of this it was powerless.[36]

The French army, for the present, has returned to silence. It has, willingly on the part of some officers, resignedly on the part of others, again accepted the concept of the instrumental, obedient state servant. Will it remain so, particularly after Charles de Gaulle passes from the scene? There are many factors which lead to a sanguine view of the prospects for civilian control in France. In the first place, the officers who were the most politically involved, the minority we have referred to as the "activists," are generally gone from the ranks of the army.

As Jean Planchais warns us, "it is necessary not to confuse those who betray . . . [the country] and those who serve it."[37] Gone are the betrayers; those that remain in the army are the officers who chose loyalty, who chose obedience, who believed in the army's traditional role. To these men France offers the task of creating a modern armed force, and in the new military functions to be instituted and learned, recent prejudices, ideas, and sorrows may be forgotten.

In 1958, Maurice Duverger wrote that the danger of military dic-

[35] James H. Meisel, *The Fall of the Republic* (Ann Arbor: The University of Michigan Press, 1962), p. 263.

[36] Samuel E. Finer, *The Man on Horseback* (New York: Frederick A. Praeger, 1962), p. 96.

[37] *Le Monde*, March 2, 1962.

tatorship for France was a short-term danger which would not survive "the exceptional circumstances which have generated it."[38] Chief among these circumstances was the Algerian war, which was seen by some as a barrier to the resumption of civilian control as long as it lasted.[39] However, De Gaulle brought the army to obedience *before* the war ended. How else could he ever have ended it?

With the close of the Algerian war, military men could reflect and recognize the fact that it was to France that they owed their allegiance, that it was to France that they took their first oaths, that it was to France that they belonged. The Algerian war was part of a painful past and so were the fifth bureaus, which disappeared even before peace appeared.

The failure of psychological war doctrines was demonstrated in Algeria. Not content with that failure, the practitioners of psychological action attempted through the OAS to "intoxicate" France. Again they failed. The neo-Fascists and National Communists who preached the techniques of psychological warfare, who were further influenced by preachings of men like Georges Sauge, discovered that France preferred the De Gaulle Republic to the authoritarian implications of their schemes and actions.

The Algerian war has become a memory and joined Indochina and Vichy in history. Officers now serve in the French army who never experienced the 1940 crisis of conscience engendered by the renegade General in London, who never fought in the jungles of Indochina, who never experienced the spell of Algeria. With each passing year, their number increases, while the roll of men who held most firmly to these memories and the fear of abandoning Algeria decreases. As has been pointed out elsewhere, even in the April, 1961, putsch the rebellious generals did not take into consideration that "the youngest officers, even on active duty, are no longer centurions."[40] Already the military schools were producing officers who could see "a little further than the end of their *djebels*" (mountains in Algeria).[41]

The "exceptional circumstances" through which the army passed caused it to lose contact with France. With the conclusion of the

[38] *Le Monde*, September 2, 1958.

[39] See Phillip Williams and Martin Harrison, *De Gaulle's Republic* (New York: Longmans, Green, and Co., 1961), pp. 211–12; Roy C. Macridis and Bernard E. Brown, *The De Gaulle Republic* (Homewood, Illinois: The Dorsey Press, 1960), p. 332.

[40] Jacques Fauvet and Jean Planchais, *La Fronde des généraux* (Paris: Arthaud, 1961), p. 64.

[41] *Ibid.*

colonial wars, France and its army, for the first time in years, have a chance to come together and become one again. The air force Chief of Staff, General Paul Stehlin, in December, 1962, wrote to the men of the air force:

> The operations of Algeria are ended, in our country the menaces of division have been avoided, calm has come to minds, hope reborn in hearts, friendship and mutual respect again assure our unity. . . .
> For the first time in twenty-four years, a year is going to begin without our armed forces finding themselves engaged, somewhere, in combat.[42]

In the final analysis, the continuance of civilian control will depend upon the civilian leaders of France. If they are able to provide their country with a viable government they will continue to be the army's masters. If they cannot, then the army will be in a position to influence again the course of French political life. An army, whatever its tasks, whatever its ethos, is still the most powerful organization in a state and in the most advantageous position to take the situation in hand when civilians have lost control. France has a long tradition of civilian control of the military, but it will be up to the civilians to determine whether the army's intervention into French political life was a brief hiatus in that tradition, or whether it set a precedent.

[42] *Le Monde*, December 25, 1962.

Appendix

Trials and Sentences of Participants in the April Putsch and the Paris Plot

Sentences of leading participants in the April putsch and the Paris plot:

	Sentence	*Date*
General Salan	Death *in absentia*	July 11, 1961
	Life imprisonment	May 23, 1962
General Jouhaud	Death *in absentia*	July 11, 1961
	Death	April 13, 1962
	(commuted, November, 1962, to life imprisonment)	
General Challe	15 years	June 1, 1961
General Zeller	15 years	June 1, 1961
General Gardy	Death *in absentia*	July 11, 1961
General Bigot	15 years	June 6, 1961
General Petit	15 years	June 7, 1961
General Nicot	12 years	June 19, 1961
General Gouraud	7 years	June 20, 1961
General Faure	10 years	September 21, 1961
Colonel Vaudrey [1]	10 years	September 21, 1961
Colonel Roca	acquitted	August 2, 1961
Colonel Ceccaldi	5 years, suspended	July 5, 1961
Major de Saint-Marc	10 years	June 5, 1961
Major Forhan	5 years	July 12, 1961
Major Camelin	3 years, suspended	July 20, 1961
Lieutenant Durand-Ruel	2 years	July 8, 1961
Colonel Argoud	Death *in absentia*	July 11, 1961
Colonel Broizat	Death *in absentia*	July 11, 1961
Colonel Gardes	Death *in absentia*	July 11, 1961
Colonel Godard	Death *in absentia*	July 11, 1961
Colonel Lacheroy	Death *in absentia*	July 11, 1961

[1] Colonel Vaudrey escaped on September 25, 1961, and became a leader in the OAS. He died in Brussels, Belgium, on January 15, 1965.

As of February, 1963, the whereabouts of these five colonels were reported as:[2]

Broizat: unknown

Gardes: in Madrid

Godard: perhaps in Switzerland

Lacheroy: in the Balearic Islands

Argoud: captured February 26, 1963. The circumstances of his capture are clouded in intrigue. A telephone call to Paris police headquarters announced that Argoud was outside in a truck. The caller informed the police that Argoud had "betrayed us" in failing in his duties, particularly in the unsuccessful attempts to assassinate De Gaulle. The conclusion was that the OAS was surrendering one of its chiefs. The police found him as indicated, bound and beaten.

Argoud had been taken in Germany, and investigation by the police there has led to speculation that he had been the victim of special agents of the French government known as the *barbouzes*, or bearded ones. Such rumors circulated in Paris shortly after his capture. At one investigation Argoud expressed his satisfaction "to be in the hands of the official police." Argoud was sentenced to life imprisonment on December 30, 1963.[3]

SUMMARY of the trials that extended from May 29, 1961, to February 2, 1962, known as the trial of the Putsch of Algiers and the Paris plot.

Grade	Acquitted	0–4 yrs.	5–9 yrs.	10–15 yrs.	suspended sentence	death in ab.	total
General	0	0	2	5	1	3	11
Colonel	6	0	3	1	7	5	22
Major	8	0	2	1	9	1	21
Captain	10	1	1	0	21	1	34
Lieutenant[4]	5	0	0	0	7	0	12
Sergeant	0	0	0	0	1	0	1
Total	29	1	8	7	46	10	101
Civilians	12	6	2	1	8	0	29
Total	41	7	10	8	54	10	130

[2] *Le Monde*, February 28, 1963.

[3] *Le Monde*, February 28, 1963; *New York Times*, February 27, 1963, p. 1:2; March 1, 1963, p. 2:7–8; March 2, 1963, p. 2:8; March 6, 1963, p. 2:7; March 13, 1963, p. 3:1; December 31, 1963, p. 3:3.

[4] One of these lieutenants was Guillaume, the only navy man tried. He was given a four-year suspended sentence.

In December, 1963, De Gaulle began pardoning and reducing the sentences of the imprisoned, including those convicted for OAS activity, with the number so favored increased each Christmas, Easter, and Bastille Day. As of December, 1966, fewer than 70 of the 1,769 civilians and military men who were found guilty of crimes against the security of the state arising out of the Algerian situation and incarcerated were still in prison, including Salan, Jouhaud, and Argoud. Among those pardoned were ex-Generals Zeller and Challe (freed in 1966 on the eve of Bastille Day and Christmas Eve respectively), Bigot, Petit, Nicot, and Gouraud, and ex-Majors de Saint-Marc and Forhan.[5]

[5] *Keesings Contemporary Archives*, September 11–18, 1965, pp. 20955–62; *Le Monde Weekly*, July 7–13, 1966; *New York Times*, July 14, 1966, p. 12:4; December 24, 1966, p. 4:3.

Select Bibliography

BOOKS

ALBORD, TONY, *et al. La Défense nationale*. Paris: Presses Universitaires de France, 1958.

ALLEG, HENRI. *The Question*. New York: George Braziller, 1958. Reprinted by Belmont Books.

ALQUIER, JEAN-YVES. *Nous avons pacifié Tazalt*. Paris: Robert Laffont, 1957.

———, *et al. Ceux d'Algérie*. Paris: Plon, 1957.

AMBLER, JOHN S. *The French Army in Politics*. Columbus: Ohio State University Press, 1966.

ANDREWS, WILLIAM G. *French Politics and Algeria*. New York: Appleton-Century-Crofts, 1962.

ANDRZEJEWSKI, STANISLAW. *Military Organization and Society*. London: Routledge and Kegan Paul, 1954.

ARGOUD, COLONEL ANTOINE. *Sans commentaire*. Paris: Editions de Minuit, 1961.

ARON, RAYMOND. *France, Steadfast and Changing*. Cambridge: Harvard University Press, 1960.

———. *France: The New Republic*. New York: Oceana Publications, 1960.

AZEAU, HENRI. *Révolte militaire*. Paris: Plon, 1961.

BARBEROT, ROGER. *Malaventure en Algérie avec le général Paris de Bollardière*. Paris: Plon, 1957.

BEHR, EDWARD. *The Algerian Problem*. New York: W. W. Norton, 1962.

BLOND, GEORGES. *La Légion étrangère*. Ottawa: Le Cercle du Livre de France, 1965.

BONNET, COLONEL GABRIEL. *Les guerres insurrectionnelles et révolutionnaires*. Paris: Payot, 1958.

BOUDOT, PIERRE. *L'Algérie mal enchaînée*. Paris: Gallimard, 1961.

239

BRACE, RICHARD, AND JOAN BRACE. *Ordeal in Algeria*. New York: D. Van Nostrand Company, 1960.

BROMBERGER, MERRY AND SERGE; GEORGETTE ELGEY; and J-F. CHAUVEL. *Barricades et colonels*. Paris: Arthème Fayard, 1960.

BROMBERGER, MERRY AND SERGE. *Les 13 complots du 13 mai*. Paris: Arthème Fayard, 1959.

CARRIAS, EUGENE. *La Pensée militaire française*. Paris: Presses Universitaires de France, 1960.

CHALLENER, RICHARD D. *The French Theory of the Nation in Arms 1866–1939*. New York: Columbia University Press, 1955.

CHALMIN, PIERRE. *L'Officier français de 1815 à 1870*. Paris: Marcel Rivière et Cie., 1957.

CHANDESSAIS, CHARLES. *La Psychologie dans l'armée*. Paris: Presses Universitaires de France, 1959.

CHAPMAN, GUY. *The Dreyfus Case*. New York: Reynal and Co., 1955.

CHEVALLIER, J-J. *Histoire des institutions politiques de la France de 1789 à nos jours*. Paris: Dalloz, 1952.

CHORLEY, KATHERINE. *Armies and the Art of Revolution*. London: Faber and Faber, 1943.

CLARK, MICHAEL K. *Algeria in Turmoil*. New York: Frederick A. Praeger, 1959.

COLES, HARRY L., ED. *Total War and Cold War*. Columbus: Ohio State University Press, 1962.

Colloque de Vincennes sur l'Algérie française. Paris: Comité de Vincennes, 1960.

CONGAR, R. P. Y., AND JOSEPH FOLLIET. *Armée et vie nationale*. Lyons: Chronique sociale de France, 1962.

DARBOISE, JEAN-MICHEL, *et al. Officiers en Algérie*. Paris: François Maspero, 1960.

DELMAS, CLAUDE. *La guerre révolutionnaire*. Paris: Presses Universitaires de France, 1959.

DÉON, MICHEL. *L'Armée d'Algérie et la pacification*. Paris: Plon, 1959.

DUFRESNOY, CLAUDE. *Des officiers parlent*. Paris: Julliard, 1961.

DUSQUESNE, JACQUES. *L'Algérie ou la guerre des mythes*. Paris: Desclée de Brouwer, 1958.

DUVERGER, MAURICE. *La Cinquième République*. Paris: Presses Universitaires de France, 1960.

———. *The French Political System*. Chicago: University of Chicago Press, 1958.

EARLE, EDWARD MEAD, ED. *Modern France: Problems of the Third and Fourth Republics*. Princeton: Princeton University Press, 1951.

ELGEY, GEORGETTE. *La République des illusions, 1945–1951*. Paris: Arthème Fayard, 1965.

ELY, GENERAL PAUL. *L'Armée dans la nation.* Paris: Arthème Fayard, 1961.

EULOGE, ANDRÉ, AND ANTOINE MOULINIER. *L'Envers des barricades.* Paris: Plon, 1960.

FAUCHER, JEAN-ANDRÉ. *Les Barricades d'Alger.* Paris: Editions Atlantic, 1960.

FAUVET, JACQUES, AND JEAN PLANCHAIS. *La Fronde des généraux.* Paris: Arthaud, 1961.

FELD, M. D. "A Typology of Military Organization," in Carl J. Friedrich and Seymour E. Harris, eds. *Public Policy*, Vol. VIII. Cambridge: Graduate School of Public Administration, 1958.

FINER, SAMUEL E. *The Man on Horseback.* New York: Frederick A. Praeger, 1962.

FREEMANTLE, ANNE, ED. *Mao Tse-tung: An Anthology of His Writings.* New York: The New American Library, 1962.

FURNISS, EDGAR S., JR. *France: Troubled Ally.* New York: Harper and Brothers, 1960.

———. *De Gaulle and the French Army.* New York: The Twentieth Century Fund, 1964.

GAULLE, CHARLES DE. *The Edge of the Sword.* New York: Criterion Books, 1960.

———. *The Call to Honour.* New York: The Viking Press, 1955.

———. *Vers l'armée de métier.* Paris: Editions Berger-Levrault, 1934.

GERIN, PAUL. *L'Algérie du 13 mai.* Paris: Gallimard, 1958.

GILLESPIE, JOAN. *Algeria: Rebellion and Revolution.* New York: Frederick A. Praeger, 1960.

GIRARDET, RAOUL. *La Société militaire dans la France contemporaine, 1815–1939.* Paris: Plon, 1953.

——— et al. *La Crise militaire française, 1945–1962.* Paris: Armand Colin, 1964.

GOGUEL, FRANÇOIS. *France Under the Fourth Republic.* Ithaca: Cornell University Press, 1952.

GORCE, PAUL-MARIE DE LA. *The French Army: A Military-Political History.* New York: George Braziller, 1963.

HATCH, ALDEN. *The De Gaulle Nobody Knows.* New York: Hawthorn Books, 1960.

HAURIOU, MAURICE. *Principes de droit public.* Paris: Recueil Sirey, 1910.

HERZOG, WILHELM. *From Dreyfus to Pétain.* New York: Creative Age Press, 1947.

HOFFMAN, STANLEY, et al. *In Search of France.* Cambridge: Harvard University Press, 1963.

HOWARD, MICHAEL, ED. *Soldiers and Governments.* London: Eyre and Spottiswoode, 1957.

HUNTINGTON, SAMUEL P., ED. *Changing Patterns of Military Politics.* New York: The Free Press of Glencoe, 1962.

———. *The Soldier and the State.* Cambridge: The Belknap Press, 1957.

———. "Civilian Control of the Military: A Theoretical Statement," in Heinz Eulau, Samuel J. Eldersveld, and Morris Janowitz, eds. *Political Behavior: A Reader in Theory and Research.* Glencoe: The Free Press, 1956.

JANOWITZ, MORRIS. *Sociology and the Military Establishment.* New York: Russell Sage Foundation, 1959.

———. *The Professional Soldier.* Glencoe: The Free Press, 1960.

KELLY, GEORGE A. *Lost Soldiers: The French Army and Empire in Crisis, 1947–1962.* Cambridge: The M.I.T. Press, 1965.

KING, JERE CLEMENS. *Generals and Politicians.* Berkeley and Los Angeles: University of California Press, 1951.

———. *Foch versus Clemenceau.* Cambridge: Harvard University Press, 1960.

KRAFT, JOSEPH. *The Struggle for Algeria.* Garden City: Doubleday and Co., 1961.

KUNTZ, FRANÇOIS. *L'officier français dans la nation.* Paris: Charles-Lavauzelle et Cie., 1960.

LAGAILLARDE, PIERRE. *On a triché avec l'honneur.* Texte intégral de l'interrogatoire et de la plaidoirie des audiences du 15 et 16 novembre, 1960. Paris: La Table Ronde, 1960.

LARTÉGUY, JEAN. *Les Prétoriens.* Paris: Les presses de la Cité, 1961.

———. *The Centurions.* New York: E. P. Dutton and Co., 1962.

LATOUR, PIERRE BOYER DE. *Le martyre de l'armée française.* Paris: Les presses du Mail, 1961.

LENTIN, ALBERT-PAUL. *L'Algérie des colonels.* Paris: Petite bibliothèque républicaine, 1958.

LERNER, DANIEL, AND RAYMOND ARON, EDS. *France Defeats EDC.* New York: Frederick A. Praeger, 1957.

LEULLIETTE, PIERRE. *St. Michael and the Dragon.* Boston: Houghton Mifflin Co., 1964.

LUETHY, HERBERT. *France Against Herself.* New York: Meridian Books, 1958.

MACRIDIS, ROY C., AND BERNARD E. BROWN. *The De Gaulle Republic.* Homewood, Illinois: The Dorsey Press, 1960.

———. *Supplement to the De Gaulle Republic.* Homewood, Illinois: The Dorsey Press, 1963.

MAURIENNE [PSEUD.]. *Le Déserteur.* Paris: Editions de Minuit, 1960.

MÉGRET, MAURICE. *L'action psychologique.* Paris: Arthème Fayard, 1959.

MEISEL, JAMES H. *The Fall of the Republic*. Ann Arbor: The University of Michigan Press, 1962.

MONTEILHET, JOSEPH. *Les institutions militaires de la France (1814–1932)*. Paris: Felix Alcan, 1932.

MUS, PAUL. *Guerre sans visage*. Paris: Editions du Seuil, 1961.

NAVARRE, GENERAL HENRI. *L'Agonie de l'Indochine*. Paris: Plon, 1957.

PAILLAT, CLAUDE. *Dossier secret de l'Algérie*. Paris: Le Livre Contemporain, 1961.

———. *Deuxième dossier secret de l'Algérie*. Paris: Les presses de la Cité, 1962.

PARET, PETER. *French Revolutionary Warfare from Indochina to Algeria: The Analysis of a Political and Military Doctrine*. New York: Frederick A. Praeger, 1964.

PERRAULT, GILES. *Les parachutistes*. Paris: Editions du Seuil, 1961.

PICKLES, DOROTHY. *The Fifth French Republic*. New York: Frederick A. Praeger, 1960.

PLANCHAIS, JEAN. *Le Malaise de l'armée*. Paris: Plon, 1958.

———. *L'Armée*. Paris: Buchet Chastel, 1959.

Le Procès des généraux Challe et Zeller: texte intégral des débats. Paris: Nouvelles Editions Latines, 1961.

Le Procès d'Edmond Jouhaud: compte rendu sténographique. Paris: Editions Albin Michel, 1962.

Les Procès du putsch d'Alger et du complot de Paris. Edited by Maurice Cottaz. Paris: Nouvelles Editions Latines, 1962.

Le Procès de Raoul Salan: compte rendu sténographique. Paris: Editions Albin Michel, 1962.

RAISSAC, GUY. *Un soldat dans la tourmente*. Paris: Editions Albin Michel, 1963.

RÉMOND, RENÉ, *et al. L'Armée et la nation*. Paris: Arthème Fayard, 1960.

RIBEAUD, PAUL. *Barricades pour un drapeau*. Paris: La Table Ronde, 1960.

ROY, JULES. *The War in Algeria*. New York: Grove Press, 1960.

SCHOENBRUN, DAVID. *The Three Lives of Charles de Gaulle*. New York: Atheneum, 1966.

SÉRIGNY, ALAIN DE. *La Révolution du 13 mai*. Paris: Plon, 1958.

———, ED. *Un Procès*. Interrogatoires, depositions, réquisitoires, plaidoiries, extraits de la sténographie et pièces authentiques du procès des "Barricades." Paris: La Table Ronde, 1961.

SERVAN-SCHREIBER, JEAN-JACQUES. *Lieutenant in Algeria*. New York: Alfred A. Knopf, 1957.

SIMON, PIERRE-HENRI. *Portrait d'un officier*. Paris: Editions du Seuil, 1958.

STERN, FREDERICK MARTIN. *The Citizen Army.* New York: St. Martin's Press, 1957.

SULZBERGER, CYRUS LEO. *The Test: De Gaulle and Algeria.* New York: Harcourt, Brace, and World, 1962.

TERRENOIRE, LOUIS. *De Gaulle et l'Algérie.* Paris: Arthème Fayard, 1964.

THOMSON, DAVID. *Democracy in France.* 3rd ed. New York: Oxford University Press, 1958.

TOURNOUX, JEAN-RAYMOND. *Secrets d'état.* Paris: Plon, 1960.

TRINQUIER, ROGER. *La guerre moderne.* Paris: La Table Ronde, 1961.

———. *Le Coup d'état du 13 mai.* Paris: Editions l'Esprit Nouveau, 1962.

TROQUER, ANDRÉ LE. *La parole est à André Le Troquer.* Paris: La Table Ronde, 1962.

TURNER, GORDON B., ED. *A History of Military Affairs Since the Eighteenth Century.* New York: Harcourt, Brace, and Co., 1956.

VAGTS, ALFRED. *A History of Militarism.* New York: W. W. Norton, 1937.

Valeurs fondamentales du patriotisme française, Les. Paris: Georges Lang, 1962.

VIDAL-NAQUET, PIERRE. *Torture: Cancer of Democracy.* Baltimore: Penguin Books, 1963.

WAHL, NICOLAS. *The Fifth Republic.* New York: Random House, 1959.

WERTH, ALEXANDER. *France, 1940–1955.* New York: Henry Holt and Co., 1956.

———. *The De Gaulle Revolution.* London: Robert Hale, 1960.

WILLIAMS, PHILLIP. *Politics in Post-War France,* 2nd ed. New York: Longmans, Green, and Co., 1958.

———, AND MARTIN HARRISON. *De Gaulle's Republic.* New York: Longmans, Green, and Co., 1961.

WRIGHT, GORDON. *France in Modern Times.* Chicago: Rand McNally and Co., 1960.

For bibliographies on the subject of civil-military relations see:

Civil-Military Relations: An Annotated Bibliography, 1940–1952. Prepared under the Direction of the Committee on Civil-Military Research of the Social Science Research Council, New York, 1954.

FINER, SAMUEL E. *The Man on Horseback.* New York: Frederick A. Praeger, 1962. (See pp. 245–57 for a bibliography that covers national studies in the field of civil-military relations.)

GIRARDET, RAOUL. "Problèmes militaires contemporaines," *Revue française de science politique,* X (June, 1960), 395–418.

HUNTINGTON, SAMUEL P. *Changing Patterns of Military Politics.* New

York: The Free Press of Glencoe, 1962. ("Recent Writing in Military Politics—Foci and Corpora," pp. 235–66. A very complete and very valuable bibliography for the field of civil-military relations.)

LANG, KURT. *Military Sociology: A Trend Report and a Bibliography.* Oxford: Basil Blackwell, 1965.

VAGTS, ALFRED. *A History of Militarism,* rev. ed. New York: Meridian Books, 1959. See pp. 525–31 for further national studies in the field of civil-military relations.

ARTICLES

The following abbreviations are used throughout:

RDN: Revue de Défense nationale
RMI: Revue militaire d'information
RMG: Revue militaire général

"Aperçu général sur les armées," Service d'Information, d'Etudes et de Cinématographie des Armées, October, 1962.

ARBONNEAU, CAPTAIN DE. "Réflexions sur les formes non spécifiquement militaires," *RMI,* No. 328 (June, 1961), 6–17.

ARGOUD, ANTOINE. "Kidnapped," *National Review,* XV (July 16, 1963), 15–16.

"Attitudes et motivation des candidats aux grandes écoles militaires," *Revue française de sociologie,* II (April–June, 1961), 133–51.

BANKWITZ, PHILLIP. "Maxime Weygand and the Fall of France: A Study in Civil-Military Relations," *The Journal of Modern History,* XXXI (September, 1959), 225–42.

BÉDARIDA, FRANÇOIS. "L'Armée et la République," *Revue Historique,* CCXXXII (July–September, 1964), 119–64.

BEHR, EDWARD. "The French Army as a Political and Social Factor," *International Affairs,* XXXV (October, 1959), 438–46.

BERTRAND-SERRET, RENÉ. "L'Armée et le régime," *Ecrits de Paris,* July–August, 1959, pp. 63–79.

BOURDET, CLAUDE. "Les hommes de la guerre," *Les Temps modernes,* No. 93–94 (August–September, 1953), 401–25.

BROWN, BERNARD E. "The Army and Politics in France," *The Journal of Politics,* XXIII (May, 1961), 262–78.

CAPITAINES T. ET A. "Capitaines, ou bas-officiers? Essai sur la structure sociale de l'armée française," *La nouvelle critique,* No. 107 (June, 1959), 43–84.

CASAMAYOR. "Le Moral de l'armée," *Esprit,* January, 1962, pp. 1–16.

CHASSIN, GENERAL LIONEL-MAX. "Du role idéologique de l'armée," *RMI*, No. 239 (October 10, 1954), 13–19.

CLARK, BLAIR. "France's St. Cyr: 'Rise, Officers!' " *New York Times Magazine*, July 18, 1954, pp. 8, 38.

COCHE, GENERAL. "Armée et guerre subversive," *RMG*, March 3, 1959, pp. 367–99.

CROZIER, BRIAN. "The General's Generals," *Encounter*, XIV (April, 1960), 10–16.

DELMAS, CLAUDE. "La Défense nationale: réflexions sur une formule," *RMI*, No. 323 (January, 1961), 2–15.

DOGAN, MATTEI. "Les officiers dans la carrière politique," *Revue française de sociologie*, II (April–June, 1961), 88–99.

DOMENACH, JEAN-MARIE. "The French Army in Politics," *Foreign Affairs*, XXXIX (January, 1961), 185–95.

DURIEUX, MAJOR A. "Psychological Warfare," *Military Review*, XXXVI (February, 1957), 79–87.

ELY, GENERAL PAUL. "L'armée dans la nation," *RMI*, No. 297 (August–September, 1958), 7–14.

FELD, M. D. "Information and Authority: The Structure of Military Organization," *American Sociological Review*, XXIV (February, 1959), 15–22.

France and Its Armed Forces. Ambassade de France, Service de presse et d'information, December, 1964.

GARRIGOU-LAGRANGE, MADELEINE. "Intégrisme et national-catholicisme," *Esprit*, November, 1959, pp. 515–43.

GERBET, PIERRE. "Les rapports entre pouvoir civil et pouvoir militaire en France dans l'élaboration de la politique de défense." Unpublished paper delivered at the Fifth World Congress of the International Political Science Association, Paris, 1961.

GIBSON, IRVING M. "The Maginot Line," *Journal of Modern History*, XVII (June, 1945), 130–46.

GROMIER, F. "L'armée et la République," *Les cahiers de la République*, No. 7 (May–June, 1957), 91–107.

GROS, ANDRÉ, AND GEORGES GUERON. "L'Armée française et l'avenir de ses cadres," *RDN*, August–September, 1962, pp. 1284–92.

A GROUP OF OFFICERS, "La guerre du Viet–minh," *RMI*, No. 281 (February–March, 1957), 25–41.

HOGARD, MAJOR JACQUES. "Guerre révolutionnaire ou révolution dans l'art de guerre," *RDN*, December, 1956, pp. 1497–1513.

———. "Cette guerre de notre temps," *RDN*, August–September, 1958, pp. 1304–19.

———. "Guerre révolutionnaire et pacification," *RMI*, No. 280 (January, 1957), 7–24.

JACOBS, WALTER DARNELL. "Mao Tse-tung as a Guerrilla: A Second Look," *Military Review*, XXXVII (February, 1958), 26–30.

JANOWITZ, MORRIS. "Changing Patterns of Organizational Authority: The Military Establishment," *Administrative Science Quarterly*, III (March, 1959), 473–93.

KATZENBACH, EDWARD L. "The French Army," *Yale Review*, XLV (Summer, 1956), 498–513.

———. "Indo-China: A Military-Political Appreciation," *World Politics*, IV (January, 1952), 186–218.

———. "Political Parties and the French Army Since the Liberation," *World Politics*, II (July, 1950), 533–48.

KELLY, GEORGE A. "The French Army Re-enters Politics," *Political Science Quarterly*, LXXVI (September, 1961), 367–92.

———. "Officers, Politics, Ideology," *Army*, XII (January, 1962), 30–33.

———. "Algeria, the Army and the Fifth Republic (1959–1961): A Scenario of Civil-Military Conflict," *Political Science Quarterly*, LXXIX (September, 1964), 335–59.

KERR, WALTER. "The French Army in Trouble," *Foreign Affairs*, XL (October, 1961), 86–94.

KOVACS, ARPAD. "French Military Legislation in the Third Republic, 1871–1940," *Military Affairs*, XIII (Spring, 1949), 1–13.

———. "French Military Institutions Before the Franco-Prussian War," *American Historical Review*, LI (January, 1946), 217–35.

KUNTZ, FRANÇOIS. "L'officier dans la nation," *RMI*, No. 317 (June, 1960), 48–66.

MACCARTHY, LIEUTENANT COLONEL. "L'armée française et la politique, 1ère partie: de 1815 à 1870," *L'Armée*, No. 1 (February, 1960), 30–40.

———. "L'armée française et la politique, 2è partie: de 1870 à nos jours," *L'Armée*, No. 2 (March, 1960), 38–48.

MAÎTRE, JACQUES. "Le catholicisme d'extrême droite et la croisade anti-subversive," *Revue française de sociologie*, II (April–June, 1961), 106–17.

MARTIN, JEAN-MAURICE. "Soldats et citoyens," *RMI*, No. 320 (October, 1960), 39–51.

MÉGRET, MAURICE. "L'armée dans la nation," *Revue de l'action populaire*, No. 109 (June, 1957), 653–66.

MESSMER, PIERRE. "Our Military Policy," *French Affairs*, No. 155, Ambassade de France, Service de presse et d'information, May, 1963.

———. "The French Military Establishment of Tomorrow," *Orbis*, VI (Summer, 1962), 205–16.

METZ, COLONEL DE. "Du role national de l'officier," *RDN*, August–September, 1958, pp. 1320–38.

MEYNAUD, JEAN. "Les militaires et le pouvoir," *Revue française de sociologie*, II (April–June, 1961), 75–87.

MORRIS-JONES, W. H. "Armed Forces and the State," *Public Administration*, XXXV (Winter, 1957), 411–16.

NEMO, COLONEL. "The Place of Guerilla Action in War," *Military Review*, XXXVII (November, 1957), 99–107.

"La pacification," *Esprit*, January, 1961, pp. 7–24.

PADOVER, SAUL K. "France in Defeat: Causes and Consequences," *World Politics*, II (April, 1950), 305–37.

PLANCHAIS, JEAN. "The French Army: A Close-up," *New York Times Magazine*, February 18, 1962, pp. 16, 109.

———. "Histoire des quatre jours," *Esprit*, July–August, 1961, pp. 50–65.

———. "The French Army," *Atlas*, II (November, 1961), 335–38.

———. "Crise de modernisme dans l'armée," *Revue française de sociologie*, II (April–June, 1961), 118–23.

———. "The French Army: Not by Force Alone," *Reporter*, XVII (November 28, 1957), 34–36.

PLEVEN, RENÉ. "La politique militaire de la France," *RMI*, No. 224 (December 10–25, 1953), 8–14.

"A propos du role idéologique de l'armée," *RMI*, No. 242 (November 25, 1954), 19–21.

PULOCH, GENERAL L. J. DE. "Future of the French Army," *Military Review*, XLIV (November, 1964), 41–49.

RÉMOND, RENÉ. "Les anciens combattants et la politique," *Revue française de science politique*, V (April–June, 1955), 267–90.

SCHOENBRUN, DAVID. "De Gaulle Faces an Anguished Army," *New York Times Magazine*, February 14, 1960, pp. 12, 13, 90, 92, 94.

SOUYRIS, CAPITAIN ANDRÉ. "L'action psychologique dans les forces armées," *RMI*, No. 298 (October, 1958), 34–45.

———. "Réalite et aspects de la guerre psychologique," *RMI*, No. 302 (February, 1959), 7–28.

SUIRE, LIEUTENANT COLONEL. "Influence populaire sur les types de guerre: la guerre révolutionnaire," *L'Armée*, February 9, 1961, pp. 22–30.

TANNER, HENRY. "Tormented Officer in a Dirty War," *New York Times Magazine*, June 26, 1960, pp. 7, 46, 47.

TERRAINE, JOHN. "The Army in Modern France," *History Today*, XI (November, 1961), 733–42.

TOURNOUX, JEAN-RAYMOND. "A Proletarian Army," *Reporter*, XX (February 18, 1960), 19–21.

VALLUY, GENERAL JEAN. "Armée française 1961," *La Revue des deux mondes*, XII (June 15, 1961), 577–94.

VIAL, JEAN. "La Défense nationale, son organisation entre les deux guerres," *Revue d'histoire de la deuxième guerre mondiale*, XVII (April, 1955), 11–32.

WAUQUIER, MAJOR. "Les forces cuirassées dans la bataille," *Revue d'histoire de la deuxième guerre mondiale*, III (June, 1953), 150–64.

WILLIAMS, PHILLIP. "L'Affaire des Généraux," *Cambridge Journal*, IV (May, 1951). 469–80.

——. "The French Army," *Encounter*, XVII (December, 1961), 30–37.

——. "How the Fourth Republic Died: Sources for the Revolution of May 1958," *French Historical Studies*, III (Spring, 1963), 1–42.

XIMENÈS. "Essai sur la guerre révolutionnaire," *RMI*, No. 281 (February–March, 1957), 11–22.

ZELLER, GENERAL ANDRÉ. "Armée et politique," *RDN*, April 13, 1957, pp. 499–517.

NEWSPAPERS

Le Monde.
New York Times.

Index

251